THE MEASUREMENT OF JOB PERF

The Measurement of Job Performance

CATHERINE T. BAILEY
*Department of Business Administration and Accountancy,
The University of Wales Institute of Science and Technology*

Gower

Published by
Gower Publishing Company Limited,
Gower House, Croft Road, Aldershot,
Hampshire GU11 3HR, England

and

Gower Publishing Company,
Old Post Road, Brookfield,
Vermont 05036,
U.S.A.

Reprinted 1984

British Library Cataloguing in Publication Data

Bailey, Catherine
The measurement of job performance.
1. Job evaluation
I. Title
658.3'06   HF5549.5.J62

ISBN 0-566-00619-7

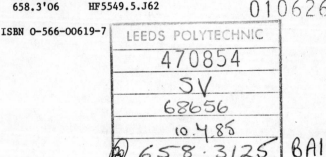
Printed and bound in Great Britain by
Antony Rowe Ltd, Chippenham, Wiltshire.

Contents

Tables

Figures

Preface

The measurement of job performance is a universal yet commonly problematic organisational activity. While there are many problems associated with performance appraisal and measurement, in the author's view, prior to any of those associated with appraisal are the problems of measurement itself. Notably, practitioners are faced with a proliferation of performance measurement methods with little clear guidance to inform their choice while researchers continue to seek a performance measurement instrument which exhibits the psychometric strengths required of a research tool but yet fail to agree on what should be measured or how. It would seem that performance measurement research has still a long way to go.

In the belief that traditional research approaches, focussing on either measurement principles or measurement techniques, have left a theoretical divide in the middle, the author's aim is to span this divide by advancing principles through to methodological implications. Given that the main impetus for research resides in the practitioner's real need for an effective performance measurement method, this decision, which necessitates a theoretical rather than a pragmatic approach, is not taken lightly. Practitioners' needs are fully recognised and guidance for the practice of performance measurement is clearly required. However, after decades of research, it is apparent that no 'wonder' technique is likely to be yielded by continued pursuit of traditional research orientations. And so, if we are not to risk the problems of performance measurement becoming an institutionalized academic concern with little hope of achieving their resolution, then we need to review our position, be prepared to question our current assumptions and reassess our orientations. By looking to basic measurement principles to inform appropriate performance measurement methodology, this is the stance adopted here.

This book is written for those who are concerned with advancing performance measurement but it is also intended to be of use to practitioners for, in the final analysis, the concerns of both are inextricable. So although the ultimate conclusions focus on appropriate methodology and research orientations in performance measurement, specific guidance for practice is derived at several points through the development of the theoretical themes and in the final chapter the author examines the changes in the practitioner's role which are implied by the theoretical conclusions.

I would like to express my gratitude to Dr. Gerry Randell for his guidance and encouragement in the research, my sincere thanks to Dr. David Butcher for invaluable discussions and for commenting so thoroughly on the final draft, and my deepest gratitude to my husband, J, not only for his help in indexing and proof-reading but for his unstinting support and encouragement. Finally, I would like to express my thanks to Kathy Hollister, who typed this book, for her cheerful perserverance and skill. Needless to say any remaining errors are the responsibility of the author.

1 Introduction: measurement in performance appraisal

A common aim of industrial, occupational and organisational psychology
is to provide an understanding of behaviour in the work environment, an
ultimate goal being to inform the decisions that are made in managing
human resources. While the behaviour of people within work environments
is an area of considerable interest and research, the traditional and
enduring concern of managers and researchers alike is the performance of
an individual in his specific work task. Specifically, concern centres
on the extent to which these work behaviours are effective, productive,
desirable, appropriate, successful in meeting objectives etc. This
focus on job performance emanates from the fact that performance is
often a critical factor in decisions made about the employment, utilization and maintenance of human resources. As the quality of these everyday decisions depends, at least, on the quality of the information on
which they are based then it is not surprising that organisations
attempt to systematize and institutionalize the ways in which individual
performance information is gathered – usually through a process of performance appraisal.

Through this introductory chapter the author seeks to establish the organisational necessity of performance appraisal, to locate performance
measurement as an essential ingredient of performance appraisal, to de-
lineate the salient problematic issues with appraisal that have been
identified and finally, to establish the need and lay the ground for a
closer study of performance measurement problems.

It is certain that performance appraisal is an essential and therefore
widely practised human resource management activity. Surveys and reviews of its practice (see, for example, Spriegel 1962, Harvard Business
Review 1973, Kane and Lawler 1979) demonstrate the large number of
decision-making purposes for which individual performance data are seemingly required and used. These include decisions concerning employee
counselling, promotion, training, development, salary administration,
bonus payment allocation, personnel auditing, potential-spotting, job
redesign, work motivation, and selection and training programme valida-

tion among others. In fact Randell (1976) argued that any major decision about the human resource necessitates performance data. These observations suggest that, for any organisation, there is no question that individual performance data need to be sought, the questions that organisations seek to answer concern the type and quality of necessary information as well as the nature of the processes by which data are acquired.

It is also evident from these surveys and reviews that performance data are used for diverse decision-making purposes. Although organisations differ in the appraisal purposes they pursue, few operate single purpose appraisal systems (Gill, Ungerson and Thakur 1973). In effect, then, most appraisal systems function to satisfy multiple and diverse decision-making needs.

The research suggests that this diversity can create problems, to the point of unsustainable stress (Yager 1981), as different purposes may place conflicting demands on the type and quality of data required.

Maier (1958) was perhaps the first to observe that by attempting to furnish diverse needs through a single information-gathering exercise the achievement of any one purpose is made that more difficult. Consequently he made a useful distinction between performance evaluation (for salary, promotion etc. decisions) and performance development (for training need diagnosis, potential etc. decisions) as the two potentially conflicting alternative basic purposes of appraisal. Not only do these purposes typically dictate a differential emphasis on quantitative and qualitative information respectively, but Maier argued that they are based on different assumptions and require different attitudes and skills for their successful achievement. Subsequent theory has reinforced this view, and in the practice of appraisal there has been a significant move towards the systems and temporal (i.e. being conducted on separate occasions) separation of activities directed at different basic purposes. So, for example, Maier (1958) himself described three types of appraisal interview, Randell, Packard, Shaw and Slater (1974) identified four, Cummings and Schwab (1973) distinguished three types of appraisal programme and Yager (1981) argued for the separation of performance appraisal, review and planning. These authors all work from the premise that the achievement of all main purposes is facilitated by setting up operationally distinct procedures so as to increase the reliability and validity of the information gathered in the pursuit of any one.

If the problems in appraisal emanate from conflicting demands on appropriate assumptions, attitudes and skills then systems and temporal separation provides the opportunity to remove this conflict. Inasmuch as these strategies achieve this separation and elaborate the different requirements of the system and appraiser, then they are valuable and provide useful guidelines for the systems designer. However, if the problems, or at least some, emanate from the nature of the very information collected or judgements made (i.e. qualitative or quantitative) then

2

temporal or system separation cannot be expected to provide a solution, for both types of information and both types of judgement are inevitably required. Graves (1982) observed that any personnel decision requires comparative evaluative data and commented that the trend towards developmental uses of appraisal overlooks the fact that evaluative information has to come from somewhere, and expressed his concern that developmental and qualitative system emphases do not obviate the need for evaluative data, they may merely force its collection by informal and uncontrolled methods. Regardless of the class of purpose of appraisal (i.e. whether evaluative or developmental) the most significant point is that both main classes presuppose performance measurement. While it is obvious that evaluative purposes presuppose performance measurement, the present author (Morrison 1980) previously argued that performance development activities also presuppose measurement as inevitably a referent is required in order to identify performance weaknesses and monitor performance improvement. In any case, as she observed, while it may be valuable to distinguish between evaluation and developmental purposes, as it provides some useful guidelines for the system designer, in practice the distinction is unlikely to be upheld for it understates the difficulty of the conceptual task faced by the practising manager who may find that reality defies such clear cut distinctions. So although the separation of appraisal practices, aimed at different purposes, requiring different techniques and different emphases in the information required, might be a useful objective, it must be recognised that this separation may never be complete. It becomes clear that any performance-based decision requires both quantitative and qualitative information and therefore that performance measurement is a fundamental feature of performance appraisal.

A Continuing Problem

The history of performance appraisal demonstrates that, while some headway has been made in attaining more effective appraisal and measurement methods, fundamental problems still exist. Intermittent reviews (Kelly 1958, Whisler and Harper 1962, Rowe 1964, Ghiselli and Dunnette 1970, Gill et al, 1973, Harvard Business Review 1973, Tilley 1974, Kane and Lawler 1979) provide evidence of shifting trends as well as bear witness to this as a perennial concern of practitioners and researchers.

The bonus schemes and merit-rating approaches of scientific management represented the earliest formal appraisal practices. The major problems encountered by such predominantly evaluation-based approaches have been outlined by Murrell (1976). Essentially, development till the 50's concentrated on instrument refinement by which time it became evident that such schemes were yet problem-ridden (McMurry 1960) and so clearly inadequate (Shimmin 1955, 1959) that this form of performance appraisal was seriously questioned. Some authors (Dailey 1961) advocated abandoning performance appraisal for anything other than performance development purposes while others (McGregor 1957, Stewart 1965) called for a reorientation towards the developmental emphasis in appraisal, with McGregor's (1960) version of MbO and, the more extreme development-only emphases of Cummings and Schwab's (1973) Developmental Action Programme as well as Randell et al's, (1974) Active Staff Development making significant contributions to appraisal practice in work organisations. Evidently the move from evaluative and quantitative to developmental and qualitative-type approaches has been of some benefit. However, recently it appears that there has been a redress of the balance. Teel's (1980) survey, for example, revealed a trend towards combining narrative and evaluative data in appraisals. Perhaps this is a reflection of organisations again trying to achieve multiple purposes under one system or, as Morrison (1980) and Graves (1982) suggested, it reflects a real need for both types of information regardless of specific purpose. Either way, this flux suggests that, despite the progress that has been made, organisational and industrial psychologists have still to solve the problems and satisfy the needs of those who require to measure and hence appraise individual job performance.

From their analysis of performance appraisal methods, which was based on the type of performance data collected, Kane and Lawler (1979) concluded that the whole range of conceivable techniques had now been investigated and yet found that none adequately met the five criteria (validity, reliability, discriminability, relevance, freedom from bias) of an effective appraisal system. As the historical development of performance measurement and appraisal methods has been hastened on by the known and often insoluble inadequacies of previous methods, then it is daunting to find that we have reached the end of the line without achieving a consensus on a valid, reliable, discriminating method which produces relevant information and which is free from bias in all situations where performance information is required. Quite clearly the problem still exists and, in line with Jacobs et al's, (1980) assertion that a new orientation to the problems of performance measurement is required, we need to reappraise our efforts and seek afresh some answers.

The universal, continuing and yet unsatisfied need for effective performance appraisal is the impetus for this book and the inextricable link between performance appraisal and measurement, as well as the issues of qualitative versus quantitative data and developmental versus evaluative processes, brings the problems of performance measurement into focus as an area where clarification is required and answers need to be sought.

There is a considerable body of research and literature concerning job performance measurement but an overview yields a divide in the pattern of academic activity. On the one hand, in continuation of a tradition, there is an active concern for the refinement and development of specific measurement techniques but in general these efforts meet with qualified success as inevitably the limits to generalizability are reached (Jacobs et al, 1980). Kane and Lawler (1979) sceptically depicted the historical development of performance measures as a cycle of technique discovery, pursuit and demise. And, in line with the author's observations, recognised that effort invested in progressing measure capability has reached a state of diminishing returns as the full range of potential types of performance data have apparently already been exploited. In short, the prognosis for this approach alone is gloomy. On the other hand, a wider and more promising perspective on methodologies, evident in the work of Guion (1961, 1965), Ghiselli (1965, 1970), Dunnette (1963, 1979), Ronan and Prien (1966, 1971) and others intent on 'cracking' the Criterion Problem, has revealed invaluable measurement principles, e.g. the concepts of criterion dynamism, dimensionality, multiplicity etc., but is yet fraught with controversy. So it is not perhaps surprising that this approach has lacked impetus in its practical applications and prescriptions.

While it is evident that both perspectives have immediate problems to overcome, an ultimate theoretical gap appears to exist between researching measurement principles and researching measurement techniques. This is the province of methodology. In this book a different orientation is taken which lies outside of these two approaches. It is an attempt to span the divide by adopting what appears to be the more promising wider perspective but by advancing measurement principles through to methodological implications.

The primary objective is to clarify some of the issues which have pervaded the search for acceptable performance measures in order that comment and recommendations may be made about fruitful research orientations and the practice of performance measurement.

Although the Criterion Problem literature has contributed substantially to our understanding of performance measurement, the aim here is to add to knowledge in this well-tilled area and so a different direction is taken through the performance measurement literature with the intention that this view can at worst only strengthen the conclusions of the criterion theorists but hopefully extend our understanding of the methodological implications. This new direction is primarily theoretical and consists of several stages which are summarised below.

At the outset Chapter 2 seeks to derive the fundamental issues in performance measure development and thus identifies the two basic theoretical themes that are subsequently explored in this book. This is achieved through an analysis of the major performance appraisal and measurement methods according to seven bases of analysis and the identification of property patterns among them. These methods are ultimately located and described with reference to a subjective-objective continuum, and a distillation of property patterns defines the underlying concerns in deriving appropriate performance measures as the issues concerned with firstly, the nature of the performance dimensions or criteria used and secondly, the role of subjective judgement and associated subjectivity.

Chapter 3 seeks to demonstrate the arbitrary nature of measurement systems and discusses the implications of this for performance measure development. Definitions of measures and dimensions are provided and explored, the differences between dimensions and criteria are analysed and issues in dimensional analysis and criterion development are identified.

Ultimately the conclusions of preceding sections are synthesised and major constraints on the choice of appropriate performance measures are elaborated, with specific limitations on the quality and quantity of appropriate performance dimensions or criteria explained.

Chapter 4 picks up subjectivity as the second major theme and, through the presentation and description of a model of the sources and effects of rater subjectivity, identifies seven major sources which contribute to rating performance, three judgemental processes of rating performance and eight characteristic measurement error outcomes differentially related to these processes. With explicit relations drawn between these sources, mechanisms of effect and outcomes, Chapter 5 identifies three general solution strategies and explores their applicability to each major source of subjectivity. Retaining the focus on subjectivity in the rating process, Chapter 6 reports a study which seeks to accentuate both general and specific theoretical conclusions by reference to empirical data.

In the final chapter the cumulative theoretical conclusions are brought into focus and discussed and specific recommendations about the development of performance measures are stated. Ultimately, wider methodological conclusions are drawn, competing research paradigms are explored and implications for the future research and practice of performance measurement are examined.

2 Properties of performance measurement methods

In this chapter the use of and problems with specific performance appraisal and measurement methods are examined. While providing a wider review than is normally undertaken, the primary objective is to lay the ground to identify fundamental problems so that a survey of all main methods and their associated problems is required. In order to achieve this the major measurement methods are identified and their characteristics systematically evaluated according to prespecified criteria of method effectiveness. While the analysis of psychometric characteristics is not a novel activity, previous research typically compares a subset of methods on a subset of characteristics whereas here the author attempts to construct a more complete picture by drawing together research on a larger array of both.

Although classifications and typologies of appraisal methods have been constructed (Cummings and Schwab 1973, Smith 1976, Anastasi 1979, Kane and Lawler 1979) the major problem has always been the selection of relevant classification variables. Because of the proliferation of performance measurement techniques and because of the diversity of method characteristics it is difficult to achieve a classification scheme which is both easily conceptualized and sufficiently detailed. As the aim here is to illuminate the perhaps complex and underlying problems of performance measurement, a choice has been made to sacrifice ease of conceptualization for greater detailed representation.

THE BASES OF ANALYSIS

Kane and Lawler (1979) suggested that appraisal method effectiveness might be judged according to the criteria of validity, reliability, freedom from bias, relevance and discriminability. Starting out with the assumption that method effectiveness is positively related to these five characteristics then they provide a convenient basis for method analysis. However, Kane and Lawler's analysis omitted several useful findings of theorists who research what is known as the Criterion

Problem. The questions they seek to answer concern the number and type of criteria required to measure job performance, questions which not only have practical significance but criterion theorists argue that such issues are critically related to psychometric characteristics. For these reasons the present review includes a consideration of the nature of criteria used by each method.

The nature and degree of appraiser judgement required is adopted as one further basis of analysis because not only is it expected to be related to findings on reliability and bias but it seems that an element of appraiser judgement is characterisic of all methods and it is one that causes problems for both practitioners and theorists. Managers are reluctant to judge others (Stewart 1965) though they prefer some judgement tasks to others. Judgement is fallible, open to interference and bias and therefore prone to inaccuracy and yet, without exception, every form of appraisal requires some degree of appraiser judgement. In order to identify methods which are more or less difficult or preferred, and more or less susceptible to factors which threaten psychometric strength, it is necessary to determine what sort of judgement is required by each method, whether required judgements differ in complexity and extent, and what freedom is given or constraints placed on the judgements made.

THE METHODS

There are probably as many performance measurement methods as there are interested theorists and resourceful practitioners and its certain that for any one method there are several variants. In this analysis the methods are classified into 6 distinct types which in some way characterize all the practices described within each. The method types to be considered are:

: Closed, Free Expression Reports which are characterized by covert performance assessments made with reference to criteria selected by the appraiser.

: Individual Standards Procedures which are characterized by performance assessments made with reference to objectives or criteria previously agreed with and specific to the appraisee.

: Comparative Standards Procedures which are characterized by performance assessments made with reference to the performance of other appraisees in similar positions or jobs.

: Absolute Standards Procedures which are characterized by performance assessments made with reference to prespecified criteria and standards.

: Performance Tests which are characterized by performance assessments made on the basis of performance at a simulated job exercise.

8

: Direct Indices which are characterized by performance assessments made on the basis of measures of job behaviour outcomes.

THE ANALYSIS

In the succeeding sections, a more detailed description of each method type and its variants is given followed by an analysis of its character- istics according to the 7 bases identified above.

Closed, Free Expression Reports

These methods are typified by the unseen appraisals of performance, called references, so commonly used in employee selection. While cir- cumstances have led to a trend away from closed reporting in the appraisal situation (Anstey, Fletcher and Walker 1976), the survey by Walker, Fletcher, Williams and Taylor (1977) found that half of the org- anisations consulted, having open reporting systems, placed some reli- ance on a parallel formal or informal closed information system too. The attraction of closed systems lies in the freedom given to the appraiser to express opinions without the need for justification. As Anstey et al, (1976) explained, this removes the fear of superior- subordinate conflict which candid performance comments may incite. How- ever, these forms of qualitative and quantitative unseen report suffer serious drawbacks. Muchinsky's (1979) review of research on the use of reference reports found it to be an under-researched area, and observed that available research provided little support for the use of refer- ences. This research is referred to below.

Validity. In reviewing the validity of reference reports Muchinsky (1979) concluded that, 'the magnitude of coefficients reported in the several validity studies range from unacceptable to mediocre' p. 292. He suggested that low predictive validity may be accounted for, in part, by severe leniency error causing restriction of range and hence reducing predictor variance. Mosel and Goheen (1959) and Browning (1968) had earlier found, however, that the validity coefficients differ according to the rater. This may be explained by the findings on reliability.

Reliability. Mosel and Goheen (1952, 1959) found the inter-appraiser reliability of reference reports to be low, a finding which could be ex- plained in part by Richardson's (1962) observation that equally com- petent executives often differ with respect to the performance aspects they consider most important. But in addition, a large amount of research concerns the opportunity for bias which closed reporting systems permit, and this seems to be a major factor influencing both their reliability and validity.

Freedom from bias. It is clear that closed reporting systems provide the opportunity for appraisers to exercise prejudice and bias. Studies by Mehrabian (1965) and Wiens, Jackson, Manaugh and Matarazzo (1969) revealed that referees write longer letters about liked persons and

9

Richardson (1962) found that the effort invested in report writing was a determinant of how high the referent was rated. It has also been suggested (Blum and Naylor 1968) that referees write over-positive evaluations of marginally performing employees in order to enhance their attractiveness to other employers. While Kryger and Shikiar (1978) noted sex differences in evaluation accuracy, finding female referees to be more subjective in their evaluation than their male counterparts, it also appears that bias is likely to occur where referee and referent are of different sex, race and nationality (Carroll and Nash 1972).

Without denying that some forms of bias may be organisationally acceptable, the likelihood of bias and the difficulty of its detection has been a major reason for the trend towards open reporting systems. Indeed, as Walker et al, (1977) remarked, the fear of bias leading to unfair appraisal has given rise to legislation enforcing open systems in countries including USA and Germany. However, the research shows that the relationship between system openness and the occurrence of bias is not a simple one. For example, Haeri (1969) found that managers think they would and do, in fact, inflate their explicitly-made evaluations, whereas Walker et al, (1977) found that in explicit evaluations, managers took more care to be fair and accurate. These suggest that open systems per se are not the complete antidote to bias.

Relevance. Appraisers differ in their ability to observe, evaluate and report accurately on individual performance (Richardson 1962, Blum and Naylor 1968) and this variance inevitably effects the relevance of information reported. Sleight and Bell (1954), studying the information content of references, found that the majority of 148 employers surveyed preferred information on personality traits such as honesty, co-operativeness etc. The traditional use of hypothetical constructs in closed free expression reports, both in the selection and appraisal situation, inevitably creates problems in establishing criterion-related validities and, as Smith (1976) suggested, leads to problems with criterion relevance. As such criterion relevance is highly variable and therefore not guaranteed by Closed, Free Expression methods of performance measurement.

Discriminability. Little evidence is available regarding the discriminability of Closed Free Expression Reports. However, assuming the individual differences cited above, Richardson (1962) concluded that such systems do not yield a form of expression which permits comparison between individuals. Muchinsky's (1979) observation of the restriction of range caused by pronounced leniency error and Myers and Errett's (1959) assertion that preselection of referees by referents in the selection situation inevitably leads to a highly positive, narrow range of opinions, both suggest that Closed Free Expression Reports suffer from low discriminability. In addition, as the level of measurement is generally nominal in the free expression form of closed system reporting, potential discriminability is necessarily limited.

Nature and degree of appraiser judgement. In Closed Free Expression

Reporting the appraiser both selects the performance criteria and evaluates individual performance relative to implicit norms, on the basis of personal impression. The appraiser's task therefore involves a high degree of subjective judgement. There is a commonly held belief that references say more about the referee than the referent. Although difficult to substantiate, Whisler and Harper (1962) cited several illustrations of the point including , for example, 'Never makes the same mistake twice but it seems to me he has made them all once' or 'Is keenly analytical and his highly developed mentality could best be used in the research and development field. He lacks common sense'. Such anecdotes demonstrate the ambiguity which uncontrolled expression permits and the (hopefully!) misguided assumptions on which uncontrolled subjective judgement can be based.

Nature of criteria used. In Closed Free Expression Reports the criteria are commonly selected by the appraiser without a check on their relevance to task performance or on the reason for their selection. But when criteria are primarily personality trait-oriented and their selection influenced by appraiser-related factors then it is not surprising that psychometric properties are poor and that their utility is reduced by lack of agreement between appraisers i.e. the criteria used are appraiser- and, quite probably, appraisee-specific.

Individual Standards Procedures

While it is typically recognised that, among the most commonly used appraisal methods, there is a distinction to be made between those which are criterion-referenced and those which are norm-referenced (Cummings and Schwab 1973), there is a further discrete category of popular methods where performance is appraised with reference to criteria and standards which are dynamic and unique to the appraisee. These Individual Standards Procedures include Drucker's (1954) Management by Objectives, McGregor's (1960) Management by Integration and Self-Control, Schleh's (1961) Management by Results, Randell's (1975) Performance Review and Cummings and Schwab's (1973) Developmental Action Programme.

With the exception of some forms of MbO which lay emphasis on the evaluation of goal achievement, these Individual Standards Procedures are distinguished from all other method types by their primary emphasis on performance development. In practice, information is gathered, checked and decisions are made about performance improvement by the appraiser and appraisee, with implied goals and action plans discussed and agreed. Method effectiveness then, relies heavily on the appraiser's ability to elicit accurate information and to help identify realistic, worthwhile and agreed means of improving performance.

The concepts of reliability and validity are not easily applied to these methods. They share a view that measurement and quantification of performance may not be the most fruitful appraisal focus and so because of their developmental and qualitative emphasis, statistical treatment and estimates of reliability and validity are difficult to achieve, if not

11

irrelevant. Secondly, the performance criteria adopted are appraisee- and situation-specific, thus unique and dynamic by their nature, again making statistical treatment difficult. However, as the interview is perhaps the critical element in any of these procedures their psychometric properties can be inferred to a certain extent from those of the interview itself, both as an information-gathering and as a decision-making medium.

Validity. There is a paucity of useful research evidence on the validity of the interview because, as Landy and Trumbo (1976) pointed out, what research exists fails to distinguish between the information-gathering and decision-making functions of the interviewer. In addition, it is often difficult to assess criterion-related validity because a) interviewers often make decisions on the basis of information collected outside the interview and b) if low validity coefficients result from comparing judgements with other job performance criteria then there is a problem in establishing whether it's the interviewer, the traits chosen or the criteria which are weak. Given this inherent difficulty, it can be suggested that as each method is aimed at behaviour change, then the incidence of desired behaviour change is the criterion against which the methods would be more appropriately validated. Within such a definition, the manager's unwillingness to tackle problems of subordinate weakness during appraisal discussion, observed by Meyer, Kay and French (1965), Fletcher (1973) and Fletcher and Williams (1976), must reflect on the validity of these procedures. Finally, as inter-interviewer reliability is typically low, the validity of the interview as an appraisal method is unlikely to be high.

Reliability. With reference to selection interviewing, Ulrich and Trumbo's (1965) review revealed that the few studies which quoted reliability estimates showed coefficients which were lower than usually accepted for prediction purposes. And later, Jessup and Jessup (1975), distinguishing between inter- and intra-interviewer reliability, found the former typified by a much larger and lower spread of estimates. While these results may not necessarily generalize to the reliability of appraisal interviews, the reasons for inter-interviewer differences should be taken into consideration. Low inter-interviewer reliability has been explained in terms of differential information coverage, differential weighting of information, inaccuracy of elicited information, and differential interviewee responses to different interviewers (Mayfield 1964) as well as individual differences in interpretation of traits/ events and lack of information standardization (Landy and Trumbo 1976). While observed in the selection situation these factors are equally likely in the appraisal situation and so they might be expected to have similar detrimental effects on reliability.

It has been argued that to evaluate any of these methods as a measurement process may be meaningless. None would claim to be a measuring instrument so a strict definition of criterion-related validity becomes meaningless. In addition, given their ultimate objective of behaviour change, the approaches consider as academic the possibility that two appraisers could arrive at different objectives with the same appraisee. This means inter-appraiser reliability may not necessarily be a meaningful concept. It seems, however, that if the interview is regarded as the core activity the methods have problems with validity and reliability and there might be something to be gained from considering factors that may influence the data-gathering and decision-making in such procedures.

Freedom from bias. The interview, the critical element in each of the Individual Standards Procedures, confers control on the interviewer. As such the quality and quantity of performance information elicited is determined by the interviewer's judgement and skill so each method has an inherent opportunity for interviewer bias to occur. The research on bias has been prolific with respect to MbO and without implying that MbO is any more or less biased than the other Individual Standards methods, it is taken as an example to illustrate the ways in which bias occurs.

Several writers (Howell 1967, Humble 1970, Koontz 1972) have noted that a major problem in MbO is the appraiser's failure to identify performance goals which adequately satisfy organisational and individual needs, and as Raia (1974) remarked, the typical imposition of organisation-only relevant goals, is a serious problem. In addition, Raia (1966) found that organisation goals over-emphasize a production orientation, an unsurprising outcome where emphasis, as in MbO, is placed on establishing goals which are easily measurable. Bias then can take the form of a dysfunctional emphasis on organisational versus individual needs and quantitative versus qualitative goals.

Relevance. The problem of criterion relevance in MbO is closely associated with that of bias. McConkey (1972) suggested that the need to write measurable objectives which are also worthwhile and meaningful creates a problem, the tendency being to sacrifice meaningful for measurable goals or vice versa. Not only is there this general difficulty of setting relevant goals but research indicates particular difficulties with respect to specific jobs. Kleber (1972), for example, identified objective-setting difficulties in the areas of public relations, engineering and research, controlling functions, educational institutions, non-profit making organisations and government agencies. In addition there is a difficulty associated with the appraisee himself. Kearney (1979) questioned the ability of some interviewees to distinguish effective from ineffective behaviour, thus influencing the relevance of objectives to the design of which they contribute. Considering this to be such a problem he proposed that, for MbO to be effective, some other support such as Behaviourally Anchored Rating Scales should be used to supplement this weakness.

In short the need to monitor desired behaviour change creates general and particular difficulties in goal-setting. What is relevant may not be measurable while what is measurable may not be relevant. Aside from this implied threat to criterion relevance, appraisee characteristics may also pose a problem to the extent that alternative measurement methods may be required in support.

Discriminability.   A weakness of Individual Standards Procedures is
their inability to discriminate consistently among individuals. If objectives are set on the basis of a unique combination of organisational
and individual needs then standardized discrimination, for comparison
purposes, is difficult to establish. The protagonists, would argue that
ultimately it is performance development rather than evaluation that is
important. However, MbO does have an explicit evaluative component, and
the difficulty of establishing a standardized system for comparing performances has been noted.   Not only is it difficult, but as Lasagna
(1971) observed, MbO programmes which attempt to cover too many management activities and impose uniform procedures on a company-wide basis,
in order to achieve standardized discrimination, often alienate managers. This means that the utility gained may be lost through the
effects of dysfunctional attitudes invoked. Finally, as the level of
measurement in these methods is generally nominal, with the exception of
some forms of MbO, discriminability is potentially limited.

Nature and degree of appraiser judgement. It is clear from the above
that these procedures require a great deal of appraiser judgement. For
these schemes to be successful the appraiser needs to exercise judgement
in interpreting organisational goals, in selecting or monitoring the
choice of relevant individual goals and in sharing the evaluation and
analysis of progress towards these.

Nature of criteria used. With each of these procedures the criteria
against which performance is either implicitly or explicitly evaluated
are objective in as much as they are usually derived from and have a
direct relation to organisational goals. The individual's contribution
to these is established by taking into account the individual's weaknesses, strengths and motivations. This 'tailoring' is what makes the
individual's objectives unique, so to an extent the criteria derived
through subjective judgement are idiosyncratic, in that they may have
little meaning to other appraisers or appraisees. But this judgement is
constrained by the need for agreement as to meaning between appraiser
and appraisee, and by a requirement that criteria are behaviourally expressed (as in Performance Review) or by a requirement that they are
measurable (as in MbO).

Comparative Standards Procedures

As the name suggests these are norm-referenced performance measurement
methods where an individual's performance is assessed in comparison to
that of other individuals (either within the same subordinate group or
engaged on the same task). Such methods are based on the idea that
while appraisers differ in their ability to describe or quantify differences between appraisee performances, all appraisers are capable of comparative discriminations.

These norm-referenced methods include:

a) Straight Ranking, which involves the rank ordering of appraisee performances starting with the best, second best and third best etc.
b) Alternate Ranking, which involves the rank ordering of appraisee performances by selecting and eliminating from the appraisee pool the best and the worst performers, the best and the worst etc.
c) Paired Comparison, which involves the evaluation of each appraisee performance relative to that of every other, the construction of a matrix of appraisee performance dyads, so that the ultimate ranking of performances is based on the frequency with which each performer is judged better than the other half of the dyad.
d) Forced Distribution, which involves ordering appraisee performances on merit and fashioning the resultant rank order to fit a normal distribution function along an interval scale.

Each of these methods has its problems. When the appraisee group is large Straight and Alternate Ranking become arduous and tedious tasks, requiring mental agility and stamina. Paired Comparison, where only two appraisees are considered at a time presents a less taxing judgement task but, by necessitating the comparison of all possible pairs, the number of judgements required is inevitably greater than that required by other methods. Each of these methods yields ordinal level data. Forced Distribution lifts measurement to the interval level by assuming appraisee performances to be normally distributed. This assumption is not only questionable on statistical grounds but a further problem is grounded in the appraiser's perspective as he might well conceive of his appraisee group, especially if personally-selected, as reasonable performers and so expect the distribution to be positively skewed.

Validity. Because validation relies on the availability of external criteria and as these performance measures have been typically adopted in the very circumstances where other criteria are not available it's not surprising that validity findings are sparse. However, as these methods permit appraiser variation in the definition or interpretation of effectiveness of job performance (Cummings and Schwab 1973), validity is likely to be appraiser-specific. And at any rate, such individual differences would make criterion-related validity difficult to establish. However with regard to descriptive validity, the commonly quoted advantage of Comparative Standards Procedures relates to the simplicity and naturalness of the task and this implies that face validity, at least, is high.

Reliability. Each of these techniques is able to claim a fair degree of reliability. Lawshe, Kephart and McCormick (1949) found a high degree of both inter- and intra-appraiser reliability with Paired Comparison techniques, while Tiffin (1951) pointed to the proven higher reliability of Forced Distribution ranking than that found with much more sophisticated systems.

Freedom from bias. While research on bias is difficult to locate, Lawshe et al, (1949) suggested that because of the time required to complete such tasks, they were susceptible to appraiser fatigue factors. In addition Cummings and Schwab's (1973) observation, that there exists differential interpretation of the global dimensions, obviously has some bearing on bias. Although Tiffin (1951) argued that global dimensions versus multi-trait systems evidenced less halo error, it is more likely that these methods permit such effects to remain undetected. In other words bias may be difficult to detect but these methods have characteristics which provide the opportunity for bias to occur.

Relevance. At the time of the major thrust in the area of Comparative Standards Procedures, it is evident that they provided more relevant information than the currently available alternatives which were personality trait-oriented measures. However, even Tiffin (1951), a main proponent, saw problems with relevance. He found it necessary to stipulate the need for an agreed checklist of traits as an aid to relevant judgement and to facilitate feedback when using Forced Distribution. Beyond this the face validity of these measures implies a degree of relevance even if this is appraiser-specific.

Discriminability. As Straight and Alternate Ranking and Paired Comparison produce ordinal data neither one takes account of absolute differences in performance. Ghiselli and Brown (1955) pointed out that the magnitude of differences between ranks on ordinal scales is not equal at different positions and so the discriminability achieved is crude and basic. In addition, the scales are anchored at either end by specific individuals and this creates problems when comparison is required between appraisees in different appraisal groups. As for Forced Distribution, while the resultant is an interval scale, the method of achieving this distorts real differences between appraisees if the assumption of normally distributed performances is not tenable.

Nature and degree of appraiser judgement. These methods derive their popularity and appeal from the apparent simplicity of the appraiser's task. As Ghiselli and Brown (1955) argued, ranking is a very natural type of evaluation which precedes any form of discrimination. In essence, at any one point of time, the appraiser is only required to make a simple dichotomous choice so the evaluation task is simple in nature and the degree of judgement required is limited. However, the global criteria used such as 'overall effectiveness' or 'job performance' are an inadequate basis on which to make such assessment judgements without some elaboration or interpretation of what effectiveness or performance means. This task is typically left to the appraiser and therefore there is a high degree of subjective judgement involved in defining the implicit criteria.

Nature of criteria used. In as much as the explicit criteria adopted are typically single and global, established by other than the appraiser, and are performance versus personality-based, they appear objective. However, these global criteria are variously but commonly unspecifically defined, and criticisms hinge on the observation that for practical purposes further implicit definition or reinterpretation is required which permits a degree of appraiser subjectivity. Finally, while the use of global criteria apparently simplifies the appraiser's task their utility may be severely restricted. Specifically, Dunnette (1963) suggested that there are few jobs for which a global evaluation is either meaningful or useful.

In summary, these methods are intuitively appealing and do show a certain amount of face validity and reliability. However, it appears that these are gained at the expense of the quality and quantity of information produced. As a rider, it should be noted that Comparative Standard Procedures became popular when the obvious alternative to global performance evaluation was a personality trait-oriented approach. It is now clear that these are not mutually exclusive alternatives. Multidimensional scaling, a recent development in statistical analysis, permits the derivation of higher quality information from the same simple dichotomous judgements, and simple ranking procedures with their characteristic reliability could be adopted with multi-dimensional criteria which are behaviour-oriented. Both of these can increase the quality and quantity of the information produced.

Absolute Standards Procedure

In contrast to the previous norm-referenced methods, these criterion-referenced methods involve the appraisal of individual performance with reference to written absolute standards established for the job. Cummings and Schwab (1973) conveniently categorised these methods into qualitative and quantitative types. Qualitative types require the appraiser to identify the presence or absence of some performance characteristic in the appraisee. Quantitative types require the appraiser to identify the degree to which the appraisee possesses certain characteristics.

Qualitative Techniques include:

a) Critical Incident Technique. First formulated by Flanagan (1949), critical incidents of job performance are obtained from supervisors after which they are examined and condensed into a small number of behavioural categories and it is then these general but critical categories of job performance that supervisors use to observe and record appraisee job behaviour. These then serve as a basis for performance evaluation as well as development.

b) Weighted Checklist. A comprehensive list of statements about the particular job performance is developed. Job-knowledgeable appraisers are asked to evaluate the favourability of each behaviour for successful performance, typically on a 7, 9 or 11 point scale, and statements are eliminated where wide variability exists between evaluations. The remaining statements are weighted according to the average scores obtained from the group evaluations. The appraiser is then provided with the final checklist, where weights are omitted, and asked to indicate the presence or absence of each behaviour in the appraisee. Appraisee performance evaluation is achieved by summing the scores of the behavioural items observed.

c) Forced Choice Procedure. Appraisers are presented with a series of groups of 3 or 4 statements about job behaviour and asked to choose an item in each which is most descriptive of the appraisee. The items are chosen on the basis of discriminability and desirability i.e. each item must distinguish between successful and unsuccessful performance and items must appear to be equally favourable statements to make about an appraisee. The evaluation is derived by summing the discrimination indices (which are unknown to the appraiser) of the items checked.

Quantitative methods include:

a) Behavioural Expectation Scales, known as BES developed by Zedeck and Baker (1971).
b) Behavioural Observation Scales, known as BOS developed by Dunnette, Campbell and Hellervik (1968).
c) Behaviourally Anchored Rating Scales, known as BARS, developed by Smith and Kendall (1963).
d) Behavioural Description Inventory, known as BDI developed by Schwind (1977).
e) Conventional Rating Scales.

BES, BOS, BARS and most recently BDI grew out of the identification of common errors with Conventional Rating Scales, the intuitive relevance and validity of the Critical Incident Technique, and a theoretical shift towards the acceptance of appraiser expertise in appraisee job-relevant areas, ideas which were originally espoused by Smith and Kendall (1963). BES, BOS and BARS differ slightly in their development procedures but result in a set of criterion scales selected and agreed upon by job-knowledgeable appraisers. Scale points are illustrated by specific incidents of behaviour, again selected and agreed by appraisers as typical of performance on that criterion and are positioned according to the degree of effectiveness illustrated.

The main difference between these methods concerns the nature of judgement the appraiser is required to make. In BES, the appraiser is asked to identify the behaviour which most closely describes that which he would expect the appraisee to exhibit. With BOS the appraiser is asked to check each incident according to the frequency with which the behaviour has actually been observed. BARS can take either of these forms, but the term is used generically in reference to the original and innovative criterion development technique from which the others derived.

Finally, Conventional Rating Scales take many forms. They may be roughly categorised as either the traditional Graphic Rating Scale where the appraiser is required to make a numerical evaluation of personality traits thought relevant to the job (or make a general evaluation on a numerical scale of job performance), or the contemporary Graphic Rating Scales on which the rater is required to make an evaluation of performance according to job-relevant factors (which are generally loosely defined, e.g. quality of work) each of which is represented by a scale labelled with evaluations such as below average/slightly below average etc. The properties of Conventional Rating Scales have been well-researched, documented and frequently reviewed (see for example, Guion 1965) so it is not the intention to repeat all the findings here. Poignant characteristics of CRS are covered by method-comparison studies and these are referred to below.

As this category of Absolute Standards Procedures encompasses many methods the discussion will focus on the main qualitative and the contemporarily popular quantitative techniques.

Validity. Whisler and Harper (1962) commented on the technical effectiveness of the Critical Incident Technique (CIT). Flanagan's innovative methodology was generated in response to the mounting discontent with conventional assessment practices and Flanagan and Burns (1957), comparing CIT to Conventional Rating Scales, found the CIT to yield superior validity of assessments, higher face validity to assessors and to be of greater utility. Andersson and Nilsson (1964), concurred that CIT provides comprehensive and valid measures of work performance. Contemporaneously with CIT development, Sisson (1948), comparing the properties of Forced Choice rating with conventional procedures, was able to show higher validity coefficients for the newer technique.

Both CIT and Forced Choice were undoubtedly able to improve on the validity of their predecessors but, as Cozan (1955) pointed out, while this may have been true, the coefficients rendered could only be called modest. Additionally, in respect of Forced Choice procedure, these early claims were not always borne out in practice. In other words, both techniques may have been an improvement on the currently available alternatives, but would probably meet with a lower level of enthusiasm nowadays.

The apparent validities of CIT, however, provided a promising base for Smith and Kendall's (1963) Behaviourally Anchored Rating Scale method. While validity studies of BARS (BES, BOS) procedures have been sporadic, Schwab, Heneman and DeCotiis (1975b) noted in their review that rater participation in scale development adds to the content and face validity of the scales generated because it ensures that the illustrative incidents are comprehensive in their coverage of the performance domain. And, Keaveny and McGann (1975), comparing BES and Graphic Ratings Scales (GRS), found BES to increase the precision in scale usage and hence to exhibit higher discriminant validity.

By and large, research has focussed on means of increasing validity rather than investigating validity per se. Borman (1974) for example, suggested BES validity to be a group-dependent phenomenon, while Dickinson and Tice (1977) found discriminant validity to be enhanced by rater training and by substituting statistical factor analysis for the intuitive factor analysis characteristic of Smith and Kendall's (1963)

BARS development procedure. They also found validity to be increased where more stringent criteria were placed on the degree of agreement required between job-knowledgeable judges in the course of BARS development and where <u>actual</u> raters participated in scale development.

<u>Reliability</u>. Andersson and Nilsson (1964) found that the stability of CIT incident categories was independent of the method of collection, that all important job performance areas were accounted for and that inter-judge agreement on critical job aspects was high, and so concluded that the 'information collected by this method is reliable' p.402. While Smith (1976) provided no hard evidence, she did question the effect on reliability of differential opportunities to observe behaviour and of selective recall of the behaviour observed.

Smith's (1976) review of Forced Choice methods confirmed that their strengths lay in validity and freedom from bias. However, she remarked that in practice the concealed scoring format often leads to a contest between the administrator and a rater intent on 'beating the system'. Such practices may well bear upon resultant reliability.

Schwab et al, (1975a) hypothesized that the use of meaningful and shared terminology in BARS would lead to higher reliabilities and this was borne out in Smith's (1976) review. Several studies (Smith and Kendall 1963, Landy and Guion 1970, and Fogli, Hulin and Blood 1971) have demonstrated the internal consistency of scales by finding high reliability coefficients where separate groups of judges allocate behavioural incidents to scale points. With respect to inter-rater reliability, studies comparing BARS with other rating methods (Williams and Seiler 1973, Borman and Vallon 1974, Bernardin 1977 and Latham and Wexley 1977) have all yielded higher coefficients for the behavioural scales.

However, inter-rater reliability may not be an inherent property of BARS. Zedeck, Imparato, Krausz and Oleno (1974) found it to be rater group-dependent, and Borman (1974) found inter-rater reliability to be higher on scales developed by the actual raters than by other job-knowledgeable judges. Such dissentions led Schwab et al, (1975b) to doubt BARS as a recipe for inter-rater reliability, but since then research has advanced to include other considerations that might question this initial conclusion. For example, Latham and Wexley (1977) were able to establish higher inter-rater reliabilities through factor-analytically derived performance dimensions. Bernardin and Walter (1977) were able to increase inter-rater reliability through rater training, and Bernardin (1977) suggested that other elements of the rating situation such as rater-ratee interaction effects, rater motivation, ratee performance and attitudinal responses to appraisal, might similarly be considered to effect reliability. This suggests that scope remains, in these areas at least, to improve on what has already been seen to be moderate inter-rater reliability.

<u>Freedom from bias</u>. While the behavioural orientation of CIT precludes the obvious effects of bias (e.g. leniency and logical rating error)

characteristic of numerical scaling methods, Smith (1976) pointed out that as CIT requires the appraiser to observe and record incidents of behaviour, it is susceptible to selective recall which is questionably accurate especially where the appraiser has insufficient opportunity to observe behaviour (as is the case with most managerial jobs). As the Forced Choice method presents an 'opaque' instrument to the appraiser, where items are equated for favourability, it has been successful in reducing deliberate rater bias (Sisson 1948). Taylor and Wherry (1951) similarly found evidence of less skew in Forced Choice than CRS ratings. Whilst agreeing that Forced Choice method clearly reduced rater bias, Cozan (1955) questioned whether, given the need to train raters, develop different tetrads for different groups, establish agreement on what constituted success and failure, and above all, to persuade raters to use an opaque evaluation instrument, this singular proven advantage warranted the time, cost and effort required for development.

While Smith and Kendall (1963) and Schwab et al, (1975b) claimed that the BARS development process is likely to lead to a reduction of rating bias, studies comparing BARS with numerically anchored scales (Campbell, Dunnette, Arvey and Hellervik 1973 and Borman and Vallon 1974) have yielded conflicting results. Keaveny and McGann (1975) found BES to display less leniency error and halo effect than GRS. However, Burnaska and Hollmann (1974) found that all levels of halo effect were still excessive and Bernardin, Alvares and Cranny (1976), comparing BES with Summated Rating Scales, while finding less halo with BES, found them to exhibit greater leniency error. In short, the results on bias are inconclusive. By way of explanation, Schwab et al, (1975b) questioned the methodologies used in comparison studies and Bernardin, Alvares and Cranny (1976) maintained that the incidence of leniency error was not an inherent characteristic of the instrument but of the rigour of instrument development. This prompted Bernardin, LaShells, Smith and Alvares (1976) to investigate the effects of different formats and development procedures and they found that aspects such as the use of performance dimension clarification statements and adherence to Smith and Kendall's (1963) original rating procedure both reduced the leniency error and increased rating variability. Schwab et al, (1975b), in pursuance of this point, strongly urged researchers to consider other sources of variance in evaluation scores, specifically, the evaluatee, evaluator and evaluation context. This is a direction which has shown great promise. Borman (1975) showed that the training of raters in reducing halo does in fact do so, a finding reinforced by Bernardin and Walter (1977) who were also able to reduce leniency in the same manner. Cascio and Valenzi (1977), investigating the effects of rater/ratee experience/ education on BARS ratings, noted significant but weak interactional effects and found that such considerations in methodology could reduce bias in ratings but halo and leniency were still evident. And, finally, the most promising development appears to be through the work of Schneier (1977) who found that cognitively complex raters, in contrast with cognitively simple raters, exhibited consistently less bias, leniency and halo errors. While he suggested that this has implications for the potential of rater training, far more important perhaps is his conclusion that characteristics of the rater (in this case, cognitive complexity) are important, and should be considered as moderating variables in the rating situation and that these previously uncontrolled variables may well account for the conflicting results of previous research where emphasis has been on the instrument.

Relevance. Flanagan and Burns (1957) emphasised the powerful effect of appraiser participation in CIT on method acceptability and utility. Smith (1976) endorsed the job behaviour orientation and relevance of CIT but with some reservation about the means of criteria determination, arguing that it is clearly possible to observe job behaviours which are remote from organisation purposes. This reflects the distinction made by Campbell et al, (1970) between behaviour at work and job performance, the point being that CIT may be more or less relevant depending on the behaviour domains on which the assessor focusses. Research on the relevance of Forced Choice Procedure is sparse. Taylor and Wherry (1951) found GRS to have more meaning than Forced Choice tetrads to the rater, but then this may be a function of the deliberate opaqueness of the instrument. However, Smith's (1976) reservations must hold here too.

The relevance of BARS has been from its inception its undisputed strength. Smith and Kendall (1963) initially stressed the need for an assessment instrument couched in assessor's terminology and Schwab et al (1975b) added that the job behaviour nature of BARS and, perhaps more significantly, rater participation in scale development, helped to ensure the choice of appropriate and relevant performance dimensions. Bernardin, Alvares and Cranny (1976) likewise concluded that BES provided the much needed behavioural specification in performance assessment. In short, relevance appears to be a major strength of these Quantitative Absolute Standards Procedures.

Discriminability. Discriminability is a strength of CIT, inherent in its behavioural specificity. Flanagan's CIT capitalized on the appraiser's ability to make finer discriminations about performance than contemporary assessment techniques permitted. Similarly, Sisson (1948) found Forced Choice Procedure to demonstrate higher discriminability than conventional methods.

In BARS research two forms of discriminability have been examined. First, and more commonly, it has been examined in the context of scale usage, i.e. the extent to which performance discriminations can be made along the continuum, and secondly, in reference to scale independence, i.e. the extent to which separate scales represent distinct performance criteria to the rater or measure different aspects of performance.

Smith and Kendall (1963) found that the 'retranslation' process in BARS development increased discriminability and reduced central tendency effect. Bernardin, Alvares and Cranny (1976) found no difference in discriminability between their BES and Summated Rating Scales but in the Bernardin, LaShells, Smith and Alvares (1976) study, the use of dimension clarification statements and the original Smith and Kendall

22

rating procedure improved discriminability. As with freedom from bias, the same pattern seems to be emerging, that is discriminability may be much more a function of the appraiser than the instrument. And, in fact, Schneier's (1977) finding that cognitively complex raters show less restriction of range, supports this contention.

As for scale dependence, results have been inconclusive. Campbell et al, (1973), comparing BARS with numerically anchored scales, found greater scale independence of BARS. In contrast, Arvey and Hoyle (1974) and Borman and Vallon (1974), in similar studies, found no significant differences in scale inter-correlations. Each of these studies was conducted in the milieu of instrument-oriented research. Perhaps by considering wider aspects of the assessment situation, such as those to have shown promise in the research of other instrument properties, more definite conclusions may be made.

Finally, comment should be made on the level of measurement attained by these instruments. The quantitative techniques, BOS, BES, BARS, BDI and Conventional Rating Scales, quite plainly strive for performance information at the interval level. Similarly, Forced Choice Procedure and Weighted Checklist provide interval level data, although the rater only makes qualitative statements. While the CIT quite clearly has interval level potential, its main strength lies in the quality of information it provides for feedback and training purposes, so in practice it may only achieve nominal level measurement.

Nature and degree of appraiser judgement. The demands on appraiser judgement made by these Absolute Standards Procedures vary considerably. Qualitative methods may or may not involve the appraiser in constructing the behavioural categories and in locating incidents on an effectiveness continuum within them. If involved, the appraiser is required to make these judgements about performance criteria and standards but these are constrained by the need for consensus among job-knowledgeable judges. As the name implies, the Qualitative methods do not require any numerical assessment to be made knowingly by the appraiser, but the appraisers are required to exercise some assessment judgement, the degree of which depends on the specific method adopted. The Weighted Checklist presents a simple judgement task, the appraiser being required to make 'does/does not exhibit behaviour' decisions. With Forced Choice Procedure, alternatives are introduced, the appraiser being asked to identify the behaviours most and least typical of the ratee, and so there is an associated increase in the judgement required. Clearly, effectiveness relies on the appraiser's observational skills and perceptual acuity. CIT adds a further dimension to the assessment judgement task. In identifying, describing and recording critical behaviours representative of the behavioural category, and locating these within the array of critical incidents presented, the appraiser's task requires not only observational powers and perceptual acuity but calls for accuracy and verbal fluency in the recall of behavioural events.

The Quantitative techniques can be conveniently divided. Conventional

Rating Scales provide the rater with explicit performance criteria and standards, thereby removing the need for these judgements. The major task for the rater is in making an assessment judgement, typically on a numerical scale with 5 to 11 points or on a loosely defined verbal scale. The onus is on the rater to interpret the scale meaning and arrive at a graded evaluation of ratee performance. The documented problems with accuracy and reliability of these scales suggests that, while apparently conceptually simple, they present an assessment judgement task which is beyond the ability of many raters.

In contrast to these, making judgements about performance criteria and standards is central to the appraiser's task with behaviourally-based scales. Appraisers provide critical performance criteria and behavioural incidents during the development of BARS, BES, BOS, and BDI. Resultant criteria and illustrative incidents are checked for clarity and relevance by a 'retranslation' procedure to ensure that scale meanings are shared and understood. So, these methods require both criterion and standard judgements from the appraiser but the resultant scales reflect only those judgements which are agreed by all appraisers. This process makes scale usage easier, i.e. the appraiser's assessment judgement task is made easier by the use of unambiguous and clearly defined scales expressed in familiar terminology, but it still relies on the observational powers and perceptual acuity of the appraiser.

As noted above, the variants of BARS place slightly different assessment judgement demands on the appraiser and it has been argued that because of this, these methods have differential utility across situations. Specifically, Latham and Wexley (1977) suggested that BOS are preferable where there is a high degree of contact between appraiser and appraisee while BES are preferable where degree of contact is low.

Nature of criteria used. The performance criteria embodied in CIT are derived through a content analysis by the instrument designer of critical incidents of performance collected from appraisers. They are therefore job-specific, behaviourally-defined and multiple. The Weighted Checklist development procedure is aimed at achieving the same behavioural and job specificity but statements are not grouped, nor are they all performance-relevant, so each statement represents a criterion of greater or lesser importance. The Forced Choice Procedure similarly produces job-specific behavioural statements which are grouped by the instrument designer into common behavioural categories and reduced to tetrads balanced for performance-relevant and -irrelevant behaviour.

While Conventional Rating Scales come in various forms they may be typified by multiple, trait-oriented or multiple/singular, performance characteristic criteria, stipulated by the instrument designer and anchored by either numerical grades or evaluative statements. Behaviourally Anchored Rating Scales embody criteria which are generated and agreed by appraisers, which are behavioural and job-task as opposed to trait-oriented, and numerical. In addition they are anchored by performance-relevant behaviours.

Work Sample Tests (applicable to semi-skilled and skilled jobs) and Situational Tests (applicable to executive and management jobs) are classified as Performance Tests as they both simulate a real work task, providing a standardized sample of job-behaviour which permits comparison between appraisees. While most widely used as predictors in employee selection, Work Sample Tests are also used as selection criteria and have been used as trainability tests (Robertson and Downs, 1979). Situational Tests are seldom used as job proficiency criteria but are used for management potential-spotting and their use as trainability measures is being extended (Gill, 1980).

Neither of these types of tests measure actual job performance so they may appear to be an unlikely inclusion were. However, they share common purposes with appraisal techniques (i.e. employee development, training need diagnosis, potential-spotting, etc.). Moreover advances are being made in extending their application and, perhaps most importantly, they provide standardized tasks upon which abilities and behaviours of job-holders at equivalent levels may be compared, so their exclusion from a consideration of performance measurement methods may be harder to justify.

Typing and stenographic tests were among the first Work Sample Tests to be developed and tests of this nature are still used in employee selection for some skilled jobs. Historically, simulations became increasingly complex, evolving to the stage where the work setting was not precisely duplicated, but rather the assessee was placed in a situation where he was asked to solve the same type of problem that he would encounter in the real work environment. The earliest reported use of such 'situational tests' was by O.S.S. (1948) and this heralded the development of the Situational Test, as the Work Sample Test for managers, which as Campbell et al, (1970) observed, takes into account the situational determinants of performance.

Situational Tests vary considerably in content and format because they are often privately developed or undergo organisation-specific modification (Finkle, 1976). However, the most popular basic formats are the individual problem-solving In-Basket Exercise, and the group problem-solving exercise, Leaderless Group Discussion (LGD).

The In-Basket Exercise was introduced in the early 50's by Frederiksen, Saunders and Wand (1957) and its industrial application reviewed by Lopez (1966). The exercise is structured round the In-Basket, which might typically include in-coming mail, memos, reports, etc., and the assessee is instructed to role-play the part of the manager and given limited time to handle the In-Basket material. The exercise is designed to simulate everyday decisions and the way these are handled is quantitatively scored on a variety of dimensions (Lopez, 1966) from which a composite evaluation of performance is developed. It may be used as a selection device, as a means of identifying potential or as a management development aid.

The Leaderless Group Discussion (LGD) exercise, initiated by Bass (1954), requires a group of assessees to discuss a given topic and arrive at a decision while assessors observe and rate the performance of each assessee according to specified criteria. Typically, the assessors are looking for the assessees' abilities to communicate effectively, overcome group or individual inertia, solve various interaction problems, meet deadlines and drive for group consensus, each of which are considered to be important in successful management performance.

Finally, it is the growing practice to combine these performance measures with other types of tests in a managerial assessment package, an idea pioneered by American Telephone and Telegraph Co. Porter, Lawler and Hackman (1975) and Finkle (1976) have identified the uses to which the Assessment Centre method is directed as potential-spotting, employee selection, performance development and counselling. This multiple assessment procedure crosses the bounds of the definition of Performance Tests but it is an accelerating growth area and Performance Tests tend to form a large and integral part.

Validity. In a study of managers attending an Assessment Centre, Bray and Grant (1966) found both In-Basket and LGD scores to be predictive of assessment ratings and of subsequent salary progression (taken as a criterion of job proficiency). This finding of internal and external validity was later reinforced by Wollowick and McNamara (1969) and Porter et al, (1975).

As Campbell et al, (1970) pointed out, the opportunity exists with In-Basket technique to elicit a rich array of behaviour samples representative of performance and this suggests that the content, construct and therefore predictive validity of In-Basket can be expected to be high. And indeed, Meyer's (1970) findings showed the results to be significantly related to job performance ratings. Likewise, Bass (1954) has demonstrated the predictive validity of LGD for a number of jobs and occupational levels.

Despite the favourable findings, the validity potential of Situational Tests appears limited. While they may satisfactorily measure managerial ability Porter et al, (1975) shared Campbell et al's, (1970) reservation that they overlook the motivational aspect of job performance and suggested that results may in fact be contaminated by motivations specific to 'test' conditions. Secondly, unlike Work Sample Tests, where perfect predictive validity is a realistic aim through careful specification of the performance domain, the potential predictive validity of Situational Tests is necessarily limited as they focus on underlying abilities and traits and are therefore less accurate reflections of the actual work situation.

Early validity studies gave favourable prognoses for the use of Assessment Centres in managerial selection but again initial results have

26

later been questioned. Wollowick and McNamara (1969) found it necessary to suggest techniques for enhancing predictive validity and Campbell et al, (1970) showed concern about possible criterion contamination, querying the accuracy of validity coefficients. Finally, Finkle (1976) argued that the validation of the Assessment Centre method is necessarily difficult because of the variety of purposes for which it is used which in turn necessitate different validation techniques. He added that validation for promotion purposes is difficult because it assumes a relatively fixed set of success-related characteristics and that the validation process for employee development purposes is so complex that it is often the practice to waive validation entirely.

In summary, Work Sample and Situational Tests have been shown to yield high predictive validity when used for selection purposes, and they are capable, to differing degrees, of high descriptive validities. While initial results on Assessment Centre method validity were encouraging, subsequent research suggests that validation for certain purposes is difficult and rarely carried out, that validity coefficients may not be accurate and that validity can certainly be improved.

Reliability. Because Work Sample and Situational Tests permit direct behaviour observation in a well-structured and standardized stimulus configuration they might be expected to exhibit high inter-rater and test-retest reliability and indeed results have been supportive of this expectation. Bass (1954) and Greenwood and McNamara (1967) found high reliabilities for LGD and Bray and Grant (1966) found similarly favourable results with In-Basket. While Landy and Trumbo (1976) observed that reliability appears to be somewhat independent of test content, there is evidence to suggest that reliability is influenced by test conditions. Bass (1954) found higher inter-rater reliabilities of LGD when descriptive behaviour checklists were provided for assessors, Bass and Norton (1951) found inter-rater reliability to be a function of LGD group size and Finkle (1976) found the inter-rater reliability of In-Basket to be higher when it is used in a highly quantified, actuarially-supported fashion than when it is treated in a subjective interview-based, almost clinical fashion.

While similarly favourable reliability estimates may be found for the Assessment Centre method, Finkle (1976) underlined the situational-specific nature of these, observing that reliability assumes a recognised set of critical success requirements as well as common knowledge of and agreement on these among assessors. Such conditions will obviously vary from one situation to the next. In summary, despite the logical reduction in error brought about by the standardization of conditions in Situational Tests, reliability estimates vary across test situations according to variations in procedure.

Freedom from bias. Because Situational Tests involve a process of inference, the assessor inferring general administrative skill from a particular sample of administrative behaviour for example, both main types provide an opportunity for assessor bias. Carlson (1972) argued

27

this may not be dysfunctional, observing that, where reliability estimates are independent of test content, it would appear that assessors can agree on ratings of general 'person-quality' and so evaluations probably involve a 'valid halo effect'. While this may be true it is evident that variations in test conditions provide the opportunities for bias which have proved dysfunctional in respect of other measurement methods already discussed.

Although Bass (1954) contended that LGD encouraged assessors to research and evaluate immediate behaviour only, Campbell et al, (1970) pointed out that assessors are often required to infer a number of assessee characteristics and to make behaviour predictions. In addition, Finkle (1976) reported that assessment interviews on In-Basket performance required the assessor to judge assessee skills and abilities according to prescribed standards and/or their own views. The admission of such implicit criteria provides the opportunity for contaminating bias. In addition, Campbell et al's (1970) criticism of Assessment Centres is that the clinical judgements which are frequently required suffer from lack of specification as to how they are made. Further, Wollowick and McNamara's (1969) finding that the statistical combination of programme variables yielded higher predictive validity than subjectively-derived overall ratings suggests that these clinical judgements are contaminated.

In summary, while these methods which involve direct observation of standardized samples of behaviour may claim some forms of psychometric superiority, in the final analysis, performance evaluations may be achieved by any of the range of techniques previously discussed and therefore they are as likely to exhibit bias as the particular technique adopted.

Relevance. It is necessary here to distinguish between the relevance of test content and that of the criteria used. Although Finkle (1976) observed that the Assessment Centre method appeals to businessmen because of its apparent relevance, and Bray and Grant (1966) found appraisers to regard Situational Tests as highly relevant, these findings only reflect the construct and content validity of the tests, not the relevance of the criteria on which test performance is evaluated. As Campbell et al, (1970) argued, the introduction of situational elements such as telephone calls, personal appearances, interruptions etc, which typify the conditions under which any executive task is done, clearly enhances the relevance of any exercise which tests managerial effectiveness. However, this does not ensure the relevance of test criteria.

It is evident that a wide variety of performance criteria are used in Situational Tests. For example, Lopez (1966) listed some dimensions on which In-Basket performance can be judged and referred to several other comparable lists. Finkle (1976) contrasted the highly explicit, quantified, actuarially-monitored performance criteria in one use of the In-Basket with the implicit subjective, clinically-monitored performance criteria in another. So there is a wide variation in the performance

28

criteria adopted. In fact, as the proponents would argue, performance criteria need to be flexible and determined for each test situation by job-level, assessment purpose, assessors' characteristics etc. in order to be effective. To draw firm conclusions then about criterion relevance is difficult, if not inappropriate, but Performance Tests are as likely to be relevant as the criteria used in any of the other measurement methods and for that reason, relevance will be a function of the rigour of criterion development.

Discriminability. As Finkle (1976) and others have pointed out, Situational Tests and Assessment Centre programmes are instrumental in achieving a variety of purposes and so may produce various kinds of data. For example, quantitative data may be combined statistically to derive an overall performance evaluation at the interval level of measurement, or qualitative data at the normative level may be sought for feedback, counselling or developmental purposes. The degree of discriminability of Situational Tests will vary with level of measurement and it would be reasonable to infer it as high where predictive validity is high.

Nature and degree of appraiser judgement. There is a wide range of judgement behaviours required of Performance Test assessors and the type of test does not necessarily define the type of judgements required. However, some broad generalizations are possible.

The Work Sample Test is perhaps the least demanding of the assessor. Criteria of speed, accuracy, quality, etc., are preset and, where in concurrent validation studies test performance is used as both criterion and predictor, then performance standards are set by current employees. The assessor is therefore relieved of making judgements about criteria or standards but required to make a performance assessment in terms of well-defined operational criteria. The task may therefore only involve the recording and reporting of time spent, number of mistakes, etc.

All of the Situational Tests place greater demands on the assessor. Campbell et al, (1970) noted that while LGD performance is purportedly assessed in terms of behavioural criteria, the assessor is often required to infer a number of assessee characteristics, i.e. inadequate criterion definition may necessitate interpretation, so in effect the assessor is required to make judgements about criteria. Secondly, the assessment judgement is somewhat speculative, as the assessor is often asked to predict future assessee behaviour in situations involving personal interaction.

The purposes of the In-Basket exercise strongly determine the assessor's judgement task. This might vary from a statistically-aided quantitative judgement, derived from an inspection of In-Basket material, to a qualitative judgement derived from a review of the assessee's reasons for his In-Basket behaviour. Clearly, these judgements differ in nature and in terms of the cognitive demands made of the assessor. As Finkle (1976) noted, in follow-up interviews on In-Basket, the assessors can be asked to rely on their own views of performance standards. By implication, the judgement that is made depends on the assessor's interviewing skill, his perceptual acuity and his conception of acceptable standards of performance. In addition, while the In-Basket criteria may be pre-specified (Lopez 1966), assessors are often invited to make criterion judgements in order to take account of different purposes and their use at different managerial levels. However, these judgements are usually subject to agreement by other job-knowledgeable assessors.

Clearly, the Assessment Centre method, embodying the above techniques, can require the entire range of assessor judgements but perhaps the most important assessor task is the judgement of appropriate performance criteria, because as Finkle (1976) pointed out, the Assessment Centre method assumes common knowledge and agreement among assessors as to the managerial and administrative skills that will indicate a capacity to meet the critical job requirements.

Nature of criteria used. Performance Test criteria are normally multiple and situation-specific. The extent to which they are behavioural and job-relevant depends on the specific test. Almost without exception, Work Sample Tests, incorporating elements of actual job performance, are both behavioural and job-relevant. With the more sophisticated Situational Tests the focus is still on behaviour but the criteria are expressed in terms of the underlying abilities or traits thought to be important in effective management. The outcome of either main type of Situational Test may be expressed in either quantitative (multiple or composite) or qualitative form. The outcome of the Assessment Centre method may be either a composite evaluation (where the multiple criteria are either subjectively or statistically weighted) or global estimates of success.

A potential problem with the criteria used in Situational Tests and the Assessment Centre method is the paradox that, while on one hand these assessment methods are built on the concept of situational determinism of performance effectiveness and therefore criterion dynamism, the notion of prediction itself presumes a relatively stable set of success-related characteristics.

Direct Indices

These are measures of job behaviour outcomes, expressed in terms which are relevant to organisational effectiveness. The adoption of Direct Indices as performance measures grew out of a general dissatisfaction with the more subjective alternatives (Cummings and Schwab 1973) and as Landy and Trumbo (1976) explained their main attraction lay in their perceived relevance to organisational goals. These direct measures of performance can be categorised as Objective or Personnel data.

Objective data include varieties of information about individual productivity or, in the case of a manager, the productivity of the subordinate group. The most widely used variables are output measures i.e. simply a count of the results of work. Such indices include sales volume, scrappage rates, standard unit processing costs, profit margins, machine down-time, or any other measures of output quality and/or quantity.

Personnel data include varieties of information about the job holder or, if taken as an index of managerial performance, information about his subordinates. These may be indices of salary level, type of salary adjustment, seniority, rate of advancement, organisational level and/or incidence of accidents, grievance, employee turnover, absenteeism, tardiness.

Validity. Campbell et al, (1970) and Landy and Trumbo (1976) seriously questioned the validity of Direct Indices as individual performance measures on the basis that they suffer from criterion deficiency (i.e. they fail to tap more than a small part of performance variance) and criterion contamination (i.e. some criterion variance is due to factors other than job holder behaviour). While directing these criticisms at the use of Direct Indices as measures of managerial performance, both groups of writers regarded this as a general problem.

Many studies (Merrihue and Katzell 1955, Stark 1959, Enell and Haas 1960, Turner 1960, Hulin 1962) have attempted to derive valid, objective measures of managerial performance. Guion's (1965) review of these concluded that Objective data were not likely to yield satisfactory measures of management performance, and, in agreement, Ronan (1970) explained that the nature of managerial work is such that immediately observable products or results are virtually non-existent. Objective measures can have a high degree of construct validity, for example, in production jobs where output is clearly definable and the worker is largely responsible for both quality and quantity but, of course, many tasks do not have these characteristics. Where outcomes are not clearly definable or attributable directly to the individual, then measures of productivity tend to be deficient indicators of performance.

In respect of Personnel data, Landy and Trumbo (1976) identified two reasons why validation is difficult and why quoted validity of these measures is suspect. With basic indices such as measures of absence or employee turnover, quoted validity coefficients vary considerably because of the variety of ways in which they are computed, e.g. different results accrue from computing absence in terms of absolute no. of days or as a no. of absences. In addition, measures may be confounded by failure to distinguish excused from non-excused absence and voluntary from involuntary turnover (recognising that the latter distinction is often difficult to make). With other Personnel data measures such as seniority, rate of advancement or type of salary adjustment, there is a high chance of criterion contamination where such factors as informal quota systems, economic conditions, etc., act as confounding variables.

In summary, despite the intuitive appeal of performance measures closely linked to organisational effectiveness, the shift from measuring behaviour to measuring behaviour outcomes is often associated with criterion contamination and even for those indices not so obviously effected by confounding variables, there can be validation difficulties.

Reliability. A major advantage of Direct Indices is their avoidance of the problems of constant errors associated with more 'subjective' measures because the measurement procedure is well-defined. This implies that Direct Indices will exhibit high inter-appraiser reliability. However, a distinction must be made between accuracy and reliability. While there may be little error in the counting process, if such measures are taken over short time periods they may not provide a representative estimate of individual output (Landy and Trumbo, 1976). This is to say that the reliability of objective measures may well depend on the time scale of measurement. Other moderating variables have also been noted e.g. Rothe and Nye (1959) discovered that 'type of pay' effected the stability of production data and Weitz and Nuckols (1953) found that sales productivity data reliability depended on adjustment being made for moderating variables such as sales territory size. Smith (1976), commenting on the reliability of Direct Indices of performance, summarized the threats to reliability as being variability in means of recording with Personnel data and the influence of situational factors (moderating variables) on Objective data.

Freedom from Bias. Because performance assessment does not rely on appraiser judgements, Direct Indices would appear to be relatively free of bias. While perhaps true of Objective data, Campbell et al, (1970) questioned this assumption with some forms of Personnel data. For example, when salary, rate of advancement or organisational level are taken as performance measures, they reflect pooled estimates of many supervisors' judgements over an individual's career, and this means that measure accuracy is limited by the quality of these previous judgements. In short, some forms of Personnel data are only quasi-objective because they ultimately rely on those subjective judgements, with their inbuilt opportunity for bias, that Direct Indices are assumed to avoid.

Relevance. Quite clearly, Direct Indices have some face validity and this is one of their major advantages. As Patton (1960) pointed out, objective measures are more readily understood by subordinates and are easier to explain because they are in quantitative terms which are part of the operating language of the business. However, as some writers have observed (Cummings and Schwab 1973, Smith 1976), this advantage may be overstated in that some aspects of organisational effectiveness are much easier to couch in objective terms than others, perhaps biasing criteria in favour of the obvious and the short term. As far as relevance is concerned, the danger lies in using deficient direct measures to the exclusion of other indices, so that the focus is on those subsets of the task that happen to be directly observable. This danger is all the more real when, for jobs which are further up the organisational hierarchy, few objective measures are meaningful. Additionally, Smith (1976) made the important point that some Direct Indices are less than directly related to organisational effectiveness. She suggested, for example, that attendance data should be regarded as of a short-term, medium-specific nature and should not be expected to relate closely to more general long-term organisational goals.

Discriminability. As Objective and Personnel data yield performance information at the interval level of measurement they are theoretically capable of high discrimination. However, discriminability also depends on the task and more specifically on the relationship between the measure and job performance such that scores achieved by effective and ineffective performers are markedly different. Locating such a measure is not easy and Landy and Trumbo (1976) observed that technological changes in the nature of work are making this task more difficult. For example, as manual operations become automated, machine operators become machine minders and, if only Objective data are considered, no differential performance data can be obtained unless the machine malfunctions. Remembering that Objective data are at their most useful in direct production jobs, this is a significant problem.

Nature and degree of appraiser judgement. As Direct Index performance criteria are set by a third-party the appraiser is relieved of the criterion judgement task, and as the appraiser typically records frequency, quality or quantity of behaviour results by a well-defined procedure the assessment judgement is simple. Cummings and Schwab (1973) typified Direct Indices as performance measures obtained without the necessity of the performance behaviour being filtered through the evaluative process of the appraiser, thereby removing the errors attributable to appraiser influence. They saw this as a major advantage but appraiser judgement is not completely obviated because performance standards need to be set, i.e. decisions need to be made about what levels of absence, turnover, production (quality and quantity) etc. constitute good performance. While standards may be set by a third party who is knowledgeable of organisational goals, it is only the job-knowledgeable appraiser, aware of the moderating and confounding variables mentioned above, who can arrive at standard judgements. Judgemental accuracy will depend on the degree to which the appraiser is aware of contaminating factors and the weighting he attributes to them. So while on one hand, Direct Indices eradicate sources of error in the important areas of criterion and assessment judgement, and make the appraiser's task easier, the standard judgement task required of the appraiser is not inconsiderable. In fact, the appraiser is asked to perform a judgement task that research has shown to be difficult.

Nature of criteria used. Objective and Personnel data are performance criteria which may be used in a direct or indirect fashion. For example, output measures may be taken to represent the performance level of an individual, while subordinate attendance, for example, may be taken as an indicator of managerial performance. Although Personnel data include singular, global measures of performance such as rate of advancement, most Direct Indices are not used in isolation. It is more common for several indices of output quality and quantity to be taken and so these methods generally assess performance on multiple criteria. The aim of some e.g. the Dollar Criterion (Brogden and Taylor 1950) is to arrive at a composite measure from these multiple criteria, normally in monetary terms. The problem however as pointed out by Dean (1957) lies in arriving at appropriate weightings of the sub-criteria. This is particularly difficult in the assessment of executive performance where facets of the executive activity are numerous and contribute to organisational performance in complex ways. For example, Dean (1957) observed that profit-determining activities may not be inherently good or bad because making most money often requires foregoing a high score in one activity in order to pursue another, e.g. achieving a high quality product at the sacrifice of a low manufacturing cost.

In contrast to other measures, the performance criteria of Direct Indices are more explicitly determined by organisational goals. However, as Landy and Trumbo (1976) noted, adequate performance criteria are based on a knowledge of how individual behaviours combine to yield certain performance profiles and how these combine with environmental factors to yield organisational outcomes, but it is often the case that the choice of Direct Index criteria over-emphasises the organisational goal-relevant data at the expense of job characteristic-relevant information. In consequence, Direct Index criteria may easily be contaminated or deficient. This commonly held view is summed up by Latham and Wexley (1977). While Direct Indices may provide good criteria of organisational performance they suffer as individual performance criteria because they neglect how and why a performance is effective, commonly neglect moderating and confounding variables and often prove to be criterion deficient.

AN ANALYSIS OF PROPERTIES AND PROBLEMS

Having described the main performance measurement methods according to the bases of analysis it now becomes possible to draw several conclusions.

First, although the method evaluations are variously favourable it is clear that each method has problems in meeting some of the effectiveness criteria. This is to say that an effective performance measurement method has yet to be found.

Second, it is evident that successive methods have tried to overcome the problems of their pedecessors but that, as Kane and Lawler (1979) suggested, the potential variety has now been exhausted. This latter assertion is supported circumstantially by a recent trend in combining methods to achieve the 'best of both worlds'. For example, Leskovec (1967) suggested a combination of superior and subordinate direct and indirect types of appraisal, Carroll and Nash (1972) recommended the use of Forced Choice technique with References, Kearney (1979) recommended the use of BARS as a supplement to MbO, similarly Randell (1978) recommended the use of BARS in Active Staff Development, and Teel (1980) argued for the combined use of narrative data and Conventional Rating Scales in performance appraisal. These developments not only recognise

34

the problems of particular methods but bear witness to the continuing
need for an effective performance measurement method. While they claim
a degree of progress towards appraisal effectiveness they appear to aim
at meeting all the appraisal purposes simultaneously and if this is so a
self-imposed ceiling on improvement is to be expected.

A special concern with respect to this trend is that despite the frequent recommendations to investigate the effect of the appraiser on the
properties of appraisal, all these attempts to improve performance
measurement are instrument-oriented. The literature witnesses a low key
but perennial recognition that factors other than the instrument are important (Campbell et al, 1970) but, with the notable exception of Smith
and Kendall's (1963) work, these have been neglected in a striving towards the psychometric decency of instruments.

Thirdly, the presentation format above provides an array of methods (see
Fig. 2.1) across which method properties can be compared and property
patterns can be perceived.

With respect to validity, it appears that both construct and content
validity increase with progression down this continuum. For example,
at one end Closed Free Expression Reports rarely focus on the full range
of job-relevant behaviours while at the other end, Performance Tests
(and some multiple Direct Indices) indirectly assess a wide range of
performance activities. Similarly, inter-appraiser reliability generally increases with downward progression. However, intra-appraiser
reliability does not necessarily conform to such a pattern, suggesting
perhaps that intra-appraiser reliability is technique-independent. Discriminability too increases with progression down the continuum in conjunction with a progression from a nominal through ordinal to an interval level of measurement.

Criterion relevance is the major problem of Closed Free Expression Reports which traditionally focus on personality. But methods at the
other end of the continuum also have relevance problems in that the emphasis is on performance-outcome characteristics rather than job-
relevant behaviours. It is more obviously the methods in the middle of
the continuum, with their focus on critical job behaviours, which satisfy the relevance criterion.

In analysing the nature of appraiser judgement involved in these
measurement methods it becomes clear that there are potentially three
types of judgement which may be required. The appraiser may be asked to
exercise his judgement in a) deciding on the appropriate performance
criteria, b) deciding on the acceptable level of criterion performance
and c) deciding on an accurate evaluation of a particular individual's
behaviour. As it will become convenient to distinguish between these
they can be labelled Criterion, Standard and Assessment judgements respectively.

As any judgement task is susceptible to subjective influence, the degree

35

FIGURE 2.1

Methods of Performance Measurement

Closed, Free Expression Reports
Individual Standards Procedures
:   Management by Objectives
:   Performance Review
:   Developmental Action Programme
Comparative Standards Procedures
:   Straight Ranking
:   Alternate Ranking
:   Paired Comparison
:   Forced Distribution
Absolute Standards (Qualitative) Procedures
:   Critical Incident Technique
:   Weighted Checklist
:   Forced Choice
Absolute Standards (Quantitative) Procedures
:   Conventional Rating Scales
:   BES
:   BARS
:   BOS
:   BDI
Performance Tests
:   Leaderless Group Discussion
:   In-basket
:   Work Sample
Direct Indices
:   Objective Data
:   Personnel Data

of judgement required by a method determines the potential for subjectivity. The effectiveness of methods which require the appraiser to choose criteria, decide on acceptable standards and assess an individual relative to these (e.g. Closed Free Expression Reports) depends to a large extent on the appraiser's judgement and so permits a high degree of subjectivity. In contrast the effectiveness of those which only require the appraiser to record presence or absence of behaviour or simply count performance output (e.g. Direct Indices) depends minimally on appraiser judgement. As such they limit potential subjectivity and may be termed objective. The array in Fig. 2.1 therefore comes to represent a subjective-objective continuum where downward progression reflects a successive reduction of the three types of judgements.

Closed Free Expression Reporting requires individual Criterion, Standard and Assessment judgements and so provides the greatest potential for subjectivity. Individual Standards Procedures also require Criterion,

Standard and Assessment judgements but these are made in joint consultation with the appraisee and so subjectivity is controlled by the need to achieve appraisee agreement. Comparative Standards Procedures apparently provide criteria but as these are often vague the appraiser in effect makes the Criterion judgement. As the procedures focus on relative work standards, no Standard judgements are required and finally the Assessment judgement amounts to a simple dichotomous worse than/ better than decision. Qualitative Absolute Standards Procedures may require Criterion and Standard judgements if the appraiser is involved in instrument development, but subjectivity is controlled by the need for inter-appraiser consensus. Some degree of Assessment judgement is required but usually constitutes a simple does/does not decision about behaviour exhibited. Quantitative Absolute Standards Procedures require Criterion and Standard judgements but, as above, these are tempered by the need for inter-appraiser consensus. Within this category, there is a range in the Assessment judgement requirements of the methods. BES require judgement of expected behaviour, BARS require decisions about extent of observed behaviour, BOS require does/does not decisions about behaviour exhibited, while BDI require observed behaviour to be recorded. In summary, each involves an amount of controlled Criterion and Standard judgement but the techniques exhibit the full range of Assessment judgements. Finally, Performance Tests and Direct Indices can remove the Criterion and Standard judgement tasks completely. Performance Tests require Assessment judgement based on behaviour observation but Direct Indices place the appraiser in little more than the technician role, recording absences, levels of productive output, etc.

A parallel to this subjective-objective continuum emerges when the freedom from bias criterion is examined across the methods. While a detailed discussion of the effects of bias and its implications is reserved for Chapter 4, three aspects are worth noting here.

First, attempts to produce methods which are free from bias have concentrated on reducing the opportunity for bias to occur. Second, the opportunity for bias has typically been associated with the degree of Assessment judgement required of the appraiser. This equation may be oversimplistic, as quite clearly any form of judgement is open to subjective influence, so Criterion and Standard judgement bias is also possible. While the reduction of the opportunity for Assessment judgement bias may be a justifiable aim, it may be premature to view the former judgement biases in the same negative light without further consideration. Thirdly, Assessment judgement bias can be deliberate and appraisee-related (e.g. prejudice and falsification) or unknowing and non-appraisee related (e.g. central tendency effect, leniency error, halo effect, etc). In relation to the method continuum described (Fig. 2.1) there appears to be a distinct trend towards removing the opportunities for appraisee-related bias by reducing the amount of any appraiser judgement, whereas the reduction of non-appraisee related bias has been the major concern of those developing and refining methods in the middle of the continuum.

The final criterion adopted in the method analysis was the nature of criteria used. Again, a pattern can be discerned in this method property which is reflected in two dimensions. First, a progression from personality-oriented measures through behaviour-description measures to behavioural outcome measures has been an evident trend in the development of measurement methods. Second, a general move from global criteria through multiple criteria to composite criteria is also evident with progression down the continuum.

FUNDAMENTAL THEMES

This analysis of properties and problems yields an explanation of current concerns in performance measure development and, perhaps more importantly, provides an overview of this complex field which permits identification of features that might account for the universally-felt unsatisfactory state of affairs.

The majority of appraisal effectiveness criteria become successfully satisfied with progression down the subjective-objective continuum. This is paralleled by an 'opportunity for bias' continuum and the historical trend in instrument development has followed the line of reducing this opportunity for bias. Quite clearly, the problems of judgement bias and subjectivity have been and are a central concern in performance measurement. While practitioners and researchers alike see great advantages in the ultimate Direct Indices methods which all but eliminate bias opportunities, these have been found to have problems with criterion contamination and deficiency. So the search is still on for methods which meet the effectiveness criteria or, in other words, which are 'methodologically pure'.

But of course, some effectiveness criteria defy this general trend. Intra-appraiser reliability appears method-independent, face validity for the user apparently decreases with progression down the continuum while relevance appears to peak at the mid-continuum methods. It would seem that criterion relevance is an especially high price to pay for greater satisfaction of other effectiveness criteria. This underlying emphasis is perhaps a concern for establishing measures which are, and are seen to be, conceptually sound.

These themes perhaps reflect the different emphases of researchers and practitioners. The practitioner, focussing on utility, needs a method which has face validity and is easy to use but which avoids the problems of high degrees of subjectivity. The researcher, focussing on effective methodology, needs a method which has favourable psychometric properties but which avoids the problems of being mathematically pure whilst conceptually unsound.

In summary, from every angle, the problem appears to be the attainment of job performance measures which are both methodologically pure and conceptually sound. Many researchers have grappled with different aspects of this problem. For example, the issues of global versus composite, multiple versus singular, behavioural versus personality versus results-oriented criteria have been argued at length, achieving varying but qualified conclusions. In the continuing search for satisfactory measurement methods, evident in the above analysis, it becomes apparent that the only real alternative left is to submit to the complexity of the performance measurement problem and tackle the underlying issues head-on.

The fundamental issues appear to be:

I. The Problems of Establishing Appropriate Performance Measures (Dimensions and Criteria) At the subjective end of the method continuum problems arise with standardization, reliability and validity because the dimensions or criteria used to assess performance are uncontrolled, differ from one assessor to another and typically focus on personality traits. At the objective end, however, there are problems of criterion deficiency and contamination and the information yielded is seen to be inadequate for some measurement purposes. In other words it would seem that one major issue in performance measurement concerns the delineation of satisfactory performance descriptors. As 'satisfactory' has now been defined in terms of methodological purity and conceptual soundness two critical questions can now be posed. Given the need for a measure which is conceptually sound, of what nature should the performance dimensions or criteria be? Given the need for a measure which is methodologically pure, how should performance dimensions or criteria be derived and what qualities should they have? These issues are tackled in Chapter 3.

II. The Problems of Relying on Subjective Judgement. Throughout the development of performance measures an explicit and implicit concern has been the reduction of the bias which subjective judgement can introduce. It is now clear that different types of judgement can be involved in measurement, i.e. that bias can be introduced in several ways, and it is also clear that, even at the objective extreme, some degree of subjective judgement is always required of the appraiser. A second major issue then concerns the apparent inevitability of subjective judgement and its associated problems in performance measurement. Bearing in mind the parameters of satisfactory performance measures, two critical questions need to be answered. Given the need for a measure which is conceptually sound, what role does subjective judgement play? Given the need for a measure which is methodologically pure, how can inevitable subjectivity be accommodated? These issues will be addressed in Chapters 4 and 5.

3 Dimensions and criteria in performance measurement

The previous chapter brought into focus the problems of establishing appropriate performance measures and the problems of relying on subjective judgement as the fundamental issues in performance measurement. As the specification of critical questions associated with these two issues makes it clear that both are complex, it would seem sensible to address these issues separately and so this chapter deals with the first of these.

Establishing the nature of appropriate measures of performance has been of course the perennial concern of those who research what has come to be known as the 'Criterion Problem' and since Bechtoldt (1947) observed that 'no subject is of greater importance than the nature of the criterion to be used in evaluating performance' p.357, many distinguished researchers (Bellows 1954, Ghiselli 1956, Guion 1961, Astin 1964, James 1973, Smith 1976) have contributed significantly to its resolution. When, however, Dunnette and Borman (1979) prefaced their performance measurement review with, 'The Criterion problem has been with us for ever...' p.486 it becomes clear that, despite this sustained activity, the Criterion Problem has yet to be solved.

Through these attempts to determine the nature of effective performance measures several critical questions have been identified and addressed. Should measures be expressed in terms of behaviours, tasks, traits or organisation outcomes? Should they be multiple, singular, global or composite? Should criteria be actual or perceived, qualitative or quantitative? Should performance dimensions be mathematically or subjectively derived? Should they be verbally or numerically defined? etc. The review in Chapter 2 illustrated the wide variety of measures that have been derived, reflecting the many potential combinations of these measure characteristics and yet it demonstrated that measures which are both conceptually sound and methodologically pure have still to be identified. In the author's view the time has now come to examine the more fundamental issues. There is a need to focus in more detail and in a way that is different from previous investigations by starting from first principles and addressing the basic questions in their fundamental form. Quite simply put, the critical questions about performance measures focus on <u>what</u> to measure and <u>how</u> to measure it.

Through this chapter the author applies a definition of measurement to the performance situation, investigates critical aspects of measurement related to dimensionality and discusses the issue of dimensional choice. The special properties of 'dimensions' and 'criteria' are distinguished in order to discuss criterion development and dimensional analysis as techniques for deriving performance measures. Ultimately, findings from the fields of measurement, criterion development and behavioural assessment are drawn together to define the limits on the number and nature of appropriate performance dimensions or criteria.

CHARACTERISTICS OF MEASUREMENT SYSTEMS

The development of measurement systems is a common feature of scientification, the transition from qualitative to quantitative descriptions of phenomena being a milestone in the advance of the physical sciences (Focken, 1953). A measurement system is indeed a powerful tool and most importantly in the performance sphere it provides a means of ordering phenomena in such a way that the descriptions, comparisons and discriminations necessary for the purpose of decision-making can be made.

While there are difficulties in applying highly mathematical definitions of measurement to social science, Jones (1976) provided a semantic convention which may be useful. He defined measurement as:

'.... a purposive acquisition of information about the object, organism or event measured by the person doing the measuring. It is the determination of the magnitude of the specified attribute of the object... in terms of a unit of measurement.. expressed by a numeral'. p.336.

Although some aspects of this definition are in a sense self-evident, they do have deeper implications which will be considered below. Within his elaborated definition, then, several features of measurement can be distinguished and their application to performance measurement explored.

Measurement implies and is implied by Purpose

A fundamental aspect of measurement is that it is purposive. As Jones (1976) explained, 'different measurements (e.g. length of a table, weight of a diamond, resistance of an electric circuit) involve not only different attributes of different objects or events but also different purposes'. p.335. In other words, the measure taken immediately defines at least a range of potential purposes. He further suggested that the purpose of measurement plays an important part in defining the appropriate measure. Taking an example from the physical sciences, a property such as volume can be conceived along a single dimension or may be conceived of as a multi-dimensional function of several more primitive dimensions. While for some purposes it would be instructive to know the spatial dimensions of a body, for others, knowledge of the volume alone might be sufficient. In other words, which measure is appropriate depends on the measurement purpose. And of course the range of potential measures includes many which are even less related. The critical point is that, without a specified purpose, any number of measures may be taken with no guarantee of an appropriate one being included.

While purpose-dependency of measure choice is fundamentally accepted in the physical sciences, the fact that the performance measurement literature rarely contains statements like 'the criteria of supervisory performance for reward allocation purposes', 'the dimensions of managerial performance for development purposes' etc., or even explicitly includes such considerations in the measure development process, suggests that purpose-dependency is not generally recognised in this sphere of measurement. This is a source of concern because these considerations are necessary to the development of relevant and valid performance measures and the explicit statement of measure purpose is a logical precedent to establishing performance measure utility and generalizability.

Measurement implies Observation Conditions

Jones (1976) explained that, 'the statement about an observation necessarily must contain specification of the conditions under which it is performed' p.337. and suggested that it is in this respect that precision of psychological measurement suffers in comparison with that of physical measurement. He thus defined measurement error as that outcome of measurement attributable to unspecified conditions. These conditions are of course difficult to identify because their specification assumes knowledge of factors effecting the measured attribute and acquiring that knowledge necessarily involves the careful documentation of conditions that may or may not ultimately prove to be critical. In the performance measurement field, where the strictures of experimental control are difficult to achieve and the attribute to be measured is complex, this process must be expected to be lengthy but it has to be regarded as necessary if measurement error is to be reduced.

There have been a few writers who have explicitly added to our knowledge of these critical conditions. Astin (1964), for example, referred to the 'ecological' nature of the criterion on observing that, 'it's difficult to speak of standards of performance without also defining the social context in which it occurs'. p.808. Borman (1974), Heneman (1974) and Klimoski and London (1974), who all found that the rater's organisational level relative to the ratee determined his frame of reference, concluded that relative appraiser-appraisee position should be regarded as a 'critical condition' of performance measurement. In the clinical sphere, Hartmann, Roper and Bradford (1979) observed that different methods of measuring the same behaviour can yield very different results and thus lead to entirely different conclusions about the behaviour. In so doing they referred to the 'behaviour/method unit', suggesting that every observation reflects the method used to make it. A similar orientation in the performance measurement field, Campbell and Fiske's (1959) multi-trait/multi-method research methodology, has been tested by Nealey and Owen (1970) and Arvey and Hoyle (1974) and has been seen to be fruitful.

It is apparent that some critical conditions have been identified but are there others? Wiggins (1973), enumerated several facets relevant to behavioural assessment which included the setting (naturalistic, controlled or contrived), the observer (participant or non-participant) and the instrument. Quite clearly, performance measurement analogies need to be actively and rigorously pursued because the notion of an assessment outcome which is context-, instrument-, and observer-dependent has significant implications for criterion validation, contamination and relevance.

Measurement implies Observation and Perception

Because the conceptual definition of a phenomenon is an essential step towards its systematic observation, the beginning of measurement is the conception of the measurable attribute (Lumsden 1976).

The definition of conceptual criteria has been long-noted as problematic. Astin (1964), for example, distinguished between the conceptual criterion and the criterion measure, stating that it is normally the sponsor's responsibility to designate the former and the researcher's to develop the latter. He observed however, that a gap often exists between the two because the conceptual criterion is inadequately or ambiguously defined and this suggests in particular that all efforts towards the clarification of conceptual criteria are to be encouraged. But note that Jones' (1976) definition of measurement includes the superficially redundant phrase 'measured by the person doing the measuring'. He suggested that the adequacy of observation is a primary antecedent to the adequacy of measurement and that what is observed depends on the observer's conceptual equipment to translate sensory experience into the notion of an attribute. While apparently obvious, the neglected but significant point is that the conceptual definition should be clear at the interface between the observer and observed. This means that, for the purpose of accurate and systematic performance measurement, conceptual criterion clarity is most important, not in the mind of the researcher, sponsor, or any other than the one who is required to observe and perceive i.e. the appraiser himself.

Whereas performance measurement methods at one end of the continuum described in Chapter 2 (e.g. Closed Free Expression Reports) satisfied this condition at the expense of standardization and those at the other end (e.g. Direct Indices) whilst invoking criterion deficiency, an important step towards satisfying this condition, taking account of both performance complexity and the need for standardization, came in the mid-continuum methods and notably with Smith and Kendall's (1963) BARS procedure. Here the definition of the conceptual criterion emanates from the appraisers themselves.

Measurement implies Quantification

The final part of Jones' (1976) definition of measurement concerns quantification. For an attribute to be measurable it must fit the specifications of a quantitative variable, i.e. differences between observations must be interpretable as quantitative differences in the property measured in order that the process be one of measurement. In more mathematical terms Ellis (1966) stated that 'the existence of a quantity entails and is entailed by the existence of a set of linear ordering relationships' p.32. In relation to performance measures three points should be made. First, these authors limit their definition of measures to those with interval or ratio scale properties, a constraint that many performance measures do not observe. Second, the specification that meaningful interpretation be given to magnitude differences suggests the need for explicit statements of performance scale gradations, a constraint that only Quantitative Absolute Standards Procedures and Direct Indices observe. And third, there is the possibility that not all attributes are measurable. If there are important but non-measurable performance attributes then performance appraisal practices need to take account of these in some other way to avoid deficient coverage of the performance domain. Perhaps the tendency towards combining methods is an implicit recognition of this fundamental point, but explicit recognition would focus attention on the identification of non-measurable attributes.

Defining an attribute in quantitative terms is a necessary but not sufficient condition for its measurement. A measurement procedure also demands that a unit of measure be established and three characteristics of units can be identified. First, Jones (1976) stated that the unit of measurement chosen is quite <u>arbitrary</u>. By way of illustration we can find length expressed in units such as inches, centimetres, hands, or even barleycorns! Second, the units of different quantitative variables need not be mutually independent but, as Focken (1953) argued, for convenience and simplicity in any measurement system a minimum number of independent units should be arbitrarily defined. So he distinguished, for example, between fundamental units (in Newtonian mechanics, those of mass, space and time) and derived units (such as those of speed, force, etc.). Third, the units chosen must be consistent <u>within</u> the measurement system so that meaningful interpretation can be given to combined quantitative variable measures. For example, it makes little sense to sum feet, metres and hands. The definition of a unit of measurement therefore, is arbitrary and the choice constrained by matters of convenience and a need for consistency.

Issues regarding quantitative variables and their units have taken such a prominent part in performance measurement research that they now become the focus here. But before proceeding, two observations can be made with respect to the characteristics so far considered. First, recent advances in performance measurement research have produced measures which adhere more closely to Jones' definition of measurement but one strikingly untilled area is the purpose-dependency of appropriate measures. Second, the fact that current developments are meeting some success through implicit pursuit of measures which merit the definition strongly suggests that explicit pursuit would be fruitful and the author has suggested what avenues might open up with explicit recognition of this goal.

THE BASES OF MEASUREMENT

The quantitative variables used in performance measurement are variously referred to as dimensions or criteria. In the succeeding sections it is the aim to explore the concept of dimension and, by investigating the properties of criterion, establish the ways in which dimensions and criteria differ. The author regards this as necessary, for two reasons. First, dimension is a central concept in measurement theory and yet it is rarely defined in the performance measurement literature despite its frequent and ambiguous use. For example, dimension and criterion are sometimes used synonymously while at others dimension is used to refer to an underlying factor in criterion scores. Second, dimensions have special properties as quantitative variables that distinguish them from criteria despite the fact that they are often used interchangeably. As these terms are unavoidable in the present pursuit some clarification of definitions is therefore required.

While there are important differences between the concepts of criterion and dimension, a less than adequate definition of both as those aspects of performance which are measured, is accepted here in order to establish the major point that criterion or dimension definition is a matter of choice, like that of unit choice, which is arbitrary and subject to matters of convenience.

Several authors (e.g. Bechtoldt 1951, Hulin 1962) have suggested that criterion validity can be evaluated in terms of intercorrelations among the measures, but the notion of validating the criterion has been questioned. Astin (1964) argued that the only method of criterion validation is through a logical analysis of its <u>relevance</u> to the conceptual criterion and he observed how frequently this is over-looked in discussions of criterion development. In short, the validity of a criterion depends on its <u>judged</u> relevance to that which is to be predicted. This ties in with the previously discussed purpose-dependent nature of measure choice. The author suggests that there will always be performance measures which are irrelevant in the light of what is to be predicted and so Astin's (1964) argument is a significant step towards alerting researchers to the context-dependency of criterion or dimension determination. We may conclude that performance dimensions or criteria, like their units of measurement, are subject to choice constrained, for one thing, by purpose. With this fundamental point of similarity in mind the basic properties of dimensions and criteria can be explored.

Dimension Properties

Dimensions have distinct properties which, when identified, may elucidate the dimensionalization process and provide guidelines for future
attempts at developing performance measures. While it would be naive to
draw major conclusions from a point by point analogy between the use of
dimensions in the physical and psychological sciences, abstraction of
general principles may provide a referent for re-evaluating our assumptions.

<u>Dimensions are unique</u>. The central condition in defining 'dimension'
appears to be the notion of uniqueness of quantity (or, in geometric
terms, direction) i.e. a dimension is a quantity the measurement of
which is independent of other measures taken. A dictionary definition
of the term, 'any of the three linear measurements, length, breadth and
depth', in contrast with the mathematical conception, can be seen to be
over-specific and perhaps overstructures our assumptions.   Length,
breadth and depth are unique directions but they only represent one set
of ways of describing an object. For example the same body could be
described in terms of its weight and its volume.

The notion of uniqueness of quantity (or direction) is embodied in the
debates surrounding the concept of uni-dimensionality. McNemar (1946)
suggested that measurement implies that one characteristic at a time is
being quantified and Lumsden (1976) claimed that uni-dimensionality is a
neglected topic where those who purport to tackle it are usually only
paying lip-service in terms of local independence.   However, as he
pointed out, there seems to be a confusion between uni-dimensionality
and theoretical singularity. While a uni-dimensional measure does have a
single attribute, the attribute may itself be complex.   For example, in
the illustration cited above it was seen that an object could be described in terms of its spatial dimensions or in terms of a single dimension of volume. The acceptability of volume as a dimension depends not
on its own dimensionality but its relation to the other dimensions used
to describe the body, i.e.   if variation in volume can be explained in
terms of any other dimension being used then volume is not a dimension
as the quantity is not unique. For example, length and volume would not
be mutually acceptable dimensions as the quantitative variable, length,
can be used to explain variance in volume.   In order to explain the
relativity of uniqueness Focken (1953) posited the idea of the 'pro-
basic' set, i.e. that a set of dimensions is only acceptable if no mem-
ber shares common variance with another.   In less mathematical terms
this means that the acceptability of a quantitative variable as a dimension depends on whether or not other designated dimensions can account
for its variance.

The main point is that a dimension is not unique in the sense of it
being fundamental or absolute.   As Dingle (1953) observed, even those
physical quantities which have been regarded as fundamental in mechanics

46

(i.e. mass, space and time) are only designated as so as matters of convenience. However, for a quantitative variable to be considered as a dimension it must represent an attribute that is not represented by other designated dimensions.

This has three points of significance for performance measurement. First, regardless of whatever other properties criteria may need to have, whether or not a criterion represents a performance dimension depends on the other criteria used. Second, attempts to derive the dimensions of performance beg the question of which dimensions are most convenient and therefore appropriate for the purpose of measurement. And thirdly, as with the volume example, under some circumstances it may be more useful and meaningful to designate a quantitative variable as a dimension, even though the variable itself could be expressed multi-dimensionally.

The use of dimensions. Defining dimensions as unique quantities within a pro-basic set which through combination can explain any other quantitative variable, confers on the concept a useful property. Focken (1953) discussed the mathematical uses of dimensions and while some are only strictly applicable or meaningful within that sphere, there are general principles which might be applied to performance measurement.

In order to perform operations with dimensions, physical quantities are reduced to dimensional expressions. These expressions then provide a conceptual equation of the properties involved in a physical equation and this can be used as a medium for doing calculations or as a means of checking the meaningfulness of calculations on physical quantitites. This latter is based on the principle of 'dimensional homogeneity' (Focken 1953) and derives from his earlier observation that only quantities of the same kind can be added, subtracted or have a ratio. In effect, for an equation between quantities to have meaning all terms which are added or subtracted must have the same dimensions. This principle is frequently used by physical scientists as a simple check on the intelligibility of an experimentally or theoretically derived formula. Disregarding constants, a necessary condition for a physical equation to be correct is that both sides of its dimensional expression balance.

The notion of being able to check the intelligibility of equations and formulae involving complex quantities by a reduction to a simple conceptual expression, is an appealing one. As pure speculation then, how might the analogue of such a principle look in performance measurement terms?

If Maier's (1955) conceptual equation of performance, $P = [M] \ [A] \ [O]$ is assumed, where P = performance, and Motivation, Ability and Opportunity are designated as the fundamental performance dimensions, then, by the principle of dimensional homogeneity, any expression in a performance equation (i.e. any performance measure), must be expressible in some or all of these basic terms but no other.

Alternatively, and once again speculatively, this conceptual check on intelligibility might be applied to the relationship between a performance measure and the purpose to which it is put. For example, where the purpose is to evaluate training effectiveness and if training outcome is defined in terms of qualitative changes in amounts of various specific abilities then by the argument of dimensional homogeneity, a relevant performance measure would also be multi-dimensional in ability. This would lead to the rather obvious conclusion that performance measures selected to identify training needs require to focus on specific abilities rather than motivational or opportunity variables. This hypothetical argument can be extended tentatively one stage further to performance measures which are required for reward allocation purposes, for example. Rewards are commonly distributed on a uni-dimensional scale (monetary) and, in theory, allocated according to individual worth. To construct an intelligible equation between performance and reward, the principle of dimensional homogeniety would require a uni-dimensional expression of performance outcome, i.e. contribution to organisational goal. Perhaps this would provide an explanation for the appeal of Direct Index measures and global measures of performance, and, if substantively argued, might also provide a rationale.

These arguments are highly speculative but they have been included to demonstrate, by analogy with the physical science uses, the potential utility of the methods which proceed from the properties of those quantities designated as dimensions.

Dimensions are abstractions. The central dimensional characteristic of uniqueness has been explored in an attempt to isolate a major constraint on dimension choice. The fact that a choice exists has to this point been summarily treated and the importance of the notion of choice has been understated. Ellis (1966) wrote that, 'certain metaphysical presuppositions... have played havoc with our understanding of many of the basic concepts of measurement, and concealed the existence of certain more or less arbitrary conventions', p.3. It appears that one such presupposition is that fundamental dimensions of job performance in some sense exist. Eysenck (1967) described factor analysis, a commonly used dimensional method, as the identification of scientific artefacts i.e. dimensionalization is an attempt to identify a unifying system of abstractions to describe and/or explain real world events. And similarly Focken (1953) regarded dimensionalization as a process of convenient choice and the notion of real world existence of dimensions as a misconception.

Several pieces of research strongly support the abstract and non-fundamental nature of dimensions, as well as suggest situational aspects which might guide dimensional choice. Jones (1976) made the point that the choice of uni- or multi-dimensional constructs is purpose-related. But to this, must be added the proviso that where multi-dimensional constructs are designated they should be unique within their dimension set. Dunnette and Borman (1979) made a case for appraiser perspective-dependent dimensionality. Ghiselli (1956) and Hulin (1962) observed that, at any point of time, job success could be defined in several ways so Ghiselli (1956) coined the term 'static criterion dimensionality'. Further, he defined the need for 'individual criterion dimensions' (i.e individual-dependent dimensionality) from his observation that different people may achieve job success in quite different ways. And finally, Fleishman and Ornstein (1960) found that six dimensions were needed to explain variance in merely manoeuvring an aircraft, a small part of pilot performance and, being concerned at the implications for the explanation of total pilot performance, they suggested that dimensional choice may be related to the scope of the conceptual criterion.

With the exception of a few such studies, the view that dimensionalization is a matter of convenient choice has not been commonly recognised in the performance measurement literature. Rather there has been a tendency to seek out dimensions which are in some sense definitive. This is most evident where factor analysis is used as the dimensionalization technique and is illustrated by a study, where the dimensionalization process is made explicit, in the closely related area of job characteristics.

Dunham (1976) found that the most parsimonious factorial solution of job characteristic measures was a single factor solution which he designated 'job complexity'. However, he noted that it was possible to adequately define 3 of the 5 a priori task characteristic scales cleanly and concluded that both a single and a four factor solution should be considered i.e. through dimensional analysis two dimensional sets were identified. Dunham then argued that the results were insufficient to abandon a multi-dimensional job characteristics construct. But to address this question is only meaningful if it is assumed that job characteristics can only be described in one way i.e. that fundamental dimensions exist. As criterion validity depends on judged relevance to the conceptual criterion the 'correctness' of either solution can only be gauged in the light of its purpose. Importantly, Dunham suggested several alternative explanations for his 'conflicting' findings. Although the majority still focussed on means of identifying the best solution, he ultimately suggested that dimensionality may be sample-dependent. From the author's perspective this last alternative provides another clue to constraints on dimensional choice.

DIMENSIONS AND CRITERIA

It is clear that to define a quantity as a dimension confers on it special and powerful properties and so the use of the term dimension indiscriminately to denote a performance measure connotes characteristics which may not necessarily be valid. It would seem therefore that, until criteria can be shown or created to exhibit these properties, using the terms criterion and dimension interchangeably may only mislead.

This is all the more important in light of the fact that criteria themselves have special properties. To designate a quantitative variable as the criterion creates a status difference between it and all other quantitative variables, (Bechtoldt 1959). Dunham (1976), like others, found that scales designated as criteria were not dimensions since the application of factor analysis yielded underlying dimensions. In what way then, do criteria and dimensions differ? It is useful to start by defining criteria.

Definitions of Criterion

'... - a canon or standard by which anything is judged or
estimated... - a characteristic attached to a thing, by which
it can be judged'. (Shorter Oxford English Dictionary, 1973)

'- a comparison object, or a rule, standard or test for making a
judgement... - a behavioural goal by which progress is judged..
the variance, comparison with which constitutes a measure of
validity.' (English and English, 1958, p.130)

'- a behaviour or condition which is or can be described in terms
of an ideal... - a goal ... behaviour which is considered
desirable and towards which one works.'
              (Jensen, Coles and Nestor, 1955, p.58)

'- a description of performance of individuals on a success
continuum'. (Bechtoldt, 1947).

'- an evaluative standard which can be used to measure a
person's performance, attitudes etc'. (Blum and Naylor, 1968).

Although these definitions vary with regard to their specificity and the implied properties of criteria, several common themes can be identified and four distinctions can be made in comparing these with the dimensional characteristics discussed above and those that are stated in the Shorter Oxford English Dictionary as:

'a measurable extent of any kind... - a mode of linear
measurement or extension in a particular direction... a term
for the (unknown or variable) quantities contained in any
product as factors'.

The critical nature of criteria. 'Goals', 'ideals', 'success', 'standards', and 'desirability' suggest that criteria are measures of critical performance aspects. In contrast, there is no such constraint on performance dimensions. Uniqueness of contribution to performance description does not imply that the dimension is critical in determining job success. In this sense, criteria might be regarded as a subset of performance dimensions. However, there is evidence to suggest that, in constructing job performance measures, apparently non-critical factors should be included.

Finding that aspects of job behaviour which are irrelevant to job proficiency, but annoying to management, can influence performance judgements, Otis (1971) argued for their inclusion in the measurement process so as to prevent contamination of critical factor assessment. Ghiselli (1956), noting the variety of ways in which different individuals achieve good performance, advocated the use of a range of measures, implying that some will be non-critical for any one performer. Ronan and Prien (1971), extending this argument to intra-individual variation in means of achieving good performance, added more weight to the need for the inclusion of occasionally non-critical factors. So, there does appear to be an argument for the inclusion of some non-critical factors (perhaps dimensions) in job performance measures.

The criterion as a discriminator. 'Progress towards an ideal', 'continuum of success' and 'evaluative standard' each characterize the criterion as a continuum which locates poor and good performance at opposite extremes, where intermediate levels represent increasingly good performance.

While dimensions have the characteristic of continua, that they comprise meaningful quantitative gradations, there is no condition that one extreme is any more or less desirable than the other. In fact, as a general condition it can be argued to be unlikely. Eysenck (1967) explained that, if you imagine dimensions as structuring space (in this case the performance domain) then, 'good' for example will not necessarily be located at the 'positive' ends of all dimensions. Again, it appears that criteria are a subset of dimensions, i.e. those for which progression along the continuum is associated with successively good performance. But, as before, the issue isn't necessarily clear cut. Not all critical aspects of performance need exhibit this bi-poloar characteristic. For example, it is conceivable that excessively high or low levels of a performance characteristic may detract from performance and in that case a linear scale of attribute amount would not parallel a scale of degree of good performance. By implication, limiting measures to those that do may lead to measure deficiency.

Criterion dimensionality. Whether or not criteria are or should be unidimensional is a subject of much controversy. Lumsden (1976) argued that criteria should be uni-dimensional but that the attribute can be complex. There is an obvious case for requiring performance criteria to be theoretically independent, as this is assumed to precede greater explanation of performance variance. However, bearing in mind the condition on a measure that it be observable and capable of conceptualization, it may be that multi-dimensional attributes are more useful and meaningful. For example, it is easier to conceptualize pressure than it is to conceptualize poundalls per square foot. So while dimensions by definition are uni-dimensional, criteria need not be so and in some circumstances this property may detract from their utility.

One final point that should be reiterated here is that dimensions represent quantitative variables, but critical aspects of job performance may of course include non-quantitative variables. Theoretically speaking then, some criteria may lie outside the class 'dimension' and this may be a significant area of investigation in attempting to reduce criterion deficiency.

The dual nature of the criterion. The above definitions help to explain the ambiguity, noted by Astin (1964), in the use of the term criterion. On the one hand it means the quantitative variable to be observed (cf. 'the standard by which', 'the comparison object', 'the rule'). So, for example, body height might be used as a job selection criterion. On the other hand criterion denotes the acceptable level of the quantitative variable (cf. 'the goal', 'the ideal', 'that which is considered desirable'). In this sense a specific body height might be quoted as a job selection criterion. As Weitz (1961) pointed out, two questions to be asked in criterion development are, firstly, which performance measures should be selected? And, secondly, what performance level is to be considered acceptable? So while as a 'comparison object' the criterion may share properties with a dimension its dual meaning and this inbuilt standard raise it to a higher status.

In conclusion, criteria and dimensions are distinct concepts, having distinct properties as variables. It is therefore misleading to use the terms synonymously and there are good reasons for their standardized usage. With these differences in mind it is now possible to discuss and compare criterion development and dimensional analysis processes as methods of establishing performance measures.

DERIVING PERFORMANCE MEASURES

As the definition of a measure is in some respects arbitrary, a choice necessarily being made as to what is measured, subject to matters of convenience and consistency, we have gone part way to answering the question of 'what to measure'? The measures themselves may, if they have the requisite properties, be termed performance dimensions, or if they are critical, bi-polar and embody a standard, may be termed criteria. In either case, how can such measures be developed? Some answers are yielded by a review of the issues that have been identified in criterion development and dimensional analysis.

Issues in Criterion Development

The large variety of criterion development methods have been well documented (Bechtoldt 1947, Guion 1961, 1965, Blum and Naylor 1968, Smith 1976 and many others). These range from the job-analytic approaches of Flanagan (1949) and Nagle (1953), through the performance factor-analytic approaches suggested by Guion (1961) to the more recent appraiser-generated approaches initiated by Smith and Kendall (1963). While all three approaches are still actively pursued, which is the better remains to be established. This can only be decided once it is clear what is expected of a criterion measure and this has been a subject of much controversy. The major issues are summarized below.

Multiple versus composite criteria. The first issue concerns whether job performance can or should be represented by multiple or singular measures. Ghiselli (1956) was probably the first to advocate the use of multiple job performance criteria and others have provided a variety of reasons why multiple criteria should be the aim. Guion (1961, 1965) argued on a point of logic, suggesting that the composite criterion falsely assumes a general factor in criteria accounting for all the important performance variance. Meanwhile, Hulin (1962) argued on a point of theoretical utility, advocating the need for multiple measures in order to determine the underlying structure of performance. Dunnette (1963) arguing for the acceptance of the 'real and complex world of success dimensionality', advocated 'junking' the criterion, suggesting that the issue isn't just about the numbers of criteria used but about the implied recognition of performance complexity. And finally, Astin (1964), arguing in terms of measurement theory, pointed out the difficulty of and error in composite score interpretation where separate elements measure relatively independent factors. In short, there appear to be various and convincing arguments for the use of multiple criteria.

Alternatively, in some quarters the logic of the composite criterion is difficult to deny. Toops (1944) and Nagle (1953) were the early advocates but more recently Blum and Naylor (1968) argued, in support, that if you ask supervisors about a worker's worth and get an agreed answer then this suggests that sub-criteria are additive into a composite, and that judges have some agreement as to sub-criteria weighting even if it can't be verbally expressed. Apart from the implied criticisms above, the major problem with the composite criteria, then, is that of combining a collection of various success measures into one evaluative index.

Recently, two suggestions have been made for the resolution of this multiple versus singular/composite issue. Clearly, Jones' (1976) argument for purpose-dependent measure choice provides one answer. In some circumstances a composite or singular measure will be appropriate whilst in others multiple measures may be more fitting, i.e. both may have their uses. A second answer comes from Hartmann, Roper and Bradford (1979) who suggested that while composite measures are required to test individual measure reliability, they can be misleading if measures aren't equivalent. On the other hand they argued that multiple measures are more appropriate to behavioural research but noted that the use of multiple measures can lead to the temptation to interpret each measure as error-free. They concluded that it is important for assessors to find some middle ground between the two extremes. Perhaps Smith's (1976) suggestions that, 'when several dimensions are involved several sets of criteria or composites will be required', p.748, might give researchers a direction in which to pursue this point.

Dynamic versus static criteria. Ghiselli (1956), finding correlations between some sub-criteria to be a function of practice or experience, argued that performance criteria should not be considered as static.

Fleishman and Hempel (1954) and Fleishman and Fruchter (1960) likewise found the same measures to have different factorial structures at different points of time. So, as Smith (1976) suggested, time appears to have an important influence on criteria. The significance of criterion dynamism lies in its practical implications. Specifically, criterion measures may suffer deficiency unless they are up-dated and so, by implication, purely practical constraints are placed on the acceptability of a criterion development method.

Behavioural versus personal criteria. Campbell et al, (1970) distinguished between performance measures which focus on behaviour and those that focus on personal qualities. While Dunnette and Borman (1979) documented the argument for a behavioural orientation, Hartmann et al, (1979), comparing personality trait assessment to behavioural assessment in the clinical sphere, provided a useful analysis of the implied differences.

Briefly, personality trait assessment assumes behaviour to be a function of enduring underlying causes, and therefore to be consistent across time and situations. The measures of personality traits therefore serve as a basis for inferring the individual's personality and behaviour across settings (Goldfried 1977). The implied practical focus is on diagnosis, classification and prediction and therefore a greater emphasis is placed on inter-individual differences. Because of their inferential nature the measures are indirect and since they focus on stable underlying traits, a small number of global measures are appropriate.

In contrast, behavioural assessment focusses on what a person does (Mischel 1968), assuming behaviour to be largely a function of current and specific environmental conditions, where behavioural stability depends on environmental stability. As such, descriptions of response patterns to particular situations are appropriate and predictions about non-test behaviour are made directly from representative and relevant samples of behaviour. The implied practical focus is on treatment (in this context, training and development) and therefore a greater emphasis is placed on intra-individual differences over time and situations. The methods are direct, characterized by a focus on specific behaviours and stimulus conditions, and therefore involve the measurement of several variables. Finally, the underlying assumptions of behavioural change imply the need for continuous measurement.

In short, the use of behavioural measures rather than personality-oriented measures represents far from a nominal distinction. It is associated with more realistic assumptions about the complexity and environmental determinancy of performance and it has considerable implications for the methods, scope and timing of measurement. In particular, it has major implications for the appropriate dimensionality of performance measures and these will be discussed in the final sections of this chapter.

<u>Scale independence of criteria</u>. While some support has been found for
Lumsden's (1976) argument for scale independence, Hackman and Oldham
(1975) suggested that criterion interdependence, measured by scale
inter-correlations, is to be expected. Concerned primarily with job
characteristics, they argued that as 'good' jobs tend to be 'good' in a
variety of ways, moderate inter-correlation between otherwise unrelated
job characteristics is somewhat inevitable. This suggests that when
unique quantitative variables (dimensions) are value-related (i.e.
acquire a criterion property) then their independence may be confounded
by the influence of the evaluative component. In other words, the
uniqueness of contribution of even empirically-determined dimensions may
change when the dimension gains the evaluative status of a criterion.

<u>Who determines performance criteria?</u>. This final issue has focussed on
whether it should be the researcher or management who should determine
performance criteria.   Campbell et al, (1970), noticed the research
tendency to emphasise traits and processes in criteria and so called
for a move away from 'expert' insights. Meanwhile Otis (1971) argued
that as psychologists are becoming more involved in organisations their
ability to participate effectively in establishing criterion measures is
increasing, allowing them to reduce their dependency on management for
both data and explanation. The former authors provided a resolution of
this conflict in suggesting that the gap between industrialists' and
researchers' emphases needed to be bridged by an empirically-determined
relationship between personal traits, job behaviours and organisational
outcomes.

A different move to qualify this controversy came from the BARS method-
ologists. Smith and Kendall (1963) argued for criteria generated by the
appraisers themselves believing that such a move would lead to better
appraiser understanding and commitment, and supportive evidence is consistently found (Schwab et al, 1975b, Jacobs et al, 1980, Kingstrom and
Bass 1981).

Issues in Dimensional Analysis

As has been seen, dimensions are abstract and the determination of dimensionality is constrained by convenience and the need for consistency.
The process of dimensional analysis then, is one of establishing a form
of abstractions which satisfy the determinants of convenience. In as
much as dimensional analysis aims to establish a measurement system, it
is concerned with providing an ordering of observed phenomena which is
parsimonious, purpose-related, standardized and, arguably, open to visualization.

Scientific description of any phenomenon implies the reduction of the
number of facts about the phenomenon to a significant few (i.e. underlying dimensions) so as to facilitate comparison, explanation and prediction.   The rationale for dimensional analysis then, is to reduce
descriptions of phenomena to the lowest possible dimensionality whilst
maintaining optimal power for explaining variance.   This search for the

lowest possible dimensionality consistent with the data means that each parameter is based on a larger subset of data and is therefore likely to be more statistically reliable. Secondly, if dimensionality is sufficiently low then a model of the measurement system is more accessible to visualization, and therefore more easily conceptualized. And finally, as is argued above, the choice of appropriate performance dimensions is linked to the purpose of measurement.

These concepts of parsimony, standardized description which permits comparison, purpose-relatedness and visualization merely provide guidelines for dimensional analysis techniques and the weight afforded to them may, of course, be situation-specific.

A Dichotomy of Methods

Dimensionalization is the process of creating a unified system for describing real phenomena, where the component dimensions are abstract and judged valid according to convenience. So, any dimensional analytic solution can only reflect real world order and this reflection can take one of two forms. If real world order is defined by nature's design and mapped onto real space then a distinction can be made between subjective world order as defined by personal constructs and mapped onto psychological space and objective data order which is defined by scientific constructs and mapped onto mathematical space.

In an attempt to describe real world events, the subjective orientation is preferred by some cognitive psychologists, implying an ideographic approach concerned with perceived ordering. Phenomenologists and Personal Construct theorists (among them, Kelly 1955 and Fransella 1977) justifying such an orientation, maintain that dimensionalization is a characteristic process of cognitive functioning and thus develop ipsative measures using techniques such as Repertory Grid. The objective orientation is preferred by operationalists and implies a nomothetic approach concerned with actual data ordering. Eysenck (1967) and Cattell (1967), for example, maintained that real world order can be sampled by observations the statistical treatment of which yields a patterning of phenomena. Their tendency is towards developing normative measures using factor-analytic techniques.

If these two approaches yielded similar solutions then choice would be a matter of personal preference, but if resultant dimensional solutions differ then the question arises as to which is more appropriate. As factor analysis appears to be the most widely used dimensional analysis technique a summary review of selected research is presented that may answer this question.

Jones (1976) believed factor analysis to be a promising technique for determining factor scores which would meet the requisites of measurement and Sims et al, (1976) found that the factor analytically-derived dimensions of their task design construct could be empirically differentiated. Similarly, Perry and Friedman (1973) and Bem and Allen (1974) found that attitudes/cognitive sets were highly dimensionalized and firmly structured and that factor analysed responses yielded dimensions equivalent to these cognitive sets. Dunham (1976) examining job characteristic dimensionality through factor analysis maintained that different techniques (e.g. multi-dimensional scaling) would yield the same solution. These, among others, would appear to suggest that factor analysis is capable of producing psychologically meaningful constructs that parallel those derived by other methods.

However, Peel (1953) argued that there was a difference between the mathematical and psychological uses of factor analysis. He claimed that factor analysis yielded underlying dimensionality in the mathematical space in which the observations are located, but that it is face validity that is important (i.e. meaning in the psychological space), and indeed, some investigators have noted this problem. For example, Distefano and Pryer (1975), using factor analysis to dimensionalize questionnaire responses identified 6 factors which accounted for 50% of the variance but found the major problem to be dimension delineation. This not uncommon problem of deriving dimensions which are mathematically pure but are difficult to conceptualize becomes critical where the aim is to establish criteria which are meaningful to the user. It seems then, that preference for techniques which map onto mathematical or psychological space may underpin the issue of how to determine methodologically pure but conceptually sound performance measures.

Not only does there appear to be this argument on conceptual grounds but there are statistical arguments against factor analysis as a criterion development tool. Astin (1964) maintained that in the common practice of retaining elements which have the highest factor loadings as the best measures of criterion factors, the data must satisfy two conditions. First, no significant amount of variance relevant to the conceptual criterion must be specific to any one element and second, the proportion of common factor variance among separate elements which is 'error' variance must be negligible. Importantly, he claimed that these conditions cannot be assumed in the criterion development situation.

Factor analysis, then, providing certain assumptions are tenable, is clearly capable of yielding performance dimensions but whether they are meaningful and therefore useful as criteria is debatable. It was seen in Dunham's (1976) study, for example, that a single dimension, termed job complexity, was the most parsimonious solution but how readily can this dimension be conceptualized? And, therefore, how useful would it be as a criterion?

There is also cause to question the purity of factor analytically-derived dimensions. For one thing the activity of verbal identification of dimensions is itself subject to personal construction, perceptual acuity etc. And for another, as in the case of Eysenck's three dimensional model of personality (1952) there can never be absolute determinancy because no individual could be accurately described along one dimension only, for observed behaviour consistencies are always contaminated by consistencies in other dimensions. So as Eysenck suggested, the way we choose to call these syndromes or consistencies is purely arbitrary. This means that even those dimensions yielded by factor analysis may not be as pure as they are regarded.

Characteristic of factor analysis are the rigid assumptions that are made about linearity, this being consistent with meaningful interpretations in mathematical space. By implication, significant non-linear groupings which may be most meaningful in psychological space are not necessarily detected. A more flexible, non-linear method of dimensional analysis may yield solutions which are perhaps more meaningful. For example, cluster analysis is a technique which identifies significant groupings of observations, and as Jones (1976) suggested, multidimensional scaling (MDS), which like factor analysis provides coordinates of n points in a space of several dimensions, holds dramatic promise. Jones' comment was based on the capacity of MDS to transform ranked data into distance measures but perhaps what is more important is that the initial data takes the form of judged similarities and differences between phenomena, i.e. MDS provides statistical manipulation of subjective data in psychological space. While its most frequent use has been in attitude and market research, its application has been extended to research in social cognition (see for example Funk et al, 1976, Wish, Deutsch and Kaplan, 1976, Butcher, 1982) and perhaps it could be usefully applied to criterion development.

The problem of developing theoretically sound measures of performance which have meaning to the observer has been the task of dimensional analysis. However, current methods tend to favour either methodological purity (e.g. factor analysis) or conceptual soundness (e.g. repertory grid). The former operates within what has been termed mathematical space, while the latter concentrates on individual psychological space so that a gap exists where solutions of the former may not be meaningful in the latter. Quite plainly factor analysis is a successful dimensional analysis technique but the extent to which it is a satisfactory criterion development technique has yet to be proven and is perhaps questionable as psychologically meaningful solutions are not to be guaranteed.

This dichotomy somewhat reflects the traditional conflict between theoretical and pragmatic approaches to measure development. The definition of appropriate measures established above quite clearly calls for the satisfaction of both implied goals and so what appears to be required are techniques of criterion development which bridge this gap. Fortunately, there are some recent techniques which may serve this purpose. Conceiving of a continuum of criterion development techniques ranging from those which are objective and mathematically-oriented to those which are subjective and psychologically-oriented then MDS may provide the link from the mathematical side, whereas Behaviourally Anchored Rating Scales may provide the bridge from the subjective, psychologically-oriented side.

LIMITATIONS ON APPROPRIATE PERFORMANCE MEASURES

This chapter has attempted to clarify our conceptions concerning the measurement of job performance so as to answer questions about what should be measured, and how these measures should be established.

Dimensions and criteria, as bases for performance measurement, have been distinguished and the measure solutions obtained by common techniques have been briefly examined. While measure choice may be arbitrary, the derivation of appropriate dimensions or criteria is subject to issues of convenience, and so choice is subject to constraints which place upper and lower limits on the number of appropriate measures as well as determine the nature of the dimensions or criteria chosen. Three sets of considerations appear to place limits on appropriate performance measures: the requirements of criteria, the requirements of a measure and the requirements of behavioural assessment.

Requirements of Criteria

The criterion development literature suggested conditions which acceptable performance measures must satisfy. Criteria should be relevant (i.e. should accurately reflect the criterion job performance) and they should be comprehensive (i.e. include all important performance components delineated by the definition of success). Criteria should be uncontaminated, dynamic and discriminating, and may often need to be multiple and behavioural in nature.

Requirements of a Measure

The measurement literature also suggested conditions which acceptable performance measures must satisfy. As measurement purpose implies and is implied by the measures taken, the nature of the measure is constrained by measurement purpose. For example, Hartmann et al, (1979) suggested that different types of measures (e.g. behavioural or traditional) have purpose-dependent utility (e.g. development or evaluation) and Messick (1975) suggested that criterion-referenced as opposed to norm-referenced assessment is more in keeping with treatment-focussed behavioural assessment. That is to say, treatment (training or development) purposes require direct as opposed to comparative measures which emphasise intra-individual as opposed to inter-individual differences, and focus on gauging levels of attainment of relatively narrow as opposed to broad performance objectives.

As measurement accuracy is influenced by the specification of observation conditions and critical facets of the measurement situation have been generally identified as the appraiser, the setting and the instrument itself, appropriate performance measure choice is partly defined and constrained by conditions including the method used, the person using it and the measurement context.

As the conceptual definition of the observed attribute is important in determining the extent to which accurate observation is possible, accurate measurement is a function of the observer's conceptual equipment. One important way of describing the observer's conceptual equipment is in terms of cognitive complexity. Perry and Friedman (1973) and Kafry et al, (1979) observed that an individual's psychological space is highly and firmly structured and these structural characteristics are associated with cognitive complexity. With reference to performance measurement, Schneier (1977) found individual and domain-specific differences in these structural characteristics to effect an individual's ability to assess, his preference for type of rating scale, and his tendencies to make different types of rating errors on particular scales. Dunnette and Borman (1979) also commented on the influence of appraiser characteristics, finding that factors such as organisational level, intelligence, personal adjustment and detail-orientation influenced measurement accuracy and reliability. All of these effect the utility of different measures and so place limitations on appropriate measure choice as they are significant factors in observation conditions.

While the satisfaction of constraints imposed by individual cognitive complexity may be necessary it is not sufficient to guarantee appropriate performance measures. A common performance measurement problem is the lack of comparability of results from different judges which usually develops from the absence of a single set of reference meanings which can be applied in evaluating performance, and so for a measurement system to be convenient and appropriate there must be common understanding of its meaning.

Finally, attribute measurement requires that the attribute be expressible in quantitative terms and that quantitative differences in the attribute measure represent real and perceptible differences in the attribute. Performance measures should therefore be quantitatively expressed and unit measure definition is limited by the least perceptible change in the attribute. This latter is an appraiser-specific variable and therefore this aspect of appropriate performance measure choice will be subject to appraiser cognitive characteristics.

Requirements of Behavioural Assessment

As the purpose of performance measurement may often require measures to be expressed in behavioural terms these measures are subject to the constraints evoked by the validity requirements of behavioural assessment. Where behaviour is directly observable and the 'test' situation and criterion situation are the same, then no construct validation is required (Goldfried 1977, Goldfried and Linehan 1977, Cone 1978) but there is a need for construct validation wherever behavioural categories and discriminations such as appropriate/inappropriate, effective/ineffective etc. are involved. In order to demonstrate validity it is therefore necessary to establish which behaviours belong to which criteria and at which levels. This then bears on the necessary level of behavioural specification in performance measures and therefore constrains the nature of the performance dimensions or criteria used.

Each of these major requirements constrains both the number and quality of appropriate performance measures. Although it is in some sense unrealistic to distinguish quality and quantity properties of performance measures, as undoubtedly each has some bearing on the other, for present purposes it is easier to treat these issues separately.

LIMITATIONS ON QUALITY

The quality of performance measures is determined by the nature of measure content, the nature of the continua representing performance components and the level of detail with which these continua are described.

Nature of Content

Behavioural specification. An increase in performance measure reliability and a reduction in scale ambiguity is to be expected when measures are expressed in behavioural terms (Borman and Dunnette 1975). Although certain purposes may require performance outcome measures such as Direct Indices, Messick (1975) believed behaviour-oriented assessment to be in keeping with treatment-focussed measurement. As many appraisal purposes might be so described (notably training evaluation, employee counselling, individual development, motivation etc.) behavioural information is often required and this implies that performance measure content should be behavioural in nature.

This need for behavioural content gives rise to other constraints. First, the assumptions of behavioural assessment require measures to focus on narrow and well-defined ranges of behaviour. In addition as the discriminant validity of measures can be improved with clarity of scale definition (Groner 1974, Dickinson and Tice 1977), useful performance measures may be restricted to those for which a precise and specific definition can be formulated. Second, Schneier's (1977) study implied that the level of rater cognitive complexity places limitations on the extent to which behaviourally-specific scales can be used with commitment and accuracy and so the utility of behavioural measures appears to be moderated by assessor cognitive complexity. Finally, as Campbell et al, (1970) suggested that behavioural specification may bridge the gap between the personal trait orientation of researchers and the performance outcome orientation of industrialists, and argued that measure utility relies on establishing connections between these three, this suggests that measure content should be restricted to those behaviours which have established meaning in terms of organisational outcome.

Performance domain sampled. The need for relevant and non-deficient criteria means that performance domain sampling should be done with care. As measure appropriateness depends on the measurement purpose, then the performance domain sampled will vary according to purpose. For this reason conceptual criterion clarification is invaluable. However, there need not be a direct relationship between the number of constructs required to sample the performance domain and its scope. For example, a performance measurement task may require the assessment of minute aspects of skilled behaviour (e.g. Fleishman and Ornstein's (1960) six performance dimensions used to describe the manoeuvring of an aircraft) or for a different purpose, require the assessment of gross skills (e.g. major components of pilot performance could be described in terms of administrative, technical and managerial skills). In this way, it can be argued that the scope of the performance domain to be sampled determines the specificity of the behaviours to be observed. So the measurement purpose places some constraint on the level of specificity required in performance domain sampling. However, as is likely in the above example, measurement at one level of specificity may be more easily attained by untrained observers than the other, so assessor expertise may also constrain the scope of the domain sampled.

Relationship between constructs. Nidorf (1961) and Harvey and Schroder (1963) demonstrated that cognitively complex assessors have less need for consistency between the constructs used to measure a performance domain than cognitively simple assessors, the former having a higher tolerance for ambiguity in the combination of constructs used and being better able to reconcile potentially contradictory adjectives. This suggests that the relationships between constituent constructs can effect the accuracy with which any one construct is used if such relationships are not tenable within the assessor's cognitive domain. For this reason the assessor's cognitive complexity places limitations not only on the content of individual measures but on the combination of constructs used.

Nature of Continua

Performance continua may be either uni- or multi-dimensional. The properties of a measure require that meaningful interpretation be attributable to different continuum levels and, in distinguishing between dimensions and criteria it was noted that criteria are typically bi-polar and value-laden whilst dimensions are descriptive, where good and poor performance may not necessarily appear at either continuum extreme. By implication, in the pursuit of non-deficient measures, non-bi-polar quantitative variables should not be automatically discounted.

Performance continua quality is partly determined by the type of scale anchoring and the quantitative condition placed on a measure requires the explicit statement of performance scale gradations. Conventionally, scales have been anchored either by assigned numerals or by words or statements. Bendig and Hughes (1953) found that verbal (as opposed to numerical) anchoring increased the amount of information transmitted by the scale, while Peters and McCormick (1966) found that scales constructed of job-task (as opposed to numerical) benchmarks could be used with greater reliability. In further specifying the nature of verbal anchoring, Johnson and Boldstad (1973) argued that behavioural measurement requires statements of which behaviours represent which levels of performance, and research on behavioural anchoring tends to reinforce this view. BARS have been found to exhibit less halo (Burnaska and Hollmann 1974), greater scale independence (Campbell et al, 1973) and higher inter-rater reliability (Borman and Vallon 1974, Williams and Seiler 1973) than numerically anchored scales.

In short, research supports the use of behaviourally anchored performance continua. However, the quantification condition on measures requires that continua levels be expressible in numerical terms and so behavioural anchors should have numerical correlates.

Level of Continua Detail

As the purpose of a performance continuum is to allow an appraiser to discriminate stimuli, the basic question concerns whether there is a number of scale levels beyond which there is no further improvement in discrimination. A limit then, may be placed on level of continua detail by a) the level of discrimination required by the purpose of measurement and b) the discrimination available to describe behaviour.

With regard to the former, the purpose of measurement places limitations on the number of appropriate continua levels. For example, whereas employee development purposes require a detailed expression of areas of performance achievement and deficiency as well as explicit statements of standards and performance levels achieved, reward-related purposes may only require an expression of performance level relative to a norm.

With regard to the limitation imposed by the discrimination available, Garner (1960) argued that the optimum number of scale categories is a function of the amount of discrimination inherent in the assessed stimuli, suggesting perhaps that a limit to the number of scale levels is imposed by the real or potential range of performance. Others meanwhile have concerned themselves with the limit placed on the number of scale levels by the appraiser's discriminative abilities. As the minimum unit of measurement is defined as the smallest perceptible difference between amounts of an attribute, an upper limit to the number of scale discriminations is enforced by appraiser-related factors. This has been a recurrent concern throughout rating research where differential discriminative ability has been related to poor inter-rater reliability and to error variance (Bechtoldt 1947, Bendig and Hughes 1953, Guilford 1954). More recently, Kavanagh et al, (1971) suggested that the discriminant validity of scales is limited by the rater's inability to go beyond a certain level of precision and Borman (1978) provided possible numerical indices of this error. The rater's discriminative ability clearly places an upper limit on the number of useful scale levels. However, Bendig and Hughes' (1953) pointed out that valuable discriminative ability may be wasted if the scale is too coarse. Some balance therefore needs to be found and researchers have concentrated on identifying the optimum number of scale points.

Hake and Garner (1951), using 5, 10, 20 and 50 response categories, found little increase in transmitted information above 10 scale categories, while Bendig and Hughes' (1953) results favoured 9 scale categories as an optimum number. However, given individual differences in discriminative ability such recommendations may be premature and as Garner (1960) suggested, there may be no single number of rating categories which is appropriate to all rating situations. Evidence from the cognitive complexity literature adds weight to this assertion in suggesting that individuals differ in respect of their level of discriminative ability within particular cognitive domains (Scott 1974, Crockett 1965, Harvey and Schroder 1963). Some appraisers through experience, knowledge or perhaps exposure, are able to make finer discriminations than others with respect to a particular performance domain and this effects the number of continua levels which are meaningful. If to this is added the need for mutually-agreed and understood measures, then the appropriate number of discrete continua levels is limited by the degree of discriminative ability common to the appraiser group.

Finally, the requirements of a measure dictate that the units used should be consistent across dimensions so, where multiple continua are used and results are to be combined or compared, then the meaning attributable to scale level differences across continua should be consistent.

Summary of Quality Limitations

From observed limitations on the nature of performance measure content, continua and level of continua detail, the following conclusions may be drawn.

Performance measure content should focus on narrow ranges of behaviour which can be precisely and clearly defined; which have proven relationships with organisational outcomes; which are determined by measurement purpose; which are specified according to the scope of the performance domain sampled; and which have independently tenable meaning within the cognitive domain of the appraisers. Performance measure continua need not necessarily be bi-polar, value-related criteria; should contain explicit behavioural statements representative of different levels of performance; and should be interpretable in numerical terms. Level of continua detail is restricted at its upper and lower ends by the discrimination required of the measure and the discrimination available. As such the number of appropriate scale levels is limited by the measurement purpose, the attribute being measured, common appraiser discriminative ability and unit consistency across continua.

Having examined the quality limitations it is clear that the quality of appropriate performance measures for a particular purpose and group of users is fairly closely constrained. But what of quantity issues? Is the number of continua similarly constrained? Is there an optimum number of criteria or optimum dimensionality for performance measures? These questions are addressed in this penultimate section.

The performance construct could be described with different degrees of thoroughness ranging from the inclusion of all performance-related variables to a simple good/bad evaluation. But the pursuit of such extremes is unlikely to satisfy the conditions which are imposed on measures in general or performance measures in particular. For one thing an upper limit is imposed where the amount of information potentially yielded far exceeds the potential population performance discriminations required. For example, 10 x 10 point criteria permit the identification of 10^{10} different performance profiles and it could be argued that such a wealth of potential information is wasted, there being a simpler underlying dimensional structure. At the other end, the arguments against global or composite criteria suggest that a single evaluative continuum yields insufficient data to satisfy many performance measurement purposes. An optimum number of dimensions or criteria then, is defined in terms of including nothing that is redundant and excluding nothing that is integral.

There are further qualifications on this general constraint. The aim of dimensional analysis places specific constraints on dimensionality and these will be discussed below. It was also argued that dimensional analysis aimed to achieve parsimony in performance description, the objective being to identify the lowest possible dimensionality consistent with the data, and that an aim might be to achieve dimensionality which was open to visualization. Neglecting highly sophisticated multidimensional analyses, there would be a requirement then for a 3- or 4-dimensional description of performance data. It will become apparent that such a restriction is likely to be in conflict with other constraints and so, for this reason, the weight afforded to it may well be situation-specific.

Finally, at this point it's worth considering how well the techniques of dimensional analysis discussed above, adhere to these general constraints. With cluster analysis, factor analysis and MDS, a post-facto decision is made as to what dimensions are necessary and sufficient to explain the data. In cluster analysis, it is acceptable to have as many dimensions as observations and, for this reason, the technique may be faulted as an attempt at a parsimonious description which can be visualized. With factor analysis, the researcher gathers and submits data on 'relevant' variables to correlational analyses to identify independent underlying factors which account for optimum variance, and this is then interpretable as optimum dimensionality. While satisfying the conditions of parsimony and standardization, this technique may not yield solutions which can be visualized and, in failing to take account of purpose-relatedness, may fall short of guaranteeing criterion validity. And finally, MDS analyses of subjective data frequently yield 3-dimensional solutions so this technique would appear to fulfil the conditions of parsimony and standardization and to provide solutions which can be readily visualized. However, the apparent frequency of 3- or 4-D solutions may be a result of data being forced into an evaluative and low dimensional form before analysis and so there appears to be little allowance for variation in dimension number as determined by purpose.

Situational-Specific Limitations

It was argued above that the number of useful performance dimensions or criteria depends on the complexity requirements of the performance measure and that the purpose of measurement determined the scope of the performance domain sampled, which may place further constraints on the numbers of dimensions or criteria deemed appropriate. Finally, Ghiselli (1956) and Otis (1971) suggested that, while the purpose determines the critical aspects of performance to be measured, this number should be extended to include aspects which may not be universally critical as well as to include those which are non-job-relevant but which may contaminate assessments.

Dunham (1976) mentioned sample-dependency of dimensionality and, applied to job performance, this would mean that the appropriate number of dimensions is partly determined by the performance characteristics of the people assessed. This reinforces the general argument above for a logical upper limit on quantity.

Purely practical considerations such as fatigue effects and time available may also place an upper limit on the number of appropriate dimensions or criteria. As the number which is used determines the time and effort required of the assessor, pragmatic considerations necessarily weigh heavily where the assessor is required to make many such assessments, i.e. there may be a trade-off to be made between measure comprehensiveness, assessor motivation, and measurement accuracy.

Finally, Blum and Naylor (1968) and Naylor and Wherry (1964) implied that assessors themselves have implicit notions of appropriate performance dimensions and this prompts the question about the limits placed on the number of performance dimensions or criteria by the assessor's cognitive characteristics.

The cognitive complexity literature suggests that the appraiser's ability to think about performance is limited by the number of different constructs he has available in that cognitive domain. This aspect of cognitive complexity is referred to as the degree of _differentiation_, 'the process of dividing the semantic space into two or more orthogonal or oblique bi-polar semantic dimensions' (Streufert and Streufert 1978) and the research suggests that the degree of differentiation depends on experience (Kelly 1955, Nidorf 1961, Crockett 1965), values (Crockett 1965), motivational state (Crockett 1965, Miller and Bieri 1965), and task area (Scott 1974). While there is some evidence which shows that the degree of differentiation may be increased through training (Sieber and Lanzetta 1964, Hunt 1966, Baldwin 1972), most authors agree that individual 'ceilings' exist.

The consequences of using a number of dimensions beyond the appraiser's range include a tendency to collapse extraneous dimensions to a simple good/bad continuum (Campbell 1960, Harvey and Schroder 1963) and a heightened susceptibility to influence from the characteristics which the appraiser regards as most salient (Streufert 1966, Petronko and Perin 1970). Indeed, this may explain the common rating error known as halo effect. On the other hand, the consequences of using a number of dimensions significantly lower than the appraiser implicitly uses to describe performance may be an 'averaging effect' (Streufert and Streufert 1978). All of these factors contribute to erroneous rating and therefore this appraiser characteristic places a situation-specific constraint on the upper and lower limits to the acceptable number of criteria or dimensions used. Useful measures, then, are limited by the number of commonly meaningful constructs that are available.

Attempting to establish the optimum number of criteria which are appropriate for measuring performance has been a quest which has attracted attention in the BARS research. Research (Landy and Guion 1970, Campbell et al, 1973, Keaveny and McGann 1975, Landy, Farr, Saal and Freytag 1976, Kafry et al, 1979, Jacobs et al, 1980) has concentrated on the factor analysis of ratings on subjectively-derived dimensions and showed that between four and eight latent factors could account for the majority of variability in evaluations. As it was argued above that factor-analytic solutions may not be meaningful in terms of psychological space these factor-analytic studies may not directly answer the question of the relationship between cognitive capacity and number of useful dimensions, but as Jacobs et al, (1980) suggested, requiring greater than eight ratings may commonly result in redundant information or lack of scale discrimination.

Summary of Quantity Limitations

In terms of general constraints, a logical upper limit to quantity is imposed by the potential population performance discriminations required and a general lower limit of more than one seems to apply. In reducing the range further, there is a general constraint on the number of dimensions or criteria which are necessary and sufficient to fulfil the conditions of parsimony, standardization, purpose-relatedness and visualization. The parsimony condition requires that the lowest possible dimensionality consistent with the data should be pursued and the visualization condition, in restricting dimensionality to less than three or four, was argued to be variably important as it may be over- restrictive for some purposes. Common dimensional analysis techniques each fail to meet one of these general constraints.

In terms of specific constraints, the purpose of measurement was again seen to be a determinant in that purposes requiring more complex information may require a greater number of measures. The scope of the performance domain sampled was argued to be a quantity determinant, as was the target sample. It was suggested that the number of performance measures should include job-irrelevant but assessment-contaminating aspects as well as variably critical performance aspects. In addition, upper limits were seen to be partly determined by the pragmatic considerations of appraiser time availability and potential fatigue. Finally, the 'differentiation' characteristic of cognitive complexity was argued to place upper and lower limits on the number of appropriate measures. The need for agreed measurement meaning qualifies this constraint by requiring the highest number of dimensions or criteria (level of differentiation) that is common to the assessor group. BARS research suggests that an upper limit of 8 may be a useful guideline.

SUMMARY

This chapter has examined various aspects of performance measurement in an attempt to identify the route to performance measures which are both methodologically pure and conceptually sound.

Four properties of 'measure' were examined with reference to performance measurement and it was suggested that performance measurement improvement may result from the explicit pursuit of establishing measures which exhibit these four properties. In particular, the issue of purpose-relatedness was found to be a neglected area. Descriptions of measures should include observation conditions and, because of the 'ecological' nature of performance criteria, research emphasis should be placed on investigating the critical conditions of measurement. In this pursuit, the investigation of the appraiser's perspective, the measurement method, situation and instrument appear to be promising directions but these may not be exhaustive and further research is required. In considering the observation and perception requirement of a measure the clarification of the conceptual criterion was found to be all-important at the observer level and the mid-continuum Quantitative Absolute Standards Procedures were seen to provide promise in this direction. Finally, in considering the quantification requirement of measures, it was argued that job performance criteria may well include qualitative variables and that there is a need for research to investigate the possibility of non-measurable but critical performance attributes.

Criteria and dimensions were distinguished and both were argued to be abstract and subject to matters of choice. Arguing that in performance measurement little explicit attention is normally paid to dimension properties these were examined, the central characteristic of uniqueness explored and the non-fundamental nature of dimensions stated. By implication: any specific criterion may or may not represent a dimension of performance depending on the other criteria adopted; attempts to derive the dimensions of performance overlook the question of which dimensions are most convenient for the measurement purpose; and under some circumstances it may be more useful to adopt multi-dimensional criteria.

The peculiar properties of dimensions were seen to be useful in the physical sciences. The principle of dimensional homogeniety was shown to provide a means of checking the intelligibility of equations and the potential utility of such a principle in the performance measurement situation was briefly explored. Finally, the abstract and arbitrary nature of dimensional choice was explored, the author arguing that such a conception is uncommon in performance measurement research. The author illustrated how a 'situation-specific' view of dimension determination may serve to resolve seemingly conflicting results, a view which changes the questions asked in research to ones which are more easily answered.

A need was established for agreed, selective and standardized use of the terms dimension and criterion and four distinctions were made between them. First, criteria represent crucial, important and desirable performance attributes whereas dimensions are descriptive measures which include non-critical performance attributes. However, there is a case for the inclusion of non-critical attributes in performance measures. Second, criteria are represented by discriminatory bi-polar continua associated with job success whereas dimensions are represented by linear continua associated with amount of an attribute, which do not necessarily parallel success continua. Third, while dimensions are uni-dimensional, criteria can be multi-dimensional and some multi-dimensional attributes may be more readily observable and more easily conceptualized than their uni-dimensional components. Finally, criterion has dual meaning, denoting both the quantitative variable against which comparison should be made and the desirable level of performance as measured by it. In the former sense it may share properties with a dimension but when an evaluative component is introduced, in defining an acceptable standard, the criterion is raised to a higher status.

Issues in criterion development were discussed. The multiple versus composite criterion controversy was found to be resolved by considering the measurement purpose. Research evidence strongly favours the pursuit of dynamic criteria and by implication constraints are placed on acceptable criterion development methods by the need to up-date measures. Behavioural measurement was found to be more consistent with treatment-related outcomes and associated with more realistic assumptions about the complexity and environmental determinancy of performance. These in turn gave rise to implications for the methods, scope and timing of assessment. On the issue of scale independence it was argued that, because of their value-related nature, criteria could be expected to inter-correlate and therefore even empirically-determined dimensions, which are unique by definition, may correlate when they are designated 'criteria'. Finally, in considering the issue of who should determine criteria, it was noted that a divide exists between the emphases of researchers and practitioners and that what is required is an empirically- determined relationship between personal traits, job behaviours and organisational outcomes. Further, the evidence suggests that pursuit of appraiser-generated criteria may be an advance towards conceptual soundness and criterion validity.

The aims of dimensional analysis were described as the achievement of standardized, parsimonious, purpose-related and readily visualized representations of performance, but the weight afforded to each of these may be situation-specific. Suggesting that the objective of dimensional analysis is to achieve a reflection of real world ordering of phenomena, a dichotomy of methods, ranging from the mathematically-oriented to the psychologically-oriented, was described, reflecting the traditional divide between theoretical and pragmatic approaches to developing measures of work performance. The author suggested that the preference for extremes has left a gap in the middle to be filled by methods which combine methodological purity with conceptual soundness and identified MDS from the mathematical perspective, and BARS from the psychological perspective as promising methods.

The general limitations on appropriate performance measures were identified as emanating from the requirements of criteria, requirements of measures and requirements of behavioural assessment. It was also noted that the characteristics of the assessor, in particular his cognitive complexity, play a major role. Specific limitations on the quality of performance measures in terms of the nature of content, continua and level of detail were explored and it was argued that optimum quality is determined by purpose of measurement, attribute measured, appraiser discriminative ability and differentiation capacity, clarity of attribute definition, relationship of attribute to organisational outcome, scope of performance domain sampled, expressibility in behavioural and numerical terms and unit consistency across continua. Finally, general and specific constraints on the number of performance measures was explored and it was found that optimum quantity is determined by the potential population performance discriminations required, the purpose of measurement, the scope of performance domain sampled, pragmatic considerations, and appraiser differentiation capacity.

CONCLUSIONS

Early in this chapter it was seen that the bases of measurement, i.e. dimensions and criteria, are in themselves arbitrary abstractions which by definition have no real meaning but which are selected inasmuch as they provide the means of structuring reality. The extent to which they are appropriate was argued to depend on the extent to which they satisfied various conditions, notably those imposed by acceptable measures, criteria and behavioural assessment. Among these, the properties of a measure, including purpose, observation conditions, amenability to observation, perception and quantification, were argued to place a major constraint on the choice of appropriate dimensions or criteria.

Such an argument provides a basis to reflect on the differential utility of the methods presented in Chapter 2, as their limitations might well be explained in terms of an overemphasis on certain constraints to the neglect of others. As an example, Direct Index methods with an emphasis on quantification, parsimony, standardization, amenability to observation and perception, fail where they neglect to take account of the observation conditions, the need for criterion relevance, criterion dynamism, and the behavioural specification often required for performance measurement purpose. And as it becomes evident that purpose is a major determinant of measure utility then, for any one method, only differential utility is to be expected. This analysis then provides a rationale for the acceptability of each of the methods within clearly defined circumstances. These are but two specific implications of such an argument. There are of course more general implications.

The acknowledgement of this one fundamental point, that the definition of a measurement system is arbitrary, leads to a reorientation in perspective. It does not necessarily provide answers to the questions that currently pervade research but, as the author argued, questions such as 'What are the dimensions of performance?' may not be answerable in absolute terms. Rather, an appropriate answer is determined by information about the context, frame of reference, values, etc, implicit in the measurement situation.

This reorientation changes the questions that research addresses. When research concerns itself with 'susceptibility to bias' it is presuming an unwanted interference causing error in the quest of an absolute. But within an arbitrarily-defined system, the assumptions and therefore the research questions change and may become 'What forms of bias are functional?', 'What critical conditions of observation are not accounted for?', 'How observable and perceptible is the attribute?' etc. Not only this, but a wider implication exists for a change in research emphasis from regarding situational variables as contaminating and moderating effects to viewing them as determinants of appropriate measure choice. As Hartmann et al, (1979) suggested:

'Researchers are frequently unaware of the many facets implicitly sampled in any observation. Increased awareness of these implicitly sampled facets might serve to direct attention to the limitations of any single observation and to encourage explicit sampling of facets'. p.15.

Their conclusion suggests one other specific change in orientation that is borne out by the argument presented here, notably the question of measure generalizability. Because of the multivariate determinancy of measure appropriateness, there is no logic in expecting measures to be universally appropriate. That is to say, in applying the concept of measure generalizability, we must look beyond the measurement stimulus and the instrument and take into account critical variables in the measurement situation which determine measure appropriateness such as the context, the purpose, the observer, etc.

On a much grander scale these conclusions may be considered not just as a reorientation to specific questions but as having implications for more fruitful research paradigms. Herbst (1970) compared the nature of physical and behavioural laws and argued that behavioural laws are more

likely to be situation-dependent. However, he argued that _forms_ of behavioural laws might be universal and so urged social scientists to concern themselves with identifying universal methodologies which yield
situation-specific laws. Such methodologies would be based on an examination of the properties of behavioural variables and the necessary
conditions which must exist between them to arrive at behavioural laws.
This strategy, he argued, allows the methodologist to derive limits outside of which laws cannot exist and inside of which, a variety of laws
and 'universes' can be defined. This philosophy has been a guiding
theme here. As it became apparent that the appropriateness of measurement systems, their dimensions and criteria was subject to issues of
convenience, the approach adopted in clarifying the measurement problem
was to examine the properties of measures, dimensions, criteria and behavioural assessment and from these to establish limits on appropriate
performance measures and to examine whether different techniques for developing measures produce results within these limits.

By adopting such a method it is now possible to define limits on the
answers to the critical questions initially posed. It can now be concluded that performance measures should be behavioural, dynamic,
purpose-related, observable and allow for observation conditions. In
terms of their qualities, it has been shown that performance measures
may be qualitative or quantitative, uni- or multi-dimensional and multiple or singular, the choices being situation-specific depending on
purpose and observability. And finally, in considering how performance
measures should be derived, what is required are methods which combine
the rigour and purity of statistical techniques with the conceptual
soundness of psychological techniques, i.e. which have meaning in mathematical and psychological space.

The constraining factors which have been discussed above vary as to
their situation-specificity. For this reason, although general recommendations and limits are derived here, which still permit a wide array
of methods and techniques, the specification of particular factors
immediately serves to reduce this range. For example, the specification of purpose automatically determines many aspects of measure quality
and quantity. As such, general constraints may be placed on measures
required for reward-allocation purposes, for example. On the other
hand, constraints such as appraiser cognitive complexity may need to be
established for every measurement task that the appraiser performs.

Although general constraints on measure development techniques have been
noted above, it is appropriate to comment in particular on the suitability of BARS and factor analysis here. This is because the author uses
the former in the empirical study reported in Chapter 6 and, with regard
to the latter, because the theory above suggests very specific limitations to the utility of this currently popular technique.

BARS is a methodology which yields situation-specific 'laws', it
attempts to map subjective variables into psychological space with statistical rigour, and its methodology explicitly permits the inclusion of

major constraints. That is to say, it checks out the type of continua and level of detail available, it ensures agreed meaning, perceptibility and observability of the measured attribute and it attempts interval level scaling. Because of its situation-specific focus it permits measure variability according to purpose. It provides multiple and potentially dynamic criteria. It permits seemingly job-irrelevant factors to be included where necessary and because of the situational-specific statements of behaviour which anchor the scale points, it is based on real assumptions about the environmental determinism of behaviour. In short, it may provide a way ahead to bridge the theoretical-conceptual gap.

All of this is not to say that statistical methods are not valuable. Clearly, factor analysis can be immensely useful in identifying underlying, theoretically- and statistically-unique dimensions of performance. These are much needed for certain purposes, for example, in validating performance predictors, and would be invaluable in pursuing the utility of the principle of dimensional homogeniety.

The appraiser has been shown to be an important and central variable in determining measure appropriateness. Appraiser characteristics can determine to what extent an attribute is observable, perceptible, quantifiable and therefore the appraiser plays an integral role in determining the utility of measures. Although there are numerous constraints on appropriate performance measures, appraiser characteristics pervade quality and quantity issues and as the analysis of dimensional analysis methods has shown, psychological space or subjective ordering is important. As such the issue of appropriate performance criteria and dimensions is inextricably linked to that of subjectivity in measurement and it is to this second theme that we now turn.

4 Subjectivity in performance measurement

Through the analysis of measurement methods in Chapter 2 it became clear that the reliance on subjectively-derived quantitative data posed a fundamental problem for performance measurement and, in subsequently finding that observer characteristics pervade quality and quantity issues in the choice of appropriate performance measures, attention is likewise drawn to the subjective aspects of measurement. This subjective theme can now be addressed by tackling the problems identified earlier. If performance measures are to be conceptually sound, what role does subjective judgement play? And, if measures are to be methodologically pure, how can inevitable subjectivity be accommodated?

It is the explicit aim of this and the following chapter to answer these questions by firstly examining the role of subjectivity in performance measurement and by constructing a model that identifies and relates the sources, mechanisms and effects of subjectivity. This not only provides a much needed systematic overview of the research in performance rating but provides the basis for distinguishing functional and dysfunctional forms of subjectivity. In Chapter 5 the model is used as a reference so that strategies for dealing with the sources and effects of subjectivity can be identified, compared and evaluated. Ultimately implications are drawn from both for appropriate research and practice.

THE ROLE OF SUBJECTIVITY IN PERFORMANCE MEASUREMENT

In as much as objectivity is held to be a characteristic of scientific status, subjectivity poses a threat to any scientific pursuit (Hebb 1974) and so the fact of subjectivity presents a fundamental problem for psychological science.

It is because subjective experience is fallible, imperfect, subject to illusion and unique that it is seen to threaten validity, objectivity and scientific status. As Wertheimer (1972) stated 'only those concepts which can be externalized into publicly verifiable operations are admissible into the inner sanctum of science' p.113. The traditional aim then in the pursuit of an objective psychology has been to circumvent subjective experience in order to avoid the distortion and bias which it can introduce.

However, subjectivity remains inevitable for psychology in general and dependence on personal observation (subjective experience) has been established as inevitable for measurement in particular. Not withstanding ultimate aims then, perhaps attempts at circumvention may be mistaken. Indeed some authors argue that what's required is a more realistic view of the role of subjectivity and for its inclusion in the purview of psychology. Natsoulas (1978) for example claimed that 'residual subjectivity' is a critical feature of psychology and argued that psychology needs to comprehend subjectivity _per se_. In other words, perhaps it is more appropriate to accept and explore the fact of subjectivity rather than deny or try to side-step it.

And in response to the apparent threat it poses to validity some have argued that a concept of validity need not preclude subjectivity. Hilgard and Atkinson (1967), for example, talked about inter-subjectivity (i.e. data, the meaning of which can be shared by any competent observer and which may reasonably include subject's reports about their experiences) and Einhorn (1974) claimed that inter-judge agreement provides an index of validity as well as a means of checking on criterion relevance. While Wertheimer (1972) argued against such 'democratic criteria of truth', questioning whether inter-observer agreement can ever yield non-subjective truth, some (e.g. Wolf, 1978) would argue that objective truth is an overrated pursuit in psychology. In other words perhaps, because of the very nature of psychology, a difference does and should exist between appropriate validation techniques for psychological and physical phenomena.

The issue of subjectivity is perhaps the most basic problem for psychology and debates around its validity, significance, role and implications are not going to be resolved here but there is a basis for accepting the inevitability of subjectivity in measurement and there appears to be some justification for considering its role in performance measurement without necessarily denying psychology of its scientific status.

In the field of performance measurement the inevitability of subjectivity has to an extent been accepted. Where, for example, Klimoski and London (1974) observed that people supervising others will always make subjective evaluations they recognised that the elimination of judgemental criteria and their associated subjectivity was highly unlikely. In a more positive vein, subjective judgement has been seen as a rich and valuable source of data. Poulton (1977), for example, saw subjective judgement as a means of complementing deplete or unobtainable objective measures while Landy and Trumbo (1976) argued that, as objective data only reflect behavioural results, subjective judgement is needed for information about the behaviour itself. These suggest that not only is subjective judgement inevitable, it is also potentially valuable.

However, the problem is that subjective judgement can be inaccurate. As

Jones (1976) claimed, any set of observations no matter how carefully controlled, will yield an estimate which not only is uncertain but is likely to be biased. And with particular reference to performance rating, Barrett (1966) believed there was no such thing as an ideal rater who observes and evaluates what is important and reports his judgement without bias or appreciable error.

The stumbling block in relying on subjective judgement appears to come with quantification. As Poulton (1977) suggested, quantitative subjective assessments are almost always biased and sometimes completely misleading. Likewise Ronan and Prien (1971) categorically stated that the human element is at its lowest ebb in rating performance and, in elaboration, Robinson (1975) stated that this dependence on subjective judgement typically gives rise to inaccuracies such as leniency error, logical rating error, contrast and similarity errors, central tendency and halo effects in performance rating. Clearly, as performance measurement serves as a basis for important personnel decisions, regardless of its reliance on subjective judgement, it needs to be valid, reliable and accurate. How then can the effects of subjective involvement be avoided or coped with?

To decide on an appropriate means of dealing with subjectivity information is needed about what subjective involvement entails, how subjectivity arises, how it operates and how inaccuracy is introduced and it is the specific aim of this chapter to provide this ground work. This is an area which has attracted intense and diverse research activity and relevant findings are synthesised here into an explanatory framework.

Although subjectivity could be explored in relation to any performance measurement method, performance rating is chosen as the vehicle here not only because rating is the most common form of judgement made in performance measurement (Guion 1965) but because it is where judgements are quantitative that the undesirable effects of subjectivity appear to be most prevalent and detectable.

A MODEL OF THE RATING PROCESS

There have been two previous models which are notable in their focus on appraisal and rating effectiveness. Kane and Lawler's (1979) model of appraisal effectiveness determinants which found main effects attributable to both methodology and environment and Lawler's (1967) multi-trait/multi-rater approach which brought together aspects of the rating system, the organisation and the people involved into a model of factors effecting rating validity, both highlighted influential variables and provide coherent views of the performance assessment process but neither provide sufficient detail for present purposes of how subjective variables combine to influence ratings. The model to be described here focusses on performance assessment as an exercise of subjective judgement and so attempts to define relevant factors and their relationships more closely and pertinently. As it is the purpose of this chapter to

substantiate and explain the variables and relationships depicted in the
model it is appropriate to begin by identifying and explaining its three
main components: The Ratee Performance System;   The Determinants of
Rater Performance and Rater Judgement Components and Errors.

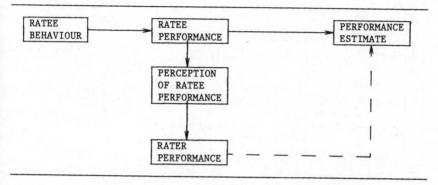

Fig. 4.1   The Ratee Performance System

The first part of the model (Fig. 4.1) draws relationships between ratee
and rater performance and the performance estimate.   Clearly the judgement process cannot be examined without defining ratee performance as
the object of judgement and without defining an accurate performance estimate as the desired outcome.   Despite the self-evidence of such definitions the qualifications which reality imposes at the outset should
be noted.   Theoretically speaking, ratee performance is a subset of
ratee work behaviours (Campbell et al, 1970) which can be observed and
measured to yield an accurate performance estimate.   However, as performance measurement is only concerned with the critical subset of performance behaviours which the rater observes and evaluates, then the link
between ratee performance and an accurate performance estimate is mediated by the rater's perception of ratee performance and by the rater's
performance at the rating task.   Ideally this observation, perception
and evaluation would be accurate but, as will be seen, there are a number of variables which influence these mediating factors and make an
accurate performance estimate an unlikely outcome.   For this reason the
relationship between rater performance and an accurate performance estimate is represented by a discontinuous line.

The second part of the model (Fig. 4.2) describes the factors which
account for rating performance variability.   Here the author takes the
view that the performance assessment can be regarded as a main outcome
of the rater's performance at the rating task.   (There are of course
other direct and indirect outcomes such as rater satisfaction, fatigue,
ratee response etc. which might be considered in a broader model of the
entire activity but which extend beyond the process emphasis required
here).   This focus on rater performance permits the identification of

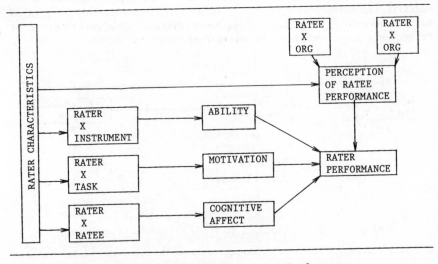

Fig. 4.2   The Determinants of Rater Performance

factors, apart from the ratee's performance, which effect rater performance and can lead to variation in the performance estimate.   Based on a
synthesis of research findings, a range of rater characteristics are
identified which interact with situational variables (including the
measurement instrument, the measurement task, the ratee himself and the
organisational context) to influence rating performance by creating systematic variance in the performance components of rater ability, motivation, cognitive affect and perception.

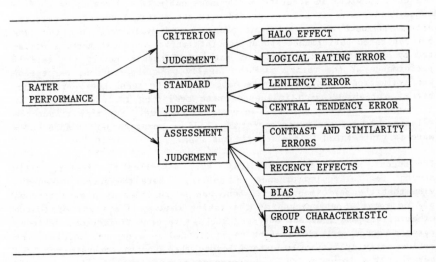

Fig. 4.3   Rater Judgement Components and Errors

The third part of the model (Fig. 4.3), in an attempt to elucidate the
relationship between subjectivity and its apparent effects, builds on
available empirical and theoretical findings and suggests the nature of
the relationship between rater performance and common rating errors.
The rating task is seen to consist of the three types of judgement (Criterion, Standard and Assessment) described in Chapter 2. The author
argues that characteristic forms of undue variance in the performance
measurement outcome arise through these differentially such that halo
effect and logical rating error are directly associated with Criterion
judgements, leniency error and central tendency error are associated
with Standard judgements, while contrast and similarity errors, recency
effects, bias and group characteristic bias are associated with Assessment judgements.

When Figs 4.1, 4.2 and 4.3 are combined with Rater Performance as the
point of contact, the ensuing model (Fig. 4.4 Rater Subjectivity:
Sources and Effects) can be seen to draw relationships between individual characteristics, situation variables, performance determinants,
judgement components and characteristic measurement errors. This description of the rating process as a subjective event allows distinct
sources of subjectivity to be identified and explored, and the mechanisms by which subjectivity effects measurement outcome to be explained.
This then provides the basis for a discussion of avoidable and inevitable, desirable and undesirable subjectivity, and lays the ground for an
examination, in Chapter 5, of potential strategies for managing subjectivity so that recommendations can be made as to appropriate strategies
for the avoidance, reduction or accommodation of its sources and
effects. With this overview of the main components of the model in
mind, the first half of the model, which is concerned with the sources
of subjectivity, can now be examined.

THE DETERMINANTS OF RATER PERFORMANCE

In the field of performance rating research it is evident that most
studies have focussed on variables included in this source end of the
model (see Fig. 4.2). However, research has typically examined the
effect of specific individual variables on indices of rater performance
(such as degree of leniency, halo etc.) while less attention has been
paid to specifying how, for example, rater characteristics interact with
situational variables and how these interactions influence rater performance. More commonplace are studies which show that raters with a particular characteristic, or (less common) in a particular situation, tend
to make a particular type of error. This essentially 'black-box'
approach to understanding the problems of performance measurement naturally limits the extent to which our understanding of the process can be
enhanced. Until both the sources and mechanisms of subjective influence
can be located and identified then it will remain difficult, if not impossible, to specify with any certainty an appropriate means of dealing
with subjectivity and its effects. The task here therefore is to syn-
thesise empirical findings and clarify the relationships that exist
between significant variables.

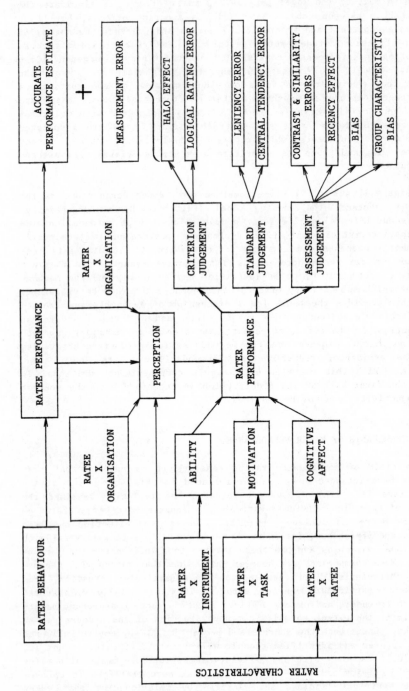

Fig. 4.4. Rater Subjectivity: Sources & Effects

80

The source end of the model is naturally anchored by rater characteristics. When Anastasi (1964) stated that 'who does the rating makes more difference in the ratings received than do characteristics of the rating scale, the rating technique employed or the conditions under which ratings are made' p.88, she drew explicit attention to the importance of the rater's personal characteristics in the rating process. This shot-in-the-arm for rating research directed attention from the traditional focus on instrument development to the rater himself, and subsequent research (Lawler 1967, Schinka and Sines 1974, Zedeck, Jacobs and Kafry 1976, Kane and Lawler 1979, Borman, 1977, 1978, 1979a) has not only reinforced the importance of rater characteristics but impressed the need for their inclusion in rating models, and urged the investigation of characteristics which determine rating ability. Given the performance-focussed view that is employed here it is clear that what is now required is detailed information about which characteristics determine rater performance (not just ability) and how. Several authors have undertaken studies which either examine particular characteristics (e.g. Schneier's, 1977, focus on cognitive complexity), or identify characteristic correlates of rating accuracy (e.g. Borman 1979a), and the results may be conveniently summarized according to whether the characteristics are associated with biography, knowledge and skills, or personality and cognitive complexity.

Biographical differences. There are a few studies which have related biographical differences to aspects of the rating activity. Cascio and Valenzi (1977) found a positive but weak correlation between education level and rating accuracy. Cline, Holmes and Werner (1977) observed that rater-ratee sex differences resulted in lower valued ratings and Fox, Hill and Guertin (1973) noted cultural differences in the perceived importance of performance criteria. And later, Lowenberg (1979) found that differences in scale perceptions and interpretation were associated with sex, major subject study and age differences and caused rating inaccuracy in their study of student evaluations.

With the exception of Cascio and Valenzi's (1977) work this sample of such studies reflects the fact that research has generally failed to show any significant direct relationship between biographic characteristics and rating performance. Typically, characteristics appear to effect rating performance through their interaction with situational variables. In particular they are characteristics which effect the rater's ability to use the instrument, his perception of performance and his perception of the performer, i.e. they contribute to Rater x Instrument, Perception of Ratee Performance and Rater x Ratee factors.

Knowledge and skills. In this area research has yielded positive correlations between physical science specialization and judgement ability (Taft 1955), technical knowledge and rating accuracy in specific performance areas (Wagner and Hoover 1974), rater skills, preferences, prejudices and rating accuracy (Mash and Terdal 1976), and rater experience and rating accuracy (Garner and Smith 1976, Borman 1978). Again, the research is sparse and, like biographical differences, main effects appear to be few.   Most common are the effects which knowledge and skills have on the rater's ability to use the instrument, his ability to perform the task with respect to a specific performance area and his perception of the performer i.e. they are variables which contribute to Rater x Instrument, Rater x Task, and Rater x Ratee factors.

Personality and cognitive complexity. Taft's (1955) investigations of judgement ability found social skill, esthetic and dramatic interests, I.Q. and academic ability to be influential personality variables while Mandell (1956) found more and less 'bright' managers to have different perceptions of subordinate performance. And much more recently, Borman (1977) found personal adjustment, dependability, stability and intelligence to be positively related to rating accuracy.   While these results are informative, the use of global concepts limits their utility for they lack the precision which might permit characteristics to be isolated and specific effects to be identified.   However, there are more specific personality characteristics which have been shown to effect the rating process.

Anastasi (1964) suggested that the rater's intellectual capacity to discriminate between performance levels and between performance aspects limits instrument choice and utility.   Likewise, Borman (1977) noted a positive relationship between detail orientation and rating accuracy, again, a Rater x Instrument factor effecting rating ability.   De Nisi and Pritchard (1978) meanwhile suggested that raters as individuals have an Implicit Theory of Performance which guides their judgements of behaviours and Gordon (1970) identified the Differential Accuracy Phenomenon (D.A.P) i.e. the tendency to recognise and rate correct behaviour more accurately than incorrect behaviour.   These mental characteristics which effect rating accuracy through Rater x Instrument and Perception of Ratee Performance factors, lead to the cognitive complexity characteristic briefly discussed in Chapter 3.   Indeed, differential discrimination and structuring of cognitive domains are essential features of this personality characteristic.   Moreover, the initial attempt by Schneier (1977) to investigate cognitive complexity variation and rating accuracy revealed that degree of complexity was associated with instrument preference and with different types of rating errors.

Much of the cognitive complexity research is based on Kelly's Personal Construct work, but specifically focusses on the effects of cognitive dimensional structure on social and interpersonal judgements. Cognitive complexity is the 'degree to which the entire and/or subsegment of a cognitive semantic space is differentiated and integrated' (Streufert and Streufert 1978) and these concepts of differentiation (the process of dividing semantic space into two or more orthogonal or oblique bipolar semantic dimensions) and integration (the process of relating a stimulus to two or more dimensions) form an agreed basis of theorists' definitions of complexity.   One other concept, variably termed discrimination (Streufert and Streufert 1978) or articulation (Bieri 1968), refers to the process of dividing semantic dimensions, where divisions are only meaningful to the extent that they can be labelled.   In other

words, differentiation refers to the process of subjective dimensionalization, integration refers to the relationships between constituent
dimensions and articulation refers to the subject's discriminative
powers with respect to specific dimensions.

Research consistently finds individual differences in this personality
characteristic and yields numerous associated differences in performance
on judgemental and decision-making tasks. The findings indicate that
cognitively simple judges and decision-makers tend to be invariant and
inflexible in their attitudes (Harvey and Schroder 1963, Streufert and
Streufert 1969), are more easily influenced by recent and salient cues
(Harvey and Schroder 1963, Mayo and Crockett 1964, Streufert 1966,
Petronko and Perin 1970), show a greater dependency on environmental
cues for responses (Harvey and Schroder 1963, Heslin and Streufert
1968), and are predisposed to respond to stimuli on a single evaluative
dimension (Campbell 1960, Harvey and Schroder 1963, Schroder, Driver and
Streufert 1967, Crockett, Mahood and Press 1975).

By comparison, cognitively complex judges and decision-makers tend to be
flexible in their attitudes (Scott 1962), seek new and broader information in decision-making (Sieber 1964, Karlins 1967, Schneider and
Giambra 1971, Watson 1971), have a greater capacity to understand and
accept potentially conflicting information (Nidorf 1961, Crockett,
Mahood and Press 1975), tend to respond to stimuli multi-dimensionally
(Schroder, Driver and Streufert 1967), and have the ability to recognise
that others might respond differently (Bieri 1955).

These characteristics have obvious implications for the rater's tasks of
gathering, perceiving, processing, recording and evaluating performance
information and might reasonably be expected to reflect on rating
accuracy through rating ability and performance. However, it would be
premature to make gross personality distinctions on the basis of cognitive complexity per se, as a unitary concept has yet to be identified.
In addition, some authors maintain that degree of complexity is domain-
specific. Scott (1974), emphasising the point, suggested that the
probable number of people having consistent cognitive structural characteristics among many areas of experience is quite small, and further,
that such individuals may well be pathological! So an individual may be
cognitively simple or complex according to the area of experience sampled. Moreover, there is a growing recognition of the influence of situational factors. Shrauger and Altrocchi (1964) drew attention to the
person-situation interaction as a determinant of complexity while Bieri
(1966) stressed the importance of environmental and situational factors
in determining the adopted cognitive style. That is to say, an individual may exhibit complex or simple characteristics depending on his
basic style, the area of experience sampled, and the judgement or
decision-making situation.

As the research reported above indicates significant differences between
cognitively complex and simple judges in their ability to meaningfully
discriminate, their ability to perform a particular judgemental task,

the flexibility of their attitudes to others and their perceptual abilities, then complexity in the cognitive domain of performance can be expected to be influential in Rater x Instrument, Rater x Task, Rater x Ratee factors and in the Perception of Ratee Performance.

In conclusion, rater differences in biography, knowledge and skills, personality, and cognitive complexity can be seen to influence rating performance differentially through Rater x Instrument, Rater x Task, Rater x Ratee factors and through the Perception of Ratee Performance. These four factors and their influence on rater performance can now be examined.

Rater x Instrument Factors and Ability

Among the attempts to improve rating accuracy, a concentration on improving scale reliability and validity through instrument-oriented research has been, till recently, the most popular. It is clear that rating system characteristics are an important factor in the validity of ratings (Lawler 1967) and several studies, including those discussed in the previous chapter, have identified salient instrument characteristics and their effects. Madden and Bourdon (1964), for example, found scale format to be a determinant of rater judgement. More specifically, trait and behavioural anchoring, as opposed to unstructured formats, display greater reliability, less halo and less leniency error (Barrett et al, 1958). Similarly, job-task, as opposed to trait-anchored scales, yield higher reliability estimates (Peters and McCormick 1966). Meanwhile, Bendig and Hughes (1953), and more recently, Lissitz and Green (1975) and McKelvie (1978) have focussed on the effect of the number of scale points on rating reliability and validity. Others still (Gravetter and Lockhead 1973 and Poulton 1977) have been concerned with the effects of the criterion range that the scale presents as a frame of reference for stimulus judgements. The major emphasis in these studies, with the exception of the latter, is on the instrument itself. But rating accuracy is not a function of the instrument per se but of how it is used and the rater may place significant constraints on scale or instrument utility and acceptability. For example, Elser and Osman (1978) attributed low inter-rater reliability to inter-rater differences in the value connotations attached to scale labels and Anastasi (1964), recognising that raters impose constraints, urged that unit choice be guided by the need for uniform interpretation by raters. In short the problem seems to lie in the meaning that measurement scales and anchors have for the rater.

The meaningfulness of scale content might be expected to be a function of rater characteristics and indeed, Schneier (1977) argued that rating accuracy is only likely to be achieved where there is a match between instrument characteristics and rater cognitive characteristics. This crystallizes a recurrent theme in personality and performance assessment literature. Several authors have sought to increase scale meaning by adopting rater-defined constructs rather than imposing their own. Research in personality assessment has specifically concerned itself with the effects of using subject-generated (rather than imposed) constructs on subjects' differentiation ability and Metcalfe (1974) found the use of generated constructs to be preferable. With respect to performance measurement, Smith and Kendall (1963) originally argued for the need to couch scale content in rater terminology and, in their Behaviourally Anchored Rating Scale methodology, produced a participative technique of scale development where raters generate performance constructs. As the BARS method has proved successful in overcoming the problems of scale meaning it may well be that rater participation in content and anchor definition ensures that resultant scales not only parallel the rater's cognitive constructs but constitute a common set of differentiated cognitive dimensions.

Clearly, rater characteristics and particularly cognitive complexity, play a part in determining rating instrument utility because they influence the meaningfulness to the rater of scale content and anchors. Therefore Borman's (1978) observation that rating problems arise out of either the lack of understanding of scale content or the lack of relevant scale anchors might be extended to conclude that both significantly effect scale utility by detracting from the rater's ability to perform the rating task. While much research has attempted to remedy the latter cause it is evident that the former should be of primary concern if the potential consequences of lack of understanding are considered.

The problem of meaning. When a rater fails to understand performance constructs or to perceive them as meaningful then he may respond to the instrument in several ways, any one of which is likely to detract from rating validity and reliability. He may, for example, reinterpret or distort construct meaning to something which is meaningful to himself. Alternatively, he may use the opportunity that lack of meaning presents to register affect, and provide ratings which reflect a single evaluation, the basis of which is unknown and so they are no more informative and perhaps less valid than global performance ratings. Or, he may accept scale meaninglessness and respond purely compliantly providing ratings that are essentially random.

Similarly, when a rater fails to understand scale gradations or to perceive them as meaningful he is likely to respond dysfunctionally. The rater may respond by imposing personally-defined gradations or by adopting a personal rating strategy (Zedeck and Kafry 1977), both of which threaten inter-rater reliability. Alternatively, he may tend towards psychometric bias through a susceptibility to salient scale characteristics in the absence of other significant cues or he may use the opportunity to register affect. All of these responses to lack of instrument meaning are likely to lead to problems with rating validity, reliability or accuracy.

The research which shows that repeated instrument exposure serves to reduce rating inaccuracy (Garner and Smith 1976, Borman 1978) suggests that raters do seek to derive meaning from the instrument and, given sufficient opportunity, are capable of overcoming poor instrument design to enhance their rating ability. And indeed, enhancing rating ability through training in instrument meaning and use has proved successful in reducing rating errors (Latham, Wexley and Pursell 1975).

Rater x Task Factors and Motivation

The second main interaction factor concerns the effect of task characteristics on rater performance. Several studies of rating situation variables (Bayroff, Haggerty and Rindquist 1954, Fiske and Cox 1979 and Kent, Kanowitz, O'Leary and Cheiken 1977) indicate that the organisational context of the performance measurement task influences rating validity, reliability and accuracy. That is to say that characteristics of the rating situation effect how well the rater performs his task. These interaction effects are referred to here as Rater x Task factors. Systematic and relevant research is lacking in this area because most studies have been conducted under experimental conditions where real organisational variables are excluded. In view of the recurrent finding that ratings obtained in research situations are more accurate and error-free than those used in practice (Sharon and Bartlett 1969, Cascio and Valenzi 1977, Warmke and Billings 1979) this is a serious lack. However a sufficient number of studies refer to these factors to allow identification of the core issues.

Task purpose. The purpose for which ratings are required may well effect the level of effort the rater is willing to invest in the task. As Landy and Trumbo (1976) suggested, where performance assessments are linked to the organisational reward and punishment system it is likely that information will be systematically gathered and carefully assessed. (For example, where performance-pay contingencies exist the ratings are likely to be more accurate). On the other hand, where information is systematically collected and equally systematically ignored, ratings are likely to exhibit low validity. It would be reasonable to suppose then that task purpose is significant because the rater's perception of task utility influences the effort he is prepared to invest in making an accurate assessment.

Social structure and pressure. Kane and Lawler (1979) explained that where organisational norms and sanctions are such that providing valid performance data is not rewarded then it is virtually impossible to obtain valid measures. Warmke and Billings (1979) similarly suggested that political and union pressures and turnover rates could prove to be significant influences on the rater's motivation to provide accurate ratings and Lawler (1971) proposed that the level of openness and trust in the organisation could significantly effect rating validity. In short, the climate surrounding the assessment task may create pressure on the rater such that self-interest is best served by providing inaccurate data. So, here the rater's perception of personal punishments or rewards associated with the task is likely to effect the effort he invests in task performance.

Time constraints. The third situation variable likely to effect rating accuracy concerns the relationship between task size (determined by the nature of the instrument), the number of such tasks required of the rater (determined by ratee group size) and the time available to perform the rating tasks. Accepting the implications of potential rater fatigue for instrument design discussed earlier, time constraints will always operate differentially on raters because of context differences. Although Warmke and Billings (1979) considered time constraints to be a potentially significant contextual factor they provided little elaboration but as the task involves accurate behavioural recall over a period, appropriate weighting of performance characteristics and their translation onto the instrument, then time pressure might be expected to effect recall, judgement and rating accuracy. In addition, as Harvey and Schroder (1963) demonstrated, the same time constraint may effect raters differently according to their cognitive characteristics. In hurried situations cognitively simple subjects are more likely than their complex colleagues to collapse differentiated categories into a simple uni-dimensional evaluation, thereby producing halo error. Under time constraints, rating accuracy appears to be a function of the rater's cognitive complexity in the performance domain and the effort he is prepared to invest in information recall and judgement.

Appraisal system requirements. What the appraisal system requires of the rater seems to be a significant Rater x Task factor effecting motivation. Warmke and Billings (1979) suggested that the need to justify ratings places a constraint on rating accuracy and McCall and Devries (1976) found that where the rater is required to discuss with the ratee the ratings given, then there is a psychological demand to provide lenient ratings. Similarly Robinson (1975) attributed central tendency effect in part to system openness, suggesting that assessments are likely to be less extreme where they may be seen by the ratee. As with social structure and pressure, this variable would appear to operate by setting up task contingencies which effect the rater's willingness to assess accurately. Where the rater is answerable to the ratee for ratings given and this is perceived as threatening then the rater's interest is best served by providing inaccurately favourable or ambivalent information.

These four Rater x Task factors place considerable and perhaps conflicting influences on the rater's motivation to provide accurate ratings. The task context can present conditions which variably enhance or detract from the rater's motivation to rate accurately.

In terms of Expectancy theory (Vroom 1964) these factors effect the expectancies and valences associated with the rating task. Performance instrumentality is reduced where ratings are ignored and enhanced where ratings are explicitly valued by the organisation (as displayed by their utility) and effort-performance expectancies are likely to be low where time constraints prevail. Finally, the task will be negatively valent where valid information is not rewarded by the oranisation, where there is a risk of attracting adverse political or social group pressure or where the system requires that the rater face potential repercussions from the ratee.

Kane and Lawler (1979), commented on the paucity of research which identifies contextual variables and documents their impact. Four contextual factors have been identified here which would appear to effect
rating performance and accuracy through the rater's motivation to do an
effective job. To further describe their mode of operation requires
further in-organisation research but it seems that an Expectancy model
of rater motivation would provide a promising theoretical framework.

Rater x Ratee Factors and Cognitive Affect

Research has identified several influences on rating accuracy which are
best described as Rater x Ratee factors. These might be conveniently
distinguished as those concerned with degree of rater-ratee acquaintance
or familiarity and those concerned with the interaction between rater
and ratee personal characteristics.

Anastasi (1964) and Freeberg (1969) found amount of acquaintance to be
positively related to rating accuracy, reliability and validity and
Fiske and Cox (1979) found target familiarity to significantly effect
the assessor's perceptual process. Cognitive complexity research can
explain this phenomenon. Crockett (1965) found that an increase in
perceiver-perceived interaction leads to an increase in the perceiver's
cognitive complexity with respect to that domain and in elaboration,
cited findings which showed that subjects exhibited greater differentiation with respect to peers versus elders. As familiar targets are likely to be more differentiated the rater would be less susceptible to
salient cues, less likely to use stereotypes and therefore more likely
to rate accurately and validly.

The second set of factors concern personal characteristics and in particular the perceived similarity between those of the rater and the
ratee. While race and sex characteristics of ratees have been shown to
significantly effect the accuracy of performance ratings (Deaux and
Emswiller 1974, Rosen and Jerdee 1973, 1974, De Jung and Kaplan 1962,
Flaugher, Campbell and Pike 1969, and Quinn 1969), Dunnette and Borman
(1979) pointed out that such results could be misleading without ensuring standardized performance across subgroups or rigorous controls on
rater sex, age and race, because ratings could be due to real differences, rating biases or a combination. Additionally,it is never
quite clear to what extent the effects are due to ratee characteristics
per se or to their perceived similarity to rater characteristics.

Although Quinn (1969) reported that ratee characteristics had a greater
influence on ratings than rater-ratee similarity, Kane and Lawler (1979)
found that rater-ratee characteristic similarity leads to more favourable ratings and, accumulated research supports this view. Campbell
(1972), Crooks (1972) and Johnson and Ronan (1979) reported a tendency
to award higher ratings to the rater's own ethnic or racial group members and indeed, the findings in this area are so strong that Anastasi

(1972) seriously questioned the validity of ratings when ethnic differences are involved. In the same vein, raters have been found to award more favourable ratings where there are rater-ratee similarities in sex (Hamner, Kim, Baird and Bigoness 1974, Cline, Holmes and Werner 1977), nationality (Borman 1974, Bigoness 1976) or attitude and personality (Nieva 1976).

These effects of personal characteristic similarity are difficult to explain in terms of rating ability or motivation but they may be partially explained in terms of cognitive affect. Newcomb (1961) and Byrne (1971) have shown that similarity between perceiver and perceived is associated with interpersonal attraction or liking, and interpersonal attraction leads to more favourable ratings, Kipnis (1960). In addition Scott (1978) suggested that where an affective dimension is introduced into the cognitive domain, attributes that correlate with liking also correlate with each other, thus reducing domain dimensionality and resulting in a halo effect. By way of contrast, those who evoke negative affect provoke greater differentiation and discrimination in the perceiver's domain (Miller and Bieri 1965, Irwin, Tripodi and Bieri 1967).

In this area of Rater x Ratee factors it appears that greater familiarity leads to greater differentiation which is associated with greater accuracy of ratings, while greater similarity and interpersonal attraction leads to less differentiation which is associated with reduced accuracy. Firm conclusions are difficult to draw because attraction may evoke familiarity but nevertheless a major factor appears to be the rater's feelings for the ratee i.e. cognitive affect.

This discussion of the first three interaction factors has identified rater ability, motivation and cognitive affect as the mechanisms by which Rater x Instrument/Task/Ratee factors effect rating performance respectively. Before discussing the effect of rater and ratee context factors on the Perception of Ratee Performance these three mechanisms can be put in the context of a rater performance model.

Rater Performance

Any task performance can be conceived as a function of the individual's ability, motivation and the opportunity provided to perform (Maier 1955, Campbell et al, 1970). Despite the issue of whether the function is additive or multiplicative (Vroom 1964, Locke 1965, Lawler 1966, Graen 1967), the central performance determinants are well-agreed. While the above analysis of factors effecting rating performance through rater ability, motivation and cognitive affect is supported by a partial congruity with this general performance model the congruence is not exact and the differences need to be accounted for.

The findings suggest that the rater's ability to perform the task depends on cognitive abilities and on the opportunity the instrument affords to differentiate and discriminate with respect to the performance domain. Inaccuracy arises where a mismatch occurs i.e. where the instrument form or content lacks interpretable meaning for the rater. The rater's motivation to perform the task depends on the perceived task utility and on the task contingencies. These are determined by task purpose, social structure and pressures, time constraints and appraisal system requirements. Inaccuracy arises where expectancy or instrumentality are low or net valences are negative. So, whereas ability and motivation are evident as direct performance determinants, opportunity appears to have an indirect effect on performance through instrument and appraisal system design.

In asking what can be done to improve accuracy then it is clear that previous attempts have focussed on specific influences only. As far as the ability component is concerned, until very recently, most research has emphasised instrument development (i.e. the opportunity factor). And as far as motivation is concerned, apart from the early concern for the manager's role in appraisal interviewing, it is only really through recent efforts to match rater and instrument constructs through BARS that the spin-off effects of rater participation on motivation have been noted and direct attempts to influence rater motivation have been made. However, the ability and motivation determinants are influenced by other variables and the identification of these sources of inaccuracy lays the ground for recommending more comprehensive and systematic strategies for improving rater performance. These are pursued in the following chapter.

The Rater x Ratee factor appears to be the other main influence on rating performance and it might be explained in terms of the rater's cognitive affect or emotional orientation towards the ratee. While cognitive affect does not fit the general performance model, its effects are strong and therefore it needs to be accommodated. When task performance centres on a social object it is reasonable to assume some emotional orientation on the performer's part and to accept that this could influence performance. Thus, an emotional component would be a necessary elaboration to the general performance model.

Finally, a distinction was made in Chapter 2 between appraisee-related and non-appraisee-related bias. This analysis suggests that non-appraisee-related bias has two major stems (rater ability and motivation) which give rise to consistent rating inaccuracy and it suggests that these sources of undue variance can be tackled through organisational and individual change strategies (to be discussed in Chapter 5).

In contrast, appraisee-related bias appears to operate through the cognitive affect factor but unlike the non-appraisee-related biases, it takes the form of intra-rater inconsistency in rating accuracy. As such, the effects are rater-specific and intermittent and so general coping strategies may be inappropriate but as the effects can be significant some consideration of possible solutions is required. Potential strategies and solutions will be discussed in the next chapter.

The Perception of Ratee Performance

Fig. 4.1 depicts the relationship between ratee performance and rater performance as mediated by the rater's perception of ratee performance. Although some major sources of undue rating variance have already been discussed, the rater's perception itself may also give rise to inaccurate rating (Zedeck, Jacobs and Kafry 1976).

While it is well-established that perception is coloured by experience, attitudes, values etc, for the purposes of isolating subjectivity sources, specific variables which influence rater perception and potentially contaminate rater performance need to be identified.

Two main factors can be distinguished here, the background against which ratee performance is perceived and the perceiver's viewpoint. Rather like the figure-ground principle of object perception, evidence suggests that the perception of ratee performance (figure) varies systematically according to the organisational context (ground) in which performance is viewed. There are several influential contextual factors and these sources of undue variance are discussed below as Ratee x Organisation factors. But perceptual distortion also results from perceiver characteristics and, in particular, aspects of the rater's organisational context. These sources of undue variance are discussed as Rater x Organisation factors.

Ratee x Organisation Factors

Characteristics of the ratee's workgroup and task appear to influence the rater's perception of ratee performance and thus rating accuracy. Group characteristic bias (see Blum and Naylor 1968) effects rater performance inasmuch as the group can define a false ceiling or floor for ratee performance and therefore resultant ratings may appear negatively or positively skewed although the perception, or the rating itself may not be inaccurate. For example, Cascio and Valenzi (1977) attributed apparent leniency error in their police officer ratings to the highly selected nature of the ratee group. However, there are ratee group factors which influence perception and result in rating inaccuracy.

Where a ratee differs in some significant way (e.g. in job experience) from other ratees then these 'chance assignment' factors can distort perception. Bechtoldt (1947) consequently noted the need to either standardize perceptual conditions or to include an index of significant factors in the rating. Grey and Kipnis (1976) found contrast effects, where the presence of a non-compliant worker enhances the ratings of compliant workers, to account for a significant amount of rating variance, and Landy and Trumbo (1976) found the ratee's organisational position to effect rating accuracy. They noted that where salary increases are based on performance ratings and where it's necessary to award larger increases to young organisation members to retain them, then longer serving members are likely to be given lower ratings as a function of age or tenure. In summary, ratee group characteristics, similarities and dissimilarities between the ratee and others, and ratee organisational position may all provide a background against which accurate performance perception is difficult to achieve and rating accuracy is likely to be effected.

The other major Ratee x Organisation factor is the ratee's task. Although there is only limited evidence, the effects of ratee job characteristics on rater perception may be substantial.

Opportunity bias.   The distortion of performance by inadequate equipment, working conditions etc. is a characteristic criterion contaminant (Robinson 1975) which distorts performance perception and has obvious implications for the comparison of ratee performances where 'opportunities' differ.

Task definition. Where the ratee position is described generally rather than in detail then raters are more susceptible to stereotyping effects (Shaw 1972) and where job definition is low (e.g. in general management as opposed to functional management jobs) then the similarity-favourability effects described above appear more strongly (Senger 1971, Nieva 1976). This suggests that where the ratee task is ambiguously defined, perception is subject to bias and rating accuracy is effected.

Job interdependence. Where the ratee job is independent of others then ratee performance is highly visible and so accurate perception and rating is relatively easy. By contrast, tasks which require cooperative effort make individual performance difficult both to distinguish and assess accurately. (Hackman and Lawler 1971, Kane and Lawler 1979).

Employee autonomy. The degree to which the ratee can control the pace, nature and method of work appears to effect the perceptibility of performance and rating accuracy. Kane and Lawler (1979) argued that high autonomy jobs are much easier to rate because they permit greater variance in performance effectiveness and allow the direct attribution of different levels of performance to the individual rather than to factors, such as machine pace, beyond the individual's control.

Intrinsic feedback.   Tasks which are high in intrinsic feedback make performance effectiveness more discernible to the perceiver (Hackman and Lawler 1971) and as such the perceiver is better equipped to assess performance on relevant grounds.

These ratee task factors including opportunity, task definition, job interdependence, employee autonomy and intrinsic feedback appear to have their main effect on rating accuracy through the constraints they place on the discernibility of the individual's contribution, the relevance of perceived stimuli, the observable range of performance effectiveness and the observability of performance effects they permit, each of which facilitate or inhibit perception of ratee performance.

Rater x Organisation Factors

Accumulated research suggests that rater organisational position, and in particular rater-ratee organisational relationship, effects both rating accuracy and relevance by influencing the rater's perception of behaviour (Miner 1968, Dubin, Porter, Stone and Champoux 1974, Schneier and

92

Beatty 1976).

Early research by Berry, Nelson and McNally (1966) found a positive correlation between similarity of rater organisational rank and similarity of subordinate appraisal, and more recent studies (Borman 1974, Heneman 1974, Klimoski and London 1974) have found low agreement to typify the ratings of raters from different organisational levels, so much so that the latter authors were able to identify, using factor analysis, the performance judgements collected from different rater groups. Concluding that inter-rater disagreements reflected systematic rater bias, they called this effect 'rater-group specific' bias. So as Dunnette and Borman (1979) observed, the evidence suggests that 'where the rater is coming from' can make a significant difference to the ratings made. But how do these biases arise and what form do they take?

Several authors have compared self versus others' ratings of performance (Dickinson and Tice 1973, Zedeck and Baker 1972, Beatty, Schneier and Beatty 1977) and found that they differ systematically with regard to the perceived amount and frequency of favourable and unfavourable behaviour. Beatty et al, (1977) explained that as self-perceptions are coloured by intentions whereas others' judgements can only be based on observed behaviour, the latter's performance estimate is likely to be more accurate than that of the ratee. However the implied accuracy is only relative and the extent to which either contains bias remains to be established.

Considering self as the rater is of course a rather special case and it is likely that the bias introduced in self-rating is of a different nature from that when the perceptual and rating bias associated with different non-self raters is considered. In this more general case, one clear cause of differential rating accuracy is the opportunity different organisational positions provide to observe ratee behaviour (Bechtoldt 1947, Landy and Trumbo 1976, Borman 1978).

As behavioural assessment relies heavily on behaviour observability, the opportunity to observe behaviour can be a source of rating differences. Zedeck and Baker (1972) demonstrated that the amount of rater-ratee contact was important in achieving accurate rating and Landy and Guion (1970) found large differences in inter-rater reliability (.24-.70) when comparing situations where rater and ratee were casually acquainted with those where they were well-acquainted respectively. Freeberg (1969) found an increase in rating validity where raters were allowed to view more ratee behaviour relevant to the rated dimensions and finally, Cascio and Valenzi (1977) attributed persistent halo effect in their police officers ratings to the low observability of relevant behaviours. Quite clearly, the opportunity to observe ratee behaviour effects the accuracy of ratings. The rater-ratee organisational relationship is a major determinant of the amount of rater-ratee contact and the effect on rating accuracy can be explained by the findings that frequency of perceiver-perceived contact is positively correlated with cognitive complexity (i.e. differentiation, integration and discrimination) and that increased complexity results in greater judgement accuracy.

But the rater's organisational position may have a significance for rating accuracy beyond the implied frequency of contact. Barrett (1966), suggested that, 'the position of the rater .... determines in part the extent and nature of his opportunity to observe, the quality of his judgement and the appropriateness of his point of view'. p.102. This implies that not only does relative position influence rating accuracy through determining observation opportunities, but that it effects what kinds of behaviours are viewed, and, as Klimoski and London (1974) also noted, what kind of judgements are made. There is substantial empirical evidence to support these hypotheses.

Zedeck, Imparato, Krausz and Oleno (1974) found that although the BARS dimensions generated by two organisational levels were similar, the behavioural anchors were valued differently , i.e. different relative positions (e.g. peer and superior) value specific behaviours differently. In addition, different raters may use different percepts or dimensions when judging performance (Guion 1965). And Norman and Goldberg (1966), observing that superiors and peers perceive different aspects of behaviour, claimed that such differential perceptions may well be valid. Accepting this view, Klimoski and London (1974) went so far as to suggest that no one position or organisation vantage point could provide the information necessary to determine a person's effectiveness while Guion (1965) argued for the use of several judges to get nearer to achieving a measure of the ultimate criterion.

These writers have proceeded beyond viewing the effects of rater position as contaminants of perception towards the view that the 'bias' is valid, as Dunnette and Borman (1979) suggested, according to the different perspectives represented. So the judgemental bias which is introduced by rater organisational position may be a source of subjectivity to be recognised and utilised rather than a contaminant to be eliminated. The utility of this view would be enhanced if it was known how rater organisational position differences in percepts are determined and this is one of the objectives of the empirical study reported in Chapter 6.

But rater organisational position is but one of the Rater x Organisation factors influencing perception. Kane and Lawler (1979) considered personal characteristics to influence the kinds of job behaviours and outcomes that raters look for and define as effective. Levy (1960), for example, found that rater job effectiveness influenced ratings given and Kirchner and Reisberg (1962) found more effective managers to value initiative, persistence, broad knowledge and planning ability in their subordinates and to exhibit a greater range of ratings when compared to less effective managers, who tended to value co-operation, company loyalty, good team work, tact and consideration and who were less capable of scale discrimination. In other words the rater's job competence was a significant factor in the performance components valued and in discriminative ability. Finally Cascio and Valenzi (1977) found job experience to be a factor influencing raters' judgements and specifically Garner and Smith (1976) found inexperienced evaluators to make greater use of stereotypes than expert evaluators. So there is some evidence to suggest that rater job effectiveness, competence and experience influence his perception, his ability to discriminate and to rate accurately.

While there may be some justification for the 'bias' introduced by rater organisational position, biases due to personal effectiveness, competence or experience are more difficult to justify, detect and isolate but nevertheless need to be considered and treated as possible contaminants of rater perception.

RATER JUDGEMENT COMPONENTS AND ERRORS

So far the concern has been to identify the sources of subjectivity and the performance determinants through which different sources operate. As the overall objective is to establish the relationship between subjectivity sources and effects, the next stage of the analysis is to build a bridge between rater performance and characteristic rating errors. In this section, therefore, the second half of the Rater Subjectivity model (see Fig. 4.4) becomes the focus in order to explain how the influences on rating performance result in rating inaccuracy and error.

Although Borman (1978) and Dunnette and Borman (1979), with well-founded convictions that new approaches to solving performance rating problems needed to be identified, called for a close examination of the processes that raters use in making performance judgements, to date there have been no specific contributions to this line of research. Given this lack of research it is now necessary to move beyond what is empirically demonstrated to some propositions as to what these linking processes might be. The author suggests that performance rating involves three judgement processes and that common rating errors (i.e. halo, logical rating error, leniency, central tendency, contrast and similarity errors, recency effect, rating and group characteristic bias) arise from these differentially.

In Chapter 2, three forms of judgement potentially required by performance measurement methods were distinguished. These were; Criterion judgement – a decision as to what performance criteria are important; Standard judgement – a decision as to what constitutes an acceptable performance level; and Assessment judgement – a decision as to what level of performance an individual has achieved. In addition, it was noted that increased objectivity was associated with a successive reduction of the requirement on the appraiser for all three forms of judgement.

While Quantitative Absolute Standards Procedures control levels of Criterion and Standard judgements and offer a wide range of types of

Assessment judgements, the findings which indicate that they do not eliminate all rating errors, the arguments presented in Chapter 3 with regard to conceptual clarity and dimensional choice, and those presented above regarding rater cognitive complexity as a determinant of rating ability, all suggest that Criterion and Standard judgement effects may be stronger than has been previously accepted.   Each of the three judgement forms is examined below and the author argues that, whether or not the rating task explicitly requires these rater judgements, they are judgements that are made by each rater and which, if not recognised and accommodated, serve to contaminate resultant ratings in the form of characteristic errors.

Criterion Judgement and Characteristic Errors

While some performance measurement methods require the appraiser to choose the performance criteria (e.g. Closed Free Expression Reports), performance rating usually stipulates the criteria against which perfor- mance is to be evaluated.   What role then can Criterion judgement poss- ibly play in the performance rating task?   In short, performance assess- ment begins with a conception and decision as to important performance components and even if the decision is implicit in instrument content it is a decision that the rater makes.   In other words, regardless of those specified by the instrument, the rater has personally-defined cri- teria.   It is suggested that these then interfere with his use of the specified criteria and result in the effects known as halo and logical rating error.

Personal Construct theory (Kelly 1955) holds that a person's cognitive processes are channelized by the way he/she anticipates events and that people differ in these cognitive processes because they are a product of the individual's unique experiences.   The function of these processes is to simplify the perceptual tasks that movement through the individual's world of people and events presents.   Within the world of performance perceptions evidence suggests that supervisors and managers develop Im- plicit Theories of Performance to simplify their everyday perceptual tasks (DeNisi and Pritchard 1978) i.e. those people who are recurrently concerned with others' performance develop dimensionalized ways of thinking about work behaviour.

That differences in these cognitive abilities are important has been argued above and the issue of rater discriminative ability, in partic- ular, has been popularly regarded as important.   Indeed perhaps the first within this particular field was Bechtoldt (1947) who commented that a major problem in achieving rating reliability lay in the differ- ential abilities of judges to make the desired discriminations (within and between criteria) and Borman (1978) argued that rating error is in- troduced because raters are selective in what behaviours they attend to due to personal construct differences and the Differential Accuracy Phenomenon (Gordon 1970).   Some research suggests that the individual's experience determines what he/she considers to be important performance domain constructs.   For example, Klimoski and London (1974) found that experience of group membership determines what performance criteria are perceived as salient (rater-group specific bias). But Criterion judgement not only involves a decision as to what is important but decisions as to how criteria are related (Guion 1965) and Einhorn (1974) argued that experiential differences between 'experts' naturally effects their perceptions of criterion relationships.

The author suggests that these structures are in effect Criterion judgements and that when presented with a priori criteria in which the relationships are defined then the rater's personal criteria interfere with his conceptualization and use of these. The paucity of relevant research makes substantiation difficult but a few studies are supportive.

Rizzo and Frank (1977) attempted to reduce rating contamination by including personally-valued but job-irrelevant performance criteria. They argued that these normally contaminated rating, producing halo effect, and found that by asking raters to evaluate personally-valued but irrelevant cues halo was indeed reduced. The study supports the idea that the rater's personal criteria are ignored at the risk of contaminating rating on specified criteria and suggests that halo effect is related to criteria content.

Secondly, Chapman and Chapman (1969), noted that in situations where objective measures of criterion relationships are given, users find these very difficult to learn if they differ from their pre-conceived ideas of what 'go-together' and Poulton (1977) also observed that a subject's 'well known rules' which do not happen to apply in the particular circumstances effect assessment accuracy. The building of construct relationships is an integral part of expert judgement and Einhorn (1974) argued that what Guilford (1954) called logical rating error is not in fact an error but a reflection of the expert's organisation of information into clusters or dimensions. Cooper (1979) likewise argued that raters apply their beliefs about criterion relationships in evaluating ratees and so apparent criterion interdependence is not necessarily a rating error. These formulations support the idea that the rater's personal conception of criterion relationships is ignored at the risk of contaminating rating on specified criteria and they suggest that logical rating error is concerned with the relationship between criteria.

It would seem that whether or not the performance rating process explicitly requires Criterion judgement it is to be expected that the rater in a supervisory position has already made such judgements because he/she is already perceiving and judging according to what he/she through experience and training as an expert has found to be a convenient conceptualization of job performance. Moreover, these conceptions are automatically invoked and difficult to ignore when he/she is requested to focus on the performance domain. It follows then that rating instrument design assumes 'carte blanche' in neglect of, and perhaps in contradiction to, what is normally expected of supervisors or managers and at the risk of criterion contamination.

To place the last link in the chain between sources and effects of subjectivity, a theoretical bridge between Criterion judgement and associated errors remains to be made. In other words why are halo and
logical rating error the expected results of conflicting 'Criterion
judgements'?

Among the common rating errors, halo effect and logical rating error are
distinguished by their association with criterion content. They are
both errors which concern what is measured and they have effects across
criteria. Halo appears to be associated with criterion salience (Rizzo
and Frank 1977) and logical rating error with criterion relations
(Einhorn 1974) and in as much as they are both concerned with what is
measured they share a common base with Criterion judgement.

Halo effect is the tendency to bias the assessment of several features
on the basis of the assessment of one. It results when certain criteria
are seen as particularly important (Landy and Trumbo 1976) and from poor
discrimination between criteria (Borman 1975). In other words it is
concerned with the salience of one or some criteria. When one or some
of the specified criteria coincide with the dimensions which structure
the rater's cognitive domain then common constructs are likely to be
perceived as more salient. The partial congruence of criteria results
in an array which is differentially meaningful and, as meaning is a
determinant of rating ability, rating is likely to be more accurate on
the more salient criteria. Non-common criteria by definition lack
meaning and, as was suggested above, the rater might be expected to respond by imposing his own meaning. Not surprisingly then, the ratings
given on non-common criteria will reflect ratings on those that are
salient. Without denying the need for empirical investigation the
suggested conclusion is that halo effect results from the partial over-
lapping of instrument-specified and personally-defined criteria, yielding an array in which some elements are easily conceptualized and used
while others lack meaning.

Logical rating error is the tendency to assess one feature in accordance
with it's perceived relationship to another. Robinson (1975) regarded
the rater's Implicit Theory of Performance to be the major cause and
Einhorn (1974) similarly argued that logical rating error reflects the
rater's way of organising information. The degree to which cognitive
dimensions are organised, stratified or ordered has been referred to as
'integration' and it was noted in Chapter 3 that care should be taken in
the selection of criteria which are to be considered to be theoretically
independent because whether or not they are conceptually independent for
the rater, and therefore independently tenable, is a function of the
degree of integration of his cognitive domain. Within a range of criteria which are designated as independent it is likely that some overlap
will occur with the rater's Implicit Theory of Performance where constructs may or may not be related and it is reasonable to expect some
interference to occur and manifest itself in correlations between
ratings on two or more specified criteria.

In conclusion, the Criterion judgement step in performance measure development can be argued to have a parallel with the natural development of the cognitive domain structure of supervisory individuals. The fact that performance rating scales specify criteria and their relationships does not prevent the rater from being influenced by his own conceptions and performing accordingly. Indeed, by definition, where specified criteria differ from those personally-defined they will lack meaning, thus detracting from the rater's ability to rate accurately and where overlap occurs, the more familiar and meaningful constructs will acquire greater salience. As a result, salient criteria are likely to display more discrimination and accuracy than others and as others lack meaning their rating is likely to display the assessment on salient criteria, accounting for what is termed halo effect. In addition the old habits of perceived relationships are notably difficult to overcome. Criteria which are specified as independent but which are related in the rater's cognitive domain are likely to be treated as non-independent and so assessed according to their perceived relationship and this would account for what is called logical rating error.

Standard Judgement and Characteristic Errors

Once the decision is made as to what to measure, a decision is required as to what amount of the critical component represents an acceptable level of performance. This is the value-related component of criterion definition and, as Poulton (1977) argued, these values are relative thus making subjective standards necessarily arbitrary and their designation, a matter of judgement. For this reason we can distinguish Standard from Criterion judgement.

Some performance measurement methods (for example, Comparative Standards Procedures) require no Standard judgement, but it is this lack of an explicit standard which makes inter-group comparison of individual performances difficult. Others (for example Closed Free Expression Reports) give free rein to the assessor in Standard judgement, while performance rating methods variously provide the standard either through democratic derivation (e.g. BARS, BES, etc.) or by implication in value-anchored Conventional Rating Scales. If the standard is explicitly provided, what role then does Standard judgement play in performance rating? It is suggested that individual raters develop personal concepts of acceptable performance levels which may not coincide with specified standards and the interference between personally-defined and specified standards gives rise to the rating errors known as leniency and central tendency.

Bechtoldt (1947), Taft (1955) and, most recently, Borman (1979b) have identified individual differences in standard perception as a neglected problem and one which has significant implications for the achievement of inter-rater agreement and performance rating accuracy. It would appear that throughout the concern for improving rating accuracy and reliability there has been an awareness that individuals do hold different personal standards that are instrumental in their assessment of performance.

Poulton (1977) and Landy and Trumbo (1976) attributed leniency error to the imposition of personal standards and noted that this is particularly likely to occur in the absence of precise and unambiguous scale points. While research partially supports the notion that detailed scale definition can overcome leniency, more recent writers (e.g. Landy and Farr 1978, Borman 1979b) maintain that the continued existence of different personal standards will always influence rating reliability and so what is required is the creation of correct and well-defined performance standards through the active development of common frames of reference between raters.

Both leniency and central tendency are errors which concern the distribution of ratings across scale points and, unlike halo or logical rating error, are intra-scale as opposed to inter-scale phenomena. While leniency error appears to be directly related to the interference of the rater's personal standards, central tendency effect, the unwillingness to use extremes of the scale, may be related to the adoption of specified standards. Poulton (1977) demonstrated that in first judgements using a new standard, the assessor 'plays safe' in selecting a response a little too close to the middle of the response range (i.e. uses a limited range of responses with an obvious middle at the standard point) and he considered these 'response range' effects to be equivalent to central tendency error.

In conclusion, the Standard judgement step required in the development of any performance measure many have a parallel with the rater's conceptual structuring of the range of ratee performances experienced. As the instrument-specified performance range and standard are normally based on a larger population of performances than the conceptual structuring of the individual rater it is likely that differences will exist between instrument-specified and personally-conceived standards and ranges. When asked to rate performance the rater's own standards may be invoked, giving rise to either positive or negative leniency errors and, when the rater adopts a new standard (i.e. where the designated standard is different from his own) he is likely to act with caution, limiting his range of responses and exhibiting central tendency error.

Assessment Judgement and Characteristic Errors

Assessment judgement, the decision as to what performance level an individual has achieved or what amount of a performance characteristic he exhibits, is the judgement most commonly associated with the rating activity. Whereas the influences on Criterion and Standard judgements appear to reside in Rater x Instrument and Rater x Organisation factors, it is in the Assessment judgement, requiring the rater to focus on a particular individual, that we might expect to see the influence of Rater x Ratee and Ratee x Organisation effects.

As a natural progression of the hypothesis that Assessment judgement is influenced by ratee factors, we would expect effects to be unsystematic because the stimulus to which the rater is responding is in itself vari-

able. For this reason, errors which are variable both in incidence and
extent are more likely to be associated with the Assessment judgement.
However, there do appear to be some systematic errors associated with
Assessment judgement.

Borman (1978) described the performance evaluation process in terms of
three steps: the observation of work-related behaviour; the evaluation
of each observed behaviour; and the weighting of observed behaviours to
arrive at a single rating on the performance dimension. He attributed
evaluation error to rater individual differences in these processes. In
particular, raters have differential opportunities to observe ratee behaviour (a Rater x Organisation effect), they evaluate behaviours un-
systematically, paying more attention to some behaviours than others
(Rater x Organisation and Perception effects) and, because they weight
behaviours observed over a time period, individual differences in susceptibility to recency effect and first impressions are likely to unduly
influence the assessment outcome. These Rater Characteristics, Perception and Rater x Organisation influences on performance rating are
likely to be relatively consistent but influences associated with the
ratee are likely to be less systematic.

Poulton (1977) maintained that any subjective assessment is influenced
by the range of stimuli to be assessed (in this case, ratee performances) and in demonstrating that once the observer has learnt the range
there is a tendency to judge each stimulus partly by its position in the
range, he provided an explanation of group characteristic bias as well
as a reason for expecting this error to be related to Assessment judgement. As each ratee has a unique group position the degree of group
characteristic bias entering the rating is likely to be moderately variable.

The effects of Rater x Ratee factors are less systematic still because
individual rater-ratee relationships tend to be variable and because relationships change over time. Contrast and similarity errors are ones
which tend to be variable and to be associated with Assessment judgement. Robinson (1975) explained that such errors emanate from the
rater's perception of his own strengths and weaknesses and the perceived
similarity of others to himself. While the rater may view his own
characteristics as stable, perceived similarity will of course be ratee-
specific and is likely to change with time and familiarity.

The effects of interpersonal attraction or liking are likely to be least
systematic of all because of all the Rater x Ratee factors, this is the
one which is determined most specifically by ratee characteristics, and
the effects of the affective components are variable. Within a certain
range of liking or disliking the effect on performance assessment is
minimal but under conditions of strong positive or negative affect, bias
may take the form of substantial over- or under-rating. In addition,
affective strength is relative and there are likely to be inter-rater
differences in the point at which affect influences judgement. Finally
as Robinson (1975) suggested, some undue rating variance may be intro-

duced by the rater's conscious efforts to overcome felt biases.

In conclusion, Assessment judgement is the final and most obvious rater process. Being the point at which the ratee and his performance become the decision foci it is to be expected that the errors mediated by Assessment judgement are those which arise from the determinants of Perception of Ratee Performance and from Rater x Ratee factors. These errors are likely to range in their consistency, those determined by stable factors in perception (e.g. organisational position and opportunity to observe) being more consistent across ratees than those determined by the specific rater-ratee personal relationship.

Implications of the Triple Judgement Formulation

In the preceding sections specific sources of rating error have been identified in an attempt to provide a rationale for discriminating among these, this being a necessary step towards developing systematic approaches to their treatment. Any performance measurement process can be described in terms of the three types of judgement which are variously required of the appraiser by common performance measurement methods. While the rating task is commonly construed in terms of the Assessment judgement it can be argued that, by virtue of his experience and expertise in perceiving subordinate performance, the rater develops cognitive structures, equivalent to Criterion and Standard judgements, which guide his ratings. Describing the rating process in this way makes it possible to explain characteristic errors in Criterion, Standard and Assessment judgement-related terms.

The three kinds of judgement provide three opportunities for sources of subjectivity to take effect. Halo effect and logical rating error arise where a mismatch occurs between the rater's conception of the performance domain and the criteria and relationships specified by the performance measurement instrument. These Criterion judgement-related errors result primarily from Rater x Instrument and Rater x Organisation factors producing a reduction in the rater's ability to use the instrument as it is intended. Leniency and central tendency errors arise where a mismatch occurs between personal and specified standards. These Standard judgement-related errors result primarily from Rater x Instrument and Rater x Organisation factors producing a reduction in the ability to use embodied scales as intended. Recency effects, contrast and similarity errors and bias in rating are associated with the Assessment judgement itself and arise from Rater Characteristics, Rater x Ratee and Ratee x Organisation factors, producing overemphasis on primary or recent events, interference by cognitive affect and misperceptions of performance respectively.

The implications of this triple judgement formulation are clear. To regard measurement error as arising from the Assessment judgement alone is an oversimplification. In attempts to reduce error, specific attention should be paid to each judgement type in the design of rating instruments and systems. Importantly, some types of subjectivity may be desirable and functional. There is a distinction to be made between subjectivity which arises from factors irrelevant to the task objective (e.g. rater preferences, job attitude and motivation, individual characteristics, personal incompetence, knowledge or skill) residing in Rater Characteristics, Rater x Instrument, Rater x Task, Rater x Ratee and some Rater x Organisation sources, and, on the other hand, subjectivity which arises from an informed view of factors relevant to the task objective (e.g. job experience, experienced observation of job performance, knowledge of what is reasonable under what circumstances, of how past ratees have performed, of specific task demands and constraints) residing in some Rater x Organisation sources and manifest in the Criterion and Standard judgements.

Clearly the sources of subjectivity which give rise to irrelevant bias need to be eliminated, changed or reduced but judgement 'bias' which emanates from informed experience is perhaps a type of subjectivity to be valued. Judgement is by its nature subjective so as long as it is required, subjectivity cannot be completely eliminated. But given this distinction neither would total elimination be particularly desirable. Rather what is needed is some control over the judgements made which will result in error reduction or elimination, increased accuracy and reliability. The Criterion and Standard judgement processes are ignored at the risk of halo, logical rating error, central tendency and leniency effects and so to deal with the effects of subjectivity, not only is there a need to control factors which effect ratee assessment but factors which effect Criterion and Standard judgements.

Methods which have deliberately excluded Criterion and Standard judgements (e.g. Direct Indices) have done so at the risk of sacrificing criterion relevance and comprehensiveness. Those which have given free rein to appraiser Criterion and Standard judgement (e.g. Closed Free Expression Reports) have done so at the risk of sacrificing standardization, reliability and validity. What appears to be required is some degree of active management of these forms of subjectivity to create standardized, relevant and reliable measures which are conceptually sound for the rater.

The rater's Criterion and Standard judgements cannot be ignored. Specifically they need to be accommodated and this has methodological implications. Either the instrument should be adapted to the rater or vice versa so as to avoid a mismatch between personal conception and instrument specification. The first implies rater involvement in criterion and standard development while the second implies that raters should be educated to develop appropriate criterion and standard awareness.

One further immediate implication of this analysis is that characteristic errors are powerful clues to the source of subjectivity in the ratings. For example, evidence of halo suggests that criterion content is differentially meaningful to the rater whereas leniency suggests that standard designation is out of line with rater experience. As subject ivity arises through different processes and from different sources, attempts at reducing its effects may require a variety of strategies and any one strategy (e.g. rater participation in criterion development) is likely to be differentially effective in reducing characteristic errors.

SUMMARY

In this and the previous chapter, the role of subjectivity in perform-ance measurement has been seen to be inevitable and subjective judge-ment, complementing objective measurement and enabling a focus on behav-iour itself, found to be a valuable source of performance data. The major problem with subjective judgement comes with quantification but as valid, accurate and reliable measurement is needed the dysfunctions of subjective involvement have to be coped with or avoided. By analysing the sources and effects of subjectivity as well as the mechanisms through which it operates this aim might be more easily addressed.

Performance rating, the most common appraisal method, provides the best potential for studying subjectivity. The model of Rater Subjectivity describes three related sets of variables:- the Ratee Performance Sys-tem, the Determinants of Rater Performance and Rater Judgement Compon-ents and Errors. In the first, rater performance was seen to be effec-ted by his perception of the critical aspects of ratee performance. In the second, rater performance was seen to be effected by rater charact-eristics which interact with the instrument, task, ratee and organisa-tional context and give rise to variation in rater ability, motivation, cognitive affect and perception. In the third, rater performance was described in terms of the Criterion, Standard and Assessment judgements which are involved whether or not they are explicitly required and which can give rise to characteristic measurement errors. In combination, these sets of variables describe the sources of subjectivity, their re-lationships to performance and their mechanisms of effect.

By describing the rating event in terms of the determinants of rating performance and the processes that constitute rating performance it be-comes clear that for an accurate, reliable and valid performance assess-ment to be a realistic expectation several conditions need to be satis-fied. Performance perception must be accurate, the rater must have the necessary and sufficient capacities to perform, rater motivation must be conducive to accurate rating, the rater's emotional orientation to all ratees should be non-extreme and equivalent, raters must understand and agree with the specified criteria and standards and be able to value and weight behavioural incidents over the rating period accurately.

These conditions are rarely, if ever, satisfied. Raters differ with respect to characteristics which effect perceptual accuracy, rating ability and emotional orientation. Ratees differ with respect to characteristics which effect the rater's emotional orientation and per-ceptual accuracy. Instruments differ with respect to characteristics which effect rating ability, and rating tasks differ with respect to characteristics which effect rater motivation. In addition, rating criteria and standards are not always meaningful to raters and individual differences exist in the evaluation and weighting of behavioural incidents. In effect there are many sources which can contribute to poor reliability, validity and accuracy of performance ratings, each one being mediated by the rater himself, the subject. As such they can be termed sources of subjectivity. These sources of subjectivity prevent the rater from recording an uncontaminated performance estimate and result in errors that reflect distortions in conception, perception and evaluation.

The conditions which produce these inaccuracies and the processes through which they effect the performance estimate have been shown to be distinct and various. As Wertheimer (1972) suggested, 'like it or not, we are stuck with subjectivity'. One form of subjectivity or another is inevitable in performance rating, making the quest for objectivity unrealistic. How then can subjectivity be accommodated such that valid and reliable ratings may still be achieved? Different strategies may be required to manage subjectivity in its many guises. It is the aim of Chapter 5 to identify and explore potential strategies so that in conjunction with the findings here, recommendations can be made for managing different types of subjectivity such that resultant measures are both conceptually sound and methodologically pure.

5 The management of subjectivity

Throughout the attempts to achieve error-free performance measures, techniques for managing the subjective contamination of ratings have proliferated but among these, three basic types of strategy can be distinguished.

As it is recognised that different rating instruments present differential opportunities for subjective contamination, one obvious strategy is to concentrate on designing instruments which prevent subjective bias. So for example, Ronan and Prien (1971) saw the way ahead in minimizing human involvement in performance measurement by keeping measures as simple as possible. A second strategy, concerned with rating conditions, recognises that the environment plays a part in contamination and so advocates changing aspects of the system in which rating takes place to eliminate subjective interference. An example of this strategy is the proposal by Madden and Bourdon (1964) that conditions which distort judgement and lead to invalid results should be identified and eliminated from the judgemental situation. Finally, as the rater himself is recognised as instrumental in subjective contamination, improving the rater's ability to rate accurately appears to be a possible strategy for reducing subjective interference. Bechtoldt (1947), for example, pointed out that rating bias could be reduced through rater training.

These distinct strategies which reflect a concern for different aspects of the performance rating process, i.e. the instrument, the environment and the rater, offer the potential for a comprehensive attack on the sources and effects of subjectivity, but the research shows that they have differed in their degree of application, have typically been used in single strategy attempts, and the full potential of each has yet to be explored.

Historically speaking, concern for instrument design was the first major area of research activity. Psychometric errors were primarily seen as indicative of a fault in instrument design and so not surprisingly research tended to examine the effects of different instrument character-

istics on the incidence of rating errors.   More recently the focus has
turned to the rater himself as the source of bias and greater attention
has been paid to rater characteristics and training raters to overcome
response biases.   However, studies examining rater training effectiveness have typically measured success in terms of rating behaviour criteria (e.g. the extent of leniency, halo, central tendency etc.) but, as
Borman (1979b) suggested, changing rating behaviour may be considerably
easier than improving reliability and accuracy and indeed the research
(Crow 1957, Borman 1975) shows that the relationship between rating behaviour criteria, inter-rater reliability and accuracy is far from consistent.   In other words, telling raters to spread their ratings or to
provide fewer high ratings may be effective but it does not necessarily
result in increased reliability or accuracy.   While perhaps a more
difficult task, rater training may well have to concern itself with
eliminating the sources of subjectivity as well as its immediate
effects.   In contrast with the other two strategies, relatively little
attention has been paid to varying the rating environment to eliminate
contamination, but recently Warmke and Billings (1979) provided a basis
for making an educated guess as to what forms of environmental or systems design may be useful in reducing rating contamination.

Each of these strategies is based on the assumption that subjectivity is
undesirable and they provide three different means of either eliminating
or reducing its sources or effects.   While instrument design and rater
training have been used successfully to overcome or eliminate specific
effects of subjectivity their potential for dealing with sources has not
been exploited.   And given a tendency to focus on particular strategies
or strategy types, the potential for a three-pronged attack on any one
source has rarely been realised.   The Rater Subjectivity model (Fig.
4.4) provides a basis for investigating the applicability of these three
strategies to each of the sources and effects and for arriving at firm
recommendations about the utility of each.   The three strategies can be
thought of as: changing the instrument through Instrument Design,
changing the rater through Rater Training, changing the rating environment through System Design.

STRATEGIC APPLICABILITY

In succeeding sections each major subjectivity source discussed in Chapter 4 is briefly reviewed, the applicability of each strategy is discussed and recommendations as to appropriate specific strategies are
made.

Dealing with Rater Characteristic Sources

Rater biography, knowledge, skills and personality were found to be
characteristics which influenced rating accuracy through their pervasive
effects on Rater x Instrument, Rater x Task, Rater x Ratee and Perception of Ratee Performance factors.

As biographical characteristics have their main influence in situations where they interact with other variables such as the ratee or the instrument, discussion of these is reserved till that of interaction factors. The rater's knowledge of the instrument, task and performer as well as task and perceptual skills were argued to be predictive of rating accuracy. While various personality factors have been found to correlate with accuracy few have done so consistently but a central theme is that of rater cognitive complexity being instrumental in rating accuracy, important in all interaction terms. The research demonstrates that rater cognitive style depends on his basic style, the area of experience sampled and the decision-making situation.

Instrument design. As rater characteristics are independent of the instrument it is unlikely that any amount of instrument design will alter these sources of variance. Therefore, subjectivity effects which arise from rater characteristics can only be dealt with in terms of changing those characteristics or changing the rating system.

Rater training. While biographical characteristics are intractable the rater's knowledge and skills can be developed through training. However, the specific training required will differ according to the interaction factor concerned, depending on whether the critical characteristic is one of ability, motivation, perception etc., and so discussion will be reserved till these factors are individually considered. While ethical issues surround the idea of changing rater personality, attempts at changing the central pervasive characteristic of cognitive complexity could be defensible. Cognitive complexity is domain-specific and, as it is reasonable to expect raters to be expert in the domain of subordinate performance, attempts to increase domain complexity might well be a target of rater training. Cognitive complexity is trainable (Hunt 1966, Baldwin 1972) and Sieber and Lanzetta (1964) demonstrated that simple reinforcement techniques can be effectively applied to increase domain-specific complexity. They found that cognitively simple subjects who were rewarded for evidence of complex characteristics when observing, reporting and evaluating behaviour, began to evidence more complex responding.

System design. Kane and Lawler (1979) suggested that raters could be selected according to individual differences in rating accuracy. In the light of the pervasive effects of rater characteristics such a system design strategy has an intuitive appeal. It is based on an acceptance of the status quo, that some people, for whatever reasons, are inherently better raters than others, and attempts to remedy the differential accuracy problem by selecting raters on accuracy. The problem with this suggestion is that it presumes that rater accuracy can be tested but neglects to say how this might be done. As has been seen, the very dependence on ratings as criteria often arises because of the lack of an alternative criterion measure. Although Arvey and Hoyle (1974) argued that Guttman scalogram analysis could be an appropriate tool for identifying poor raters, their results suggested that rather than good/poor rating being a generalized rater characteristic, rater errors appeared

to be strongly dimension- or criteria-specific and this finding
questions the basis and utility of the selection approach. As well as
this problem of rater validation some consideration must be given to
practical constraints. Unless rating accuracy is used as a job selection criterion the real need for subordinate performance information may
place a demand on rater availability which a reduced rater pool, forced
by strict rater selection criteria, may be unable to meet.

Given the problems of establishing the accuracy of raters, the non-
generalized nature of the rating accuracy characteristic plus real practical constraints, this approach loses some of its initial appeal.
Clearly there are implementation problems. Where, however, alternative
strategies are not available and where significant biographical or personality effects exist, rater selection may provide the last resort.

Dealing with Rater x Instrument Sources

Rating ability is impaired where the rater is unable to understand instrument terminology, to differentiate performance according to the
specified criteria or to discriminate at the level required. In short,
rating accuracy depends on the match between the rater's cognitive capacity and the demands of the instrument. Reducing this source of subjectivity appears to rely on ensuring that the instrument is meaningful
to the rater and each strategy provides potential solutions.

Instrument design. Borman (1978) suggested that problems of meaning
could be overcome by choosing scale anchors the relevance of which is
determined by the actual raters. This was the central idea behind
Smith and Kendall's (1963) BARS methodology and studies indicate that
rater participation in dimension definition and scale point designation
is a major step to overcoming the problem of meaning (Borman 1979b,
Dunnette and Borman 1979, Jacobs et al, 1980).

Rater training. One method of overcoming the problem of scale meaning
is to increase the rater's exposure to the instrument through training.
Latham et al, (1975) provided trainee raters with the opportunity to
practise observing and rating videotaped ratees and they found evidence
of less contrast and similarity errors, less halo effect and less first
impression bias in their ratings over the training period. However,
Borman (1979b), in an elaborated replication, found the effects of such
training to be limited to reducing psychometric errors rather than increasing rating accuracy and to depend on the job being rated. Apart
from providing the opportunity for the rater to gain familiarity with
the instrument through practice on videotaped ratees, discussions which
clarify the meaning of scale content, as well as lectures and discussions on characteristic rating errors, appear to be fruitful training
emphases. While this is likely to be costly and time-consuming, Jacobs
et al, (1980) maintained that performance evaluation should be viewed as
an integral part of the supervisor's role and one for which training is
legitimately required.

<u>System design</u>. The notable exception to the lack of research in the application of this third strategy to Rater x Instrument sources is Schneier's (1977) suggestion of selecting the instrument according to individual rater cognitive abilities.   This 'horses for courses' approach is essentially a system design solution where the rating environment (in this case the instrument) is manipulated to match the capabilities of the user.   In finding cognitively complex subjects to prefer and to provide higher quality ratings on relatively complex behaviour-type scales (in contrast cognitively simple raters prefer and provide higher quality ratings on less complex scales) Schneier demonstrated that rater-based instrument selection can overcome the problems of differential accuracy, and has provided a promising line of development. However, the strategy is not without problems. The use of different instruments which provide different levels of information and available feedback may disadvantage some subordinates, simpler instruments may not afford the information necessary for some measurement purposes and information standardization for comparison purposes may be difficult to achieve.   These difficulties need not be insurmountable but, for example, they would necessitate the development of parallel instruments.   More critical perhaps is the fact that the approach assumes that cognitive complexity can be measured and while Schneier (1977) has done so, other cognitive complexity theorists would disagree as to the appropriate measure. Clearly, other and perhaps more detailed measures might well be explored.

Dealing with Rater x Task Sources

The main effect of Rater x Task sources is on rater motivation and the author suggested that an Expectancy model might well explain the effects on specific task variables on the rater's willingness to expend effort on accurate rating. Research showed that assessment purpose, its perceived utility, social structure and pressure, time constraints, and appraisal system requirements influence rater motivation.   As these factors are essentially systems characteristics it would be reasonable to expect that systems design strategies would be useful in their treatment but other strategic suggestions that have been made should not be neglected.

<u>Instrument design</u>. Although no instrument can be expected to yield accurate ratings where the rating exercise is thought to lack utility and organisational support, those which are time-consuming or require a large amount of effort place a greater strain on the rater's motivation and are less likely to be completed accurately. So, where demotivating environmental conditions are unchangeable, attention should be paid to designing instruments in their simplest and shortest form.   In addition, where different instrument content is required for different assessment purposes (reward, promotion, development or training) and adverse environmental conditions are differentially related to these purposes (e.g. communicating appraisal results for training purposes being perceived as less threatening by the rater than communicating results for reward purposes) then design of separate instruments for separate

purposes may overcome the negative motivational effects associated with some of these.

Rater training. Expectancy theory proposes that perceptions and values which are unrealistic in terms of their organisational context can be a source of demotivation. By implication effective management might aim to realign an individual's perceptions with reality and values with attainable outcomes. Applying this theory to rater motivation, several clear implications for rater training emerge.

First, where the perceived task utility is low then counselling and information-giving on the assessment purpose may increase the perceived value of the outcome. Second, where the system requires the rater to discuss ratings with the ratee and this is seen as negatively valent, the valence may be changed by increasing the rater's confidence through training raters in feedback skills. Third, where time constraints are a critical factor, increasing the rater's ability to do the task through training would serve to reduce its onerous nature. Finally, where real negatively valent social structure or pressure contingencies exist they may be perceptibly reduced by group-based problem-sharing or through individual counselling. In short, rater training may be used, not necessarily to change real systems variables or contingencies but to make the perception of these more accurate and to increase the rater's coping ability.

One other means of rater training is through participation in instrument development. Friedman and Cornelius (1976) presented a study which manipulated full participation in scale construction as a dependent variable. While they found participation to reduce halo effect and significantly increase convergent validity, perhaps their most important finding was that these effects were maintained when raters were asked to use scales which they had not generated. They attributed the former results to a better understanding of scale use and of job components, but could only attribute the latter finding to increased rater motivation.

System design. No system can be expected to result in accurate, reliable and valid information where organisational support is lacking or where the information required lacks apparent utility, so any appraisal system must be concerned with providing consistent reinforcement and support for accurate rating behaviour. The major sources of demotivation referred to above provide immediate recommendations for systems design.

With respect to task purpose, perceived utility is likely to increase where other human resource decisions are explicitly linked to the performance rating results. By implication, where performance-pay, performance-training, performance-promotion, and performance-development contingencies exist, system developers should ensure that these links are both apparent and understood.

Second, apart from the obvious but undesirable and impractical solution of returning to closed reporting systems, social structure and pressure effects could be partially alleviated by the counter-balancing effects of formal influence. Reinforcement from superiors and organisational systems for accurate information-giving may produce a net contingency valence which is at least less negative if not positive.

Third, while appraisal system requirements could be modified so as to remove the necessity of rater-ratee discussions of ratings, the removal of the feedback element may well be robbing the system of its major benefit, which is neither desirable nor functional. It would appear then that rater training provides the major potential for overcoming the motivational problems associated with appraisal system requirements.

Finally, time constraints must be a concern in appraisal system design. No system can be sensible where its internal demands are in conflict. Setting up time constraints in competition with information quality seems to be both pointless and avoidable. System developers should pay specific attention to the task and ratee group size for each supervisor who is expected to complete ratings and set time constraints which take these factors into account.

Dealing with Rater x Ratee Sources

In the earlier discussion of Rater x Ratee sources of subjectivity, rating accuracy and favourability were seen to be mediated by rater-ratee familiarity, similarity and interpersonal attraction and it was suggested that the major problem in dealing with these sources is the difficulty of their detection and control. This is not only because their effects may be masked by more systematic ones but also because the rater is likely either to be unaware of or guarded about registering cognitive affect.

Instrument design. Rater-ratee effects are either unconscious, residing in distorted perception, or deliberate, residing in prejudice. In either case instrument design is unlikely to be an effective strategy as it can neither rectify perception nor prevent determined falsification. However, effects might well be detectable and controllable if raters were asked to provide an index of, for example, degree of ratee familiarity, perceived similarity and degree of attraction. As a means of clarifying the effects of these relationship properties this may be a worthwhile pursuit but its practical implementation may well be seen to overstep the bounds of legitimate information. For this reason instrument design strategies are unlikely to be appropriate.

Rater training. Where the rater is unaware of the biasing effects of his emotions on ratings then an increased awareness combined with the recognition of the importance of accurate rating may provide the stimulus to examine more closely the basis of his judgements. Training which alerts raters to the potential effects of perceived similarity and interpersonal attraction in terms of tendencies to be over-critical, tendencies to pay less attention and to be less systematic in observation, may well achieve this aim. However, incidence of pure bias is individual-specific and so in preference to this general approach perhaps it is more appropriate to monitor individual rater's ratings and provide individual counselling and feedback where necessary.

System design. Freeberg's (1969) study suggested that encouraging raters to have more frequent and informal performance-related discussions with ratees enhances rating accuracy and so this appears to be one effective system design strategy. Alternatively, where raters are known to have strong affective orientations towards particular individuals and are themselves aware of it then providing a 'no rating' alternative would permit some known bias to be avoided. Finally, Kane and Lawler (1979) suggested a systems design strategy which in effect masks or averages specific ratee bias by resorting to a 'higher level of collectivity'. They saw the use of group performance estimates, where groups included males/females, minorities/non-minorities to be an answer to individual similarity and attraction biases. While foregoing individual data, Lawler (1971) suggested that this sacrifice might justifiably be made in return for a greater measure of fairness and utility. This strategy implies significant systems redesign which is not without its problems, the most salient of which would be the reduction of individual information and the implied lack of individual feedback. Nevertheless, it is an attempt to temper measurement activities in line with current capabilities and may well provide a cautious intermediate step towards more accurate individual performance measurement.

Dealing with Ratee x Organisation Sources

Specific characteristics of the ratee in relation to the organisation, the work group and his task serve to influence the rater's perception of ratee job performance. As these factors are contextual it might be expected that manipulating the rating environment through system design would be the most promising strategy for their resolution but as environmental characteristics are wide-ranging other strategies may also prove useful.

Instrument design. Group characteristic bias, contrast effects and the inaccuracy attributed to imprecise job definition are all effects which might be tackled by an instrument design strategy. First, a ratee group which is preselected on the basis of past performance or significantly different in level of experience is unlikely to reflect the standards of a total ratee population and so in these circumstances a common instrument should identify standard variability. In scale development, standards for such groups should be calculated and indicated by 'banding' in order to overcome group characteristic bias and distinguish it from leniency error. Second, contrast effects, arising from a significant difference between the ratee and his group, may be tackled by collecting information on distinct differences and treating these as moderator variables. Finally, the inaccuracy arising from imprecise job definition has obvious implications for the improvement of job description and specification but perhaps more importantly reinforces the need for a symbiotic relationship between performance specification and job analysis. Instrument developers should attempt to match performance criteria with those implied in the job description and job analysts should be alert in their descriptions to critical performance requirements.

Rater training. The research on figure—ground effects in object perception demonstrates that they are notoriously difficult to overcome and that even the subject's knowledge of them does not guarantee that resultant distortions will be eliminated. This, by analogy, provides a clue to the utility of training strategies with respect to performance perception and might suggest that increasing awareness of contextual influence on perceptual accuracy, a possible training strategy, is in itself unlikely to be a particularly fruitful strategy. Instrument design to overcome the effects of such distortion and system design to remove its sources would appear to be more promising.

System design. One simple strategy suggested by Poulton (1977) for reducing, what he called, stimulus range effects is the adoption of a one—rater—one—ratee assessment procedure. Theoretically speaking any contrast, chance assignment, group bias and organisational position effects would be eliminated by the removal of a background of other ratees. In practice however, there are obvious limitations to such an approach. Standardization would be sacrificed and other sources of perceptual inaccuracy such as job inter—dependence could still be active. It would seem then that effective system design solutions need to be more sophisticated and the sources of perceptual inaccuracy suggest possible components of an effective solution.

First, contrast effects could be reduced by a design where only individuals at the same level of experience, length of service etc. are rated. Second, different instruments could be used for different assessment purposes, for example payment decisions, which produce bias according to ratee organisational position. Third, job opportunity appraisals could be introduced as a means of identifying the facilitating and inhibiting effects of equipment, job layout etc. on job performance, and the information used in the interpretation of performance ratings. Fourth, given its use in facilitating performance measurement, intrinsic feedback and employee autonomy should be an important consideration in job design. And finally, the influence of job interdependence could be overcome by rating at a higher level of collectivity (Kane and Lawler 1979). All or some of these, which range from very general tools to very specific solutions, could be part of an effective system design strategy.

Dealing with Rater x Organisation Sources

The rater's frame of reference is important in performance perception and the significant determinants were found to be the opportunity to observe performance behaviours, the rater's job experience, competence and effectiveness. These lead to differential weighting of behavioural incidents and differences between raters in the values attached to different types of behaviour. Each of the three stategies offers a means of dealing with these sources of subjectivity.

Instrument design. As behavioural rating is less falsifiable than trait or global rating when the rater is ill-informed, a behavioural emphasis in instrument construction may well stimulate the rater to seek greater opportunity to observe. Second, requiring raters to keep a diary of performance events has been shown to overcome both halo and leniency effects associated with inexperience or inadequate information (Bernardin and Walter 1977). However, as the major disadvantage of diary-keeping is the implied time commitment, other strategies may be more acceptable to the rater.

Rater training. No system or instrument alone can overcome the inexperience, ineffectiveness or sheer incompetence of the rater. Clearly there is an important role for training to increase the capacity of inexperienced and incompetent individuals to perform the rating task more effectively, and so systematic training and feedback in instrument use and on information collection should be regarded as an integral part of the induction of inexperienced supervisors. The other problems in this area, such as the effects of differential weighting and values, may however, require more sophisticated training approaches.

To agree with Borman (1979b), it is clear that training raters in standardizing behaviour observation is an important goal to which research should be addressing itself, and a training strategy which presents itself from the cognitive complexity literature is the development of shared constructs between raters through group discussion. Exposure of an individual to his colleagues' views of performance may widen his view and change the valued behaviours because, as Harvey and Schroder (1963) observed, shared concepts tend to become group norms. This activity plays an integral part in BARS methodology and Schwab et al, (1975a) found that it has the desired effect. However, whether this concept-sharing strategy should be recommended when there are reasons for a priori criterion definition, or where evidence suggests that group consensus is highly biased by one or two individuals, are questions which need to be explored and will be discussed in relation to Criterion judgement.

System design. The matching of instrument format to cognitive abilities was discussed in relation to Rater x Instrument sources and as complexity is expected to increase with job experience then it would make sense to use instruments sequentially, the rater graduating to more sophisticated instruments as he becomes more knowledgeable about and familiar with the ratee job. It is also possible to select instruments according to observation opportunity. Latham and Wexley (1977) found that Behavioural Expectation Scales were more reliable in situations where the opportunity to observe behaviour was low while Behavioural Observation Scales were more reliable where greater opportunity existed. Clearly, parallel instruments might be developed relatively easily and differen-

tial usage could be a solution to the variations in observation opportunity afforded by different organisation positions.

Other system design suggestions focus on either rater selection or the
utilization of different organisational views. Clearly, observation
opportunity problems can be overcome by selecting raters such that their
position permits optimal opportunity. As a guide Borman (1978) suggested that the choice of rater should favour peer versus supervisor or
supervisor versus 'grandfather' but other considerations obviously im-
pinge on the implementation of this recommendation. There are circumstances for example where the peer is in no better position than the
supervisor, (e.g. in relation to a field sales representative job) and,
with respect to some jobs no organisation vantage point is particularly
close, (e.g. police patrol man, doctor, lecturer etc.) In these situations, other solutions need to be sought.

Guion (1965), proposed that different rater views were valuable and advocated the collection of data from multiple sources in order to get a
comprehensive view of performance, a proposal reinforced by more recent
literature (Lawler 1967, Kavanagh et al, 1971). Whilst intuitively
appealing, this might be difficult in practice because the potential
task demands on an average organisational position are large but this
solution might be appropriate in particular types of organisations (e.g.
small, hierarchically slim etc.) or at particular organisational levels
only.

As an alternative, Klimoski and London (1974), believing ratings from
different levels to be predictive of different criteria, suggested that
choice of rater should depend on the decision-making purpose. This
strategy recognises the validity of information collected from different
vantage points and is one of few which actively capitalizes on the real
complexity of subjective performance measurement. What is now required
is systematic research to identify which vantage points are appropriate
sources of information for which decision-making purposes.

In this review of the applicability of each strategy to the elimination,
reduction or control of subjectivity sources, findings have been colla-
ted, fruitful areas of development have been identified and positive
practical methods of coping with known sources have been suggested.
But given that it is often difficult to pinpoint active sources, that
sources often operate simultaneously and that systematic attempts to
manage subjectivity may inevitably be multi-faceted, it is necessary to
consider strategic applicability to coping with subjectivity as it con-
taminates ratings through the rater judgement processes.

Accommodating Criterion Judgement

Criterion judgement was previously identified as a natural rater process
and it was found that the rater's cognitive domain in relation to subordinate performance developed in response to factors ranging from basic
cognitive style to Rater x Organisation factors such as job experience.

Halo and logical rating errors were argued to occur where there were differences between the structure and content of the instrument and the rater's cognitive domain. Against this background each of the three strategies provides a means of managing subjectivity as it operates through the Criterion judgement process.

Instrument design. Eliminating the mismatch between instrument content and the rater's cognitive domain would seem to be a means of overcoming the effects of Criterion judgement interference. Schneier's (1977) findings which show differences in cognitive structure to be predictive of rating quality on different instruments imply that instruments could be fruitfully designed to suit the rater's cognitive structure. But rater cognitive domains differ not only in terms of structure but in terms of content, and successful instrument design needs to take content into account. In recognition of this Smith and Kendall (1963) advocated the use of democratically-derived as opposed to developer-imposed performance constructs, and this BARS approach has recurrently appeared as a solution to measurement problems described in the previous two chapters and above. However, in this context, three problems are associated with it.

First, there is Wertheimer's (1972) reservation about the validity of democratically-derived criteria which cannot be denied, but if objective criteria are as yet unattainable then as Einhorn (1974) suggested, inter-subjective agreement is at least an acceptable intermediate step. Second, it is clear that under some circumstances blind adoption of rater-generated criteria would be foolish. For example, where there are strong opinion leaders then democratic concept-sharing may merely result in group adoption of one individual's norms or where group perceptions are distorted by informal pressure or shared grievance then generated constructs may be likewise biased. Such threats to the viability of this strategy are not insurmountable but they highlight the need for a high level of skill and control in managing the development of democratic criteria. Third, as it is unlikely that democratically- agreed criteria will ever totally reflect individual Criterion judgement then this solution cannot be expected to completely eliminate associated errors.

As an alternative matching strategy, performance criteria could be imposed and format could be structured in such a way as to educate raters and increase their cognitive domain complexity. It has been established that reduced halo is to be gained by increased dimension definition (Borman 1978), increased anchor point definition (Robinson 1975) and by stipulating instrument use procedure (Landy and Trumbo 1976) but the research reviewed above suggests that simply imposing criteria and format is likely to meet with limited success. If, however, this is a preferred strategy then there is a need for supportive training.

Rater training. Raters can be trained to reduce halo error, characteristically associated with Criterion judgement mismatch, through lectures and discussions about its nature (Levine and Butler 1952, Brown 1968,

Borman 1975, Latham et al, 1975 and Bernardin and Walter 1977) but effects of training deteriorate over short periods of time, (Bernardin 1978 and Ivancevich 1979), and the reduction of characteristic errors does not necessarily lead to rating accuracy and reliability (Borman 1979b). Rater training has perhaps over-concentrated on remedying symptoms as opposed to curing causes and when it is found that even symptom remedies are temporary and incomplete then training is forced to concern itself with the sources of error. In this hitherto neglected area empirically tested strategies are generally lacking but there is one important exception.

Borman (1979b) argued that, if reliability is to be a reasonable expectation then, inter-rater agreement has to be reached regarding the relative importance of different kinds of behaviour as contributors to effective performance, and indeed, Friedman and Cornelius (1976) who used scale construction participation as a training format found such training to reduce halo effect and increase convergent validity significantly. As the results generalized to the use of imposed scales they concluded that such a training format is effective in engendering a greater understanding amongst raters of job components and their importance.

While the reduction of halo effect has been a frequent aim of training little research has addressed itself to reducing logical rating error, yet this is a direction which deserves greater attention because, as Einhorn (1974) suggested, learning relationships between criteria is important in the mastery of a particular area. So the development of training techniques to enhance understanding of criterion relationships must be an aim if the incidence of logical rating error is to be reduced.

System design. As the Criterion judgement mismatch concerns the rater-instrument interface it is unlikely that systems strategies, apart from that of differential instrument utilization, will provide direct solutions. However, if the 'Democratic Criterion' method is adopted to overcome mismatch then there are significant systems implications. Notably, instrument development ceases to be a 'back-room' job and becomes an organisation-wide activity which needs to be organised, monitored and controlled. Techniques which identify homogeneous sets of subordinate jobs need to be developed, implying an integration of measure development and job analysis activities. Systems for up-dating criteria as well as techniques for the conversion of data through one criterion set to another, so that performances may be compared, need to be developed. These systems implications, provide well-defined goals for research in the implementation of democratically-derived performance measures.

Accommodating Standard Judgement

As with Criterion judgement, it was argued that raters bring their personally conceived standards to the rating situation and errors arise where personal and designated standards fail to coincide. Notably, leniency occurs where the rater persists in the use of his own judged standard and central tendency error occurs where he over-cautiously adopts the standard which is designated. As errors are likely to be reduced and rating accuracy and reliability increased by a reduction in the mismatch, two obvious approaches present themselves. Democratically-derived standards may be adopted, or standards may be imposed paralleled by an attempt to modify those of the rater. These approaches may be pursued through each of the strategies.

Instrument design. Leniency error can be reduced by increasing anchor point and dimension definition (Robinson 1975, Landy and Trumbo 1976, Borman 1978) so as to reduce scale ambiguity. This is, in effect, a re-educative strategy as the rater is provided with more information in a coherent and structured format. However, learning will only take place where the rater finds the additional information meaningful and so, without supportive training, mere proliferation of information may not achieve the objective. And indeed the favourable findings referred to above came from studies of BARS development where training in dimension and anchor meaning is implicit.

While these instrument design strategies are unconcerned with the sources of personal standards, the diary-keeping activity, which Bernardin and Walter (1977) found to reduce leniency error, assumes the difference between personal and designated standards to arise through the distorted or inadequate recall of behaviours and seeks to remove the problem at source. Clearly it is an effective solution where personal standards are strongly influenced by these factors.

Central tendency error can be reduced by forced distribution methods (Robinson 1975, Landy and Trumbo 1976), by omitting a middle scale category or by providing an unlimited number of rating categories (Poulton 1977). In that each of these strategies deny the rater the opportunity to register caution, they are remedial rather than curative. However, if an Imposed Standard approach is preferred they may be useful solutions.

If the approach to reducing mismatch is the Democratic Standard method, then performance standards must be elicited from the rater group and scaled on the instrument format. BARS methodology provides a procedure where the members of the rating group individually scale critical behavioural incidents and combines this with statistical techniques for deriving democratically-agreed standards.

Rater training. Training to overcome Standard judgement mismatch has typically focussed on informing raters about leniency and central tendency errors (e.g. Sharon and Bartlett 1969, Bernardin 1978). However, training does not always result in increased accuracy and reliability, nor are its effects permanent, so training might be more effective if it addressed itself to the sources.

Borman (1979b) saw the need for a shift of training emphasis towards securing standard agreement and the learning of correct performance standards. Specifically he suggested that raters should somehow be taught a frame of reference for defining the performance levels of different job behaviours. This might take the form of either instruction or standard-sharing. In the former case training emphasis must be placed on teaching raters the meaning of scale definitions, anchors and standards. In addition, training results could be monitored by analyses of rating performance, and feedback could be given to coach raters and reinforce their learning. In the latter case training could involve group discussion of perceived performance standards but, as was noted in relation to democratic derivation of criteria, control needs to be exercised where there are obvious opinion leaders or where emergent standards are considered to be wholly unrealistic. By implication, trainers must be skilled in handling group dynamics and discussion participants might well include all significant organisation members (e.g. union, functional representatives, etc.).

System design. Once again because the problem concerns the interface between rater and instrument, system design strategies are unlikely to yield direct solutions but the pursuance of a Democratic Standard approach has systems implications similar to those suggested in reference to the Democratic Criterion approach.

In addition, as it may be easier or more practical to accept and accommodate Standard judgement mismatch than attempt to change either the rater or the instrument, the statistical technique of normalization could be used to translate each rater's ratings into standardized 't' scores. This technique involves the summary of individual rater scale use across ratees, frequency counts of scale point usage, and a normalizing transformation of each individual rating. While providing a possible solution this is a time-consuming activity and would be costly where large numbers of raters are involved, and as personal standards are likely to change over time transformations may need to be developed anew on each rating occasion.

Finally, for some purposes commonly agreed standards may not be required. For example where the rating purpose is development-oriented then monitoring intra-ratee performance change is more important than inter-ratee comparison and so inter-rater reliability is much less a concern than intra-rater reliability. In these cases Standard judgement mismatch is not a problem as long as the system is designed such that different instruments are used for different purposes.

Improving Assessment Judgement

Rater x Ratee, Ratee x Organisation and Perception factors were seen as the major determinants of inaccuracy and unreliability of Assessment judgement. As such, the strategies proposed above in respect of these factors, as well as the diary-keeping suggestion of Bernardin and Walter (1977) for eliminating distorted recall and recency effects are similarly pertinent here. However, it was noted that perhaps the major problem with Assessment judgement is that of error detection. As Assessment judgement error is individual-specific and often unsystematic, once-only tests for these errors are likely to be unreliable. What is required is a system design that includes periodic reviews and analyses of an individual's ratings coupled with feedback given on rating performance. In short, to control Assessment judgement error, system administrators need to appraise appraiser performance.

The applicability of each strategy to the sources of subjectivity is summarized in Table 5.1 and a brief inspection allows several conclusions about strategy utility and potential to be made.

STRATEGIC CHOICE AND POTENTIAL

Through its history, performance rating research and development has evidenced a mismash of ideas and approaches have lacked coherence. In what was once unmapped territory, researchers and developers have forged various routes towards the mutual destination of improved rating accuracy, validity and reliability, guided by a preference, or sometimes a fashion, for a particular strategic, solution or error-focussed pursuit. At this stage accumulated research and experience makes it possible to distinguish arterial routes, and locate unexplored ground.

This analysis of the applicability of instrument design, rater training and system design strategies indicates that, in any systematic attempt to eliminate, reduce or control rater subjectivity: all three strategies are ultimately required; each strategy is differentially useful; combined strategies are essential for dealing with certain subjectivity sources; and that several areas of undeveloped solution potential exist.

The Strengths and Potential of Instrument Design

Instrument design can contribute little to the reduction or elimination of subjectivity arising from Rater Characteristics, Rater x Ratee or Rater x Organisation factors. It provides major solutions where subjectivity arises from Rater x Instrument factors and is essential in the pursuit of either method adopted to resolve Criterion and Standard judgement problems. It is a useful supplement to other strategies in dealing with Rater x Task and Ratee x Organisation factors and therefore for enhancing Assessment judgement. Although a frequently adopted and researched strategy, three areas of undeveloped potential emerge (RT, ReO and AJ), and of these instrument design would appear to have greatest undeveloped solution potential with respect to Ratee x Organisation factors.

Traditionally, instrument design has sought to eliminate errors by removing the opportunity for error to occur, but it could be used to control some of the sources of subjectivity that effect the rater's ability

Table 5.1

Summary of Strategic Applicability and Potential

		SOURCE										AJ
		RC	RI	RT	RR	ReO	RrO	CJ		SJ		
								IC	DC	IS	DS	
STRATEGIES	Instrument Design	−	√	+P	−	+P	−	√	√	√	√	+P
	Rater Training	√P	+P	√P	+P	−	√	+P	√	+P	√	+P
	System Design	P	P	√P	√P	√P	√P	−	−	−	−	+P

KEY

√ = major solution strategy
+ = supplementary solution strategy
P = undeveloped solution potential

ABBREVIATIONS

RC = Rater Characteristics
RI = Rater x Instrument factors
RT = Rater x Task factors
RR = Rater x Ratee factors
ReO = Ratee x Organisation factors
RrO = Rater x Organisation factors
CJ = Criterion judgement
SJ = Standard judgement
AJ = Assessment judgement

IC = Imposed Criterion method
DC = Democratic Criterion method
IS = Imposed Standard method
DS = Democratic Standard method

and motivation to perform, as well as his apparent misperceptions.

The Strengths and Potential of Rater Training

Rater training can do little to reduce or eliminate subjectivity that arises from Ratee x Organisation factors. It provides major solutions where subjectivity arises from Rater Characteristics, Rater x Task and Rater x Organisation factors and is essential in the pursuit of the Democratic Criterion and Standard methods for overcoming Criterion and Standard judgement problems. It is a useful supplementary strategy in dealing with Rater x Instrument, Rater x Ratee factors and therefore Assessment judgement problems. In addition it is a critical supplement to instrument design where criteria and standards are imposed. Rater training is a currently popular area of research and indeed the analysis indicates seven areas of undeveloped solution potential, but among these its greatest potential would appear to be with respect to Rater Characteristics and Rater x Task factors.

Rater training has typically been used to reduce error by teaching raters to avoid particular rating configurations but it could be used to control subjectivity sources by changing the Rater Characteristic of cognitive complexity and by modifying task perceptions, skills and knowledge to enhance rater motivation.

The Strengths and Potential of System Design

System design offers no direct solution to Criterion or Standard judgement problems although recommended strategies have significant implications for the encompassing system. It does, however, provide major solutions with respect to Rater x Task, Rater x Ratee, Ratee x Organisation and Rater x Organisation factors, and it can be useful in identifying Assessment judgement problems. Of the three strategies, system design has been the least systematically explored and so for source elimination it has several areas of unexploited potential (including RC, RI, RT, RR, ReO and RrO). Perhaps the most important lies in its potential for modifying rater motivation through Rater x Task factors.

In addition the analysis highlighted the importance of the relationships (both their existence and form) between what are sometimes seen as independent activities. For example, the relationships between performance rating and reward, promotion and training activities, job analysis and criterion development, job design and performance appraisal were all seen to be important. The dependence of solution effectiveness on these relationships reinforces an emphasis that is often placed on the integration of organisational sub-systems and the need for appraisal system design to be co-ordinated with other sub-system features. As such, some form of system design activity can be viewed as necessary whatever the particular subjectivity problem.

As the sources of subjectivity are more or less susceptible to different strategies, the solubility of problems arising from different sources depends on the strategy chosen. In developing performance rating systems, therefore, there is a need to be selective in strategic choice and Table 5.1. provides an aid to selection both on the basis of strategic applicability and solution availability.

One other consideration in strategic choice is the practical commitment implied by a strategy and bearing on this are those situations where the effectiveness of one strategy depends on the parallel application of another. In these cases each strategy is described in Table 5.1. as being a major contributor to solution. So, for example, the solutions to low rater motivation require both rater training and system design strategies to deal with Rater x Task factors.

A further conclusion which can be drawn from Table 5.1. is that the choice of strategy to overcome the unsystematic errors associated with Assessment judgement cannot be a clear one until research has clarified source-error links. Moreover, the strategy required depends on the source of the specific effect and each of the contributing sources are ones where it is evident that strategies are relatively undeveloped.

Finally, one point which emerged from the consideration of sources of subjectivity, which has perhaps the greatest significance in strategic choice, is that there are different forms of subjectivity. In particular some types of subjective bias can be seen as functional, so strategic choice depends on whether these differences are recognised and valued. In examining the applicability of strategies to Criterion and Standard judgement problems a choice of methods presented itself i.e. the Imposed Criteria or Standards and Democratic Criteria or Standards methods. In effect, these represent two philosophies with respect to subjective bias. The former makes no distinction between these and any other sources of subjectivity and so seeks to eliminate, reduce or change the source. The latter recognises that the rater is in some sense expert and utilizes this expertise in a controlled way. These differences in underlying philosophy imply different strategies. The choice of philosophy should be consciously made if either strategy is to be effective but the choice may be difficult because neither of the implied methods is easy. Imposing criteria and standards through instrument design alone is inadequate. Supportive training is always required and its effects need to be reinforced through rating performance analysis and feedback. So this attempt to 'keep the lid on' personal Criterion and Standard judgements in the hope of re-educating raters can be a long, hard, up-hill battle. On the other hand, Democratic Criterion and Standard development initially involve much greater time commitment, effort and expense and require fairly high level training skills. In addition, this participative approach might be seen as inconsistent with the normal management practices of the organisation. However, from the evidence, the beneficial effects of democratic derivation of criteria and standards appear considerable, consistent and relatively enduring.

In short, strategy choice depends not only on the subjectivity sources present, the relative applicability of strategies and solution availability, but on the status afforded to rater judgement and the value associated with it.

SUMMARY AND IMPLICATIONS

Through this chapter three possible strategies for managing subjectivity have been identified, discussed and their applicability to different sources of subjectivity has been examined.   This strategic analysis suggests that previous research has over-concentrated on remedying the effects of subjectivity rather than to curing causes, that overemphasis has been placed on certain strategies and solutions to the neglect of others, and that attempts at dealing with subjectivity have lacked the selective application of strategies.

From a summary of strategic applicability, the strengths and weaknesses of instrument design, rater training and system design have been identified.   The choice of appropriate coping strategy was discussed and the author suggested that this choice should be made according to the source of subjectivity to be dealt with, solution availability and the status afforded to rater judgement.

This analysis in conjunction with the research and theory bearing on rater subjectivity, its sources, mechanisms and effects, contained in Chapter 4, provides a unique opportunity to distinguish potentially fruitful directions for performance rating research and development.

Research in rater cognitive complexity. As the cognitive capabilities of the rater appear to play a central role, effecting Rater x Instrument, Rater x Ratee, Rater x Organisation, Perception factors and rater judgement processes, and as cognitive capabilities may be modified, then the development of the cognitive complexity research orientation in performance rating research would seem to be a worthwhile goal.   In particular, to enhance measurement accuracy by utilizing the critical factor of cognitive complexity it is necessary to know how to develop complexity in the cognitive domain of performance, what limits there are to its trainability and to its predictive power.

Research in real settings. As the system design strategy has multiple areas of undeveloped potential, as it shows promise in eliminating situational influences and has an essential role in motivation modification, greater attention should be paid to system design solutions.   The main reason for the lack of pursuit of this strategy has been the tendency to conduct performance rating research under experimental conditions so what is needed is more research within real organisational settings.   In addition, attention needs to be paid to developing critical sub-system relations.

A training focus on subjectivity sources. While the traditional training emphasis has been on remedying the effects of subjectivity, the strategic analysis suggests that rater training has great cause-curing potential. Clearly a shift of focus from effects to sources is required and the author suggests that rater training should combine both lecture and participation in instrument development, should take initial rater attitudes into account and should deal with organisational constraints and realities so as to deal with ability, motivational, perceptual and cognitive affect sources of subjectivity.

Research on rater participation. Rater involvement in instrument development can increase understanding of scale use (Rater x Instrument factor), increase motivation (Rater x Task factor), increase perceptual standardization (Rater x Organisation factor), and of course it is essential to the development of democratically-agreed criteria and standards. As a multiple solution it promises to be a valuable tool but full rater participation may not be essential to the achievement of these goals. Therefore it is necessary to establish what type and degree of rater involvement leads to what effects.

Selective strategy application. No one strategy for overcoming the problems of subjectivity is preferred, but rather what is required is the selective application of strategies depending on source and form of subjectivity. And, from the review, it is clear that all three are differentially required to achieve accurate, reliable and valid rating.

Clarification of rater status. Having established that different forms of subjectivity exist which have different implications for strategic choice, then it is clear that the researcher or developer has to make a conscious decision about the view taken of the rater and the value attributed to rater expertise. In the authors view the rater's Criterion and Standard judgements are features of expertise and should be valued as such. This view is based on two main observations. Firstly, in reality the rater is expected to be an expert in subordinate performance, otherwise little value could ever be attached to his assessment of performance by any judgemental method. Secondly, whether or not it is recognised, raters do behave as experts and there are strong reasons for believing that unaccommodated expert judgements can have detrimental effects on the rating outcome.

Controlling functional subjectivity. Including expert insights in criterion development is a progressive step but the subjectivity admitted needs to be controlled and actively managed in order to avoid unstandardized observations and the Democratic Criterion and Standard methods provide a means of doing so.

CONCLUSIONS

The many findings reported in this and the previous chapter bear witness to the level of attention that the search for error-free performance rating has received as well as the diversity of approaches that have been adopted in the pursuit of performance measures which are valid, reliable and accurate despite their dependence on subjective involvement and judgement. While each piece of research has contributed to a vast and growing body of knowledge about the performance rating activity, it appears that the achievement of the ultimate goal has been dogged by the lack of a coherent theory of how rater characteristics give rise to measurement error, the lack of a systematic framework within which to locate and relate research findings, the lack of a guiding theme to inform the decisions of researchers and developers and the lack of a rational set of assumptions from which to derive testable hypotheses.

The model of Rater Subjectivity presented in Chapter 4 is based on the partially substantiated assumptions that subjectivity is inevitable; originates in rater characteristics; is the prime cause of characteristic rating errors; and is mediated by rating performance. Using the research which shows that rater characteristics interact with situation variables to effect performance determinants, and the appraisal method analysis which yielded three kinds of appraiser judgement, the author arguing for their association with particular rating errors, the model provides logical relations between individual differences, situational variables, performance determinants, judgemental components of rating performance and measurement errors. In so doing the model yields some answers to major research problems. It provides a theory of subjectivity which explains how rater characteristics give rise to measurement error and it provides a systematic framework within which to locate and relate research contributions. For example, the significance of Schneier's (1977) work lies in its contribution to understanding the ability and judgemental components of rating performance while the significance of Blum and Naylor's (1968) definition of opportunity bias lies in its contribution to our understanding of the perceptual component of rating performance. In addition, through the model it is possible to identify areas where research is needed. For example, Rater x Task factors and motivation and the relationship between cognitive affect and performance are areas which immediately present themselves for further empirical enquiry.

The analysis of strategies for dealing with subjectivity also provides a guiding theme to inform the decisions of researchers and developers. Two alternative philosophies emerge in the form of the Imposed Criterion and Standards methods and the Democratic Criterion and Standards methods. The former is guided by a rationale which sees all subjectivity as undesirable and which attempts to resolve subjectivity problems by over-riding sources and preventing effects, while the latter recognises some forms of subjectivity as desirable and attempts to resolve subjectivity problems by accommodating the judgement sources of subjectivity, thereby controlling and reducing its undesirable effects whilst capitalizing on its desirable effects. Preference for either method may be dictated by personal or situational conditions but both have implications for the choice of appropriate coping strategies. And finally the model displays a set of assumptions from which to derive and test hypotheses.

Accepting subjectivity as inevitable, the crucial issue is how to manage it such that accurate, reliable and valid ratings are achieved. Essentially the alternatives appear to be those of eliminating or controlling the effects and/or the sources of subjectivity through instrument design and/or rater training and/or system design. While the strategy analysis presents the array of possible solutions, the fact that there appear to be both functional/desirable and dysfunctional/ undesirable forms of subjectivity must be a major guide to the choice of methodology if the former is not to be sacrificed by default in attempts to remove the latter. Where methodologies concentrate on eliminating sources or masking effects by instrument design and rater training they may lose the potential benefit of rater expertise and criterion relevance. What is required is the ability to distinguish one form of subjectivity from the other and the ability to deal selectively with sources and effects.

The foregoing theory and analysis go some way to developing this ability. Basically, Rater Characteristics, Rater x Instrument, Rater x Task, Rater x Ratee and Ratee x Organisation sources of subjectivity are undesirable and need to be eliminated, changed or their effects at least reduced. Meanwhile, Criterion and Standard judgement sources and some Rater x Organisation factors are desirable but need to be actively managed and controlled. The strategy analysis provides guidelines as to how these factors might be eliminated, reduced or controlled in terms of instrument design, rater training and system design.

This, in the final analysis, provides an answer to the original questions about the role that subjectivity plays in performance measurement, and the handling of it such that resultant measures are conceptually sound but methodologically pure. Subjectivity is inevitable and complex. It arises from several sources and operates through several mechanisms. It can be functional or dysfunctional depending on the source and how it is handled. In terms of coping with it such that measures meet the conceptual and methodological criteria, sources of subjectivity need to be dealt with selectively. The road to conceptual soundness appears to be through the accommodation, active management and control of Criterion and Standard judgements, while the road to methodological purity appears to be through the elimination or reduction of idiosyncratic tendencies which arise from the rater himself and his interaction with situational variables, and are predominantly manifest in the Assessment judgement.

These two chapters have pursued subjective involvement as a central concern in the determination of appropriate performance measures. Chapter 4 identified and elaborated the sources and possible effects of subjectivity and established the legitimacy of particular forms of subjectivity, while Chapter 5 derived appropriate means of achieving their elimination, reduction or control.

The main thrust of these conclusions signifies a fairly radical view of the role and significance of the rater in the measurement process which emanates from a fundamental regard for the inevitability of subjectivity and the saliency of its effects. In order to reinforce some of these conclusions Chapter 6 describes an empirical study of performance rating, conducted within a real organisational setting, which illustrates the saliency and significance of rater subjectivity.

6 An empirical illustration

In Chapter 3, where it was found that the observer determined several
limitations on the nature of accurate, reliable and valid performance
measures, the author argued that the observer has to be a major consideration in the choice of appropriate measure. In the subsequent chapter, the significance of subjectivity in measurement was underlined,
sources and effects of subjective involvement identified and the instrumentality of observer characteristics, abilities, motivations, perceptions and judgements in performance rating outcome was demonstrated. In
Chapter 5 arguing for the inevitability of observer influence as a fundamental aspect of criterion development and measurement methodology the
author identified alternative methodological responses, the choice of
which was seen to depend on the value and legitimacy attributed to observer involvement. Where observer expertise is valued his influence
needs to be actively managed and controlled at source through methodologies typified by the Democratic Criterion method. In contrast, where
this value is not held then observer influence needs to be avoided,
where possible, at source by situational management and its effects reduced or suppressed through methodologies typified by the Imposed Criterion method and criterion usage training.

While the author advocates the former approach with its focus on sources
versus effects, active management versus coping and criterion development versus criterion usage training it does have wide-ranging implications that are unlikely to be readily accepted. To envisage methodologies which actively accommodate observer influence ultimately implies
situation-specific criterion development. While such a suggestion is
likely to invoke resistance both from academics, with an interest in the
generalization of job performance theory and from practitioners, working
under constraints of time, resource and expertise, to reject this
approach out of hand may be to overreact at the expense of some worthwhile developments.

The aim of this chapter therefore is to highlight the academic and practical significance of some of these theoretical conclusions by reference

to empirical findings. The author describes a study which examines some of the effects of perceived criterion importance on rating performance and the relationship between rater organisational position, criterion selection and standard definition.

The potential significance of perceived criterion importance and of rater organisational position is first outlined and research objectives formulated. The background to the research, the procedure adopted and main features of the design are subsequently explained. The analyses are presented in three parts, relating to the themes of criterion selection, standard definition and perceived criterion importance. Ultimately, the findings are summarized and specific implications are drawn for rater organisational position choice, BARS methodology and the Rater Subjectivity model.

RESEARCH FOCI AND OBJECTIVES

The empirical foci were chosen for their potential significance. From the academic point of view the likelihood of accepting observer influence as inevitable would be enhanced if it could be demonstrated that the subjective perception of criterion salience influences rater performance. From the practical point of view, if rater organisational position influences rating performance then we need to know what the critical features are of organisational position and what aspects of rating performance it effects.

Perceived Criterion Importance (PCI).

The author has argued that observer conceptual clarity is a significant determinant of performance measure choice and utility. As the cognitive complexity research finds that individuals make conceptual distinctions according to constructs which have grown to have importance to them, it suggests that constructs which are perceived as important are likely to be conceptually distinct and clear. In Chapter 4 these conceptual distinctions with respect to performance were identified as Criterion and Standard judgements and their use or neglect in criterion development was argued to determine the occurrence of certain rating errors. Whether or not these personal conceptual distinctions are valued appears to be the methodological watershed and yet the effects of PCI is an area which has not been investigated. Even within research on the Democratic Criterion development methods (e.g. BARS) little attention has focussed on the perceived importance of individual constructs and in fact, as Jacobs et al, (1980) noted, there is an implicit assumption that generated criteria are perceived as equally important. Understanding the effects of perceived criterion importance seems fundamental to methodological choice for if it is associated with rating accuracy then there is good reason to ensure that the performance criteria used are those which are considered important by the user.

One main objective of the reported study was therefore to examine the effects of PCI on rating performance. The necessary data were collected from fifteen raters who generated, ranked in order of importance and used performance criteria developed through BARS methodology.

Rater Organisational Position (ROP)

The second theme, again chosen to emphasise the significance of observer involvement, focusses on ROP as a determinant of rater judgement which has practical significance for the development of performance measurement and for the organisational utility of performance measures.

On finding systematic relationships between ROP and rating accuracy, relevance, amount of bias, and inter-rater reliability, the author suggested in Chapter 4 that these might be explained in terms of different ROPs giving rise to systematic differences in Criterion and Standard judgement. The budding awareness that ROP-related differences in percepts have some validity (Dunnette and Borman 1979) has yielded competing views as to how these differences might be used. On one hand Klimoski and London (1974) suggested that, in performance rating, an appropriate ROP should be chosen according to the measurement purpose while Guion (1965) proposed that ratings from several ROPs should be combined as a means of capturing different facets of performance.

In order to utilize ROP differences to enhance performance measurement in either way then it is necessary to know what form ROP-related differences in perception take and what critical features of ROP determine perception. Typically ROP-related differences in rating performance have been attributed post-facto to variable opportunity to observe, differences in the kinds of behaviours observed and variable frequency of rater-ratee contact. Is differential emphasis simply a matter of differential observation or does ROP effect Criterion and Standard judgements in other ways? What is the extent of the differences between ROP perceptions? Clearly we need information about the similarities and differences between the perceptions of different organisational positions. In particular it's necessary to establish the nature of ROP differences and to investigate their sources.

The second objective therefore of this study was to investigate and account for the differences and similarities in preferred criteria and standards of raters from different organisational positions. BARS method is a means of generating preferred performance criteria and the parallel development of BARS by different ROPs for a focal job performance provides a vehicle for examining ROP-related Criterion and Standard judgement differences as well as a basis for their exploration.

While it is convenient to distinguish between the PCI and ROP research foci, they are chosen to illustrate and reinforce previous conclusions at a general and specific level respectively. As such the findings from one inevitably inform the findings of the other so the specifics, i.e. data on ROP-related differences, will be considered first in the analyses.

BACKGROUND AND PARTICIPANTS

This study was conducted within a UK tobacco processing company as a contribution to a larger project (see Makin et al, 1978), concerned with identifying selection tests for cigarette-making and -packing machine mechanics.

The Organisational Problem.

With a focus in the main project on the perceived performance inadequacy of mechanics who serviced, maintained and repaired making and packing machines, the personnel, production and training staff were interviewed and specific problems with the selection, training and assessment systems were identified.

In light of a high training drop-out rate, personnel and training staff felt that the selection criteria and predictors were deficient in validity and reliability. A poor relationship between training and production assessments of mechanics was a frequently mentioned source of discontent and it was felt that perceived omissions in mechanic training and the low utility of training assessments were due to some critical (and unknown) differences between the performance criteria used by training and production personnel. With regard to the appraisal system, personnel staff were concerned about poor rating discrimination, supervisory staff found the information obtained to be inadequate for feedback purposes and training need diagnosis, while the mechanics themselves frequently brought allegations of rating bias. In summary, the selection, training and assessment procedures were seen to be lacking by all interested parties.

This multi-faceted problem was tackled at several levels, but the singular common concern, central to each of these problems, was the inadequacy of current performance criteria. Valid and reliable, behaviourally-detailed, discriminating and quantitative criteria for mechanic performance were required and BARS methodology not only promised a means of developing criteria with these properties but their parallel development by relevant organisational groups provided a means of identifying group differences in valued performance criteria.

This partial coincidence of academic and organisational concerns provided the opportunity to investigate ROP-related differences in Criterion and Standard judgement whilst satisfying an organisational need for new performance criteria and information about the differences in trainers' and supervisors' bases of assessment. The perceived validity of the findings for organisation members also provided an additional basis on which to gauge their utility.

The Choice of Rater Groups

In response to the academic and organisational objectives three BARS-generating rater groups were chosen (Floor Managers, Technical Supervisors, Training Instructors).

The Training Instructors (TI), of which there were three, were individually responsible for the training, supervision and assessment of mechanics both during the training school period and an initial four month period on the production floor. Each TI was an experienced mechanic and gained familiarity with most of the mechanics either directly through his training function or indirectly through day-to-day contact in his trouble-shooting role. From these characteristics the TI group were judged to be job-knowledgeable.

The six Technical Supervisors (TS) had responsibility for the supervision of mechanics, machine crew and skilled craftsmen and the maintenance of production. Again as 'time-served' mechanics themselves with extensive experience of mechanic supervision these individuals constituted a job-knowledgeable group.

Finally the six Floor Managers (FM) had responsibility for the supervision and administration of each production floor. Not all were experienced mechanics nor did they have as frequent contact with individual mechanics as the other two groups. However they were chosen as the final job-knowledgeable group on the basis that they were referred to by TSs on supervision, production and technical problems and were formally required to assess mechanic performance.

These fifteen people generated the research data. While small in number these organisational members comprised the population of job-knowledgeable raters. The three groups independently participated in the development of BARS for mechanic performance.

RESEARCH DESIGN AND PROCEDURE.

For ease of reference the sequence of research activities is outlined in Table 6.1. and the major design features including independent group generation of BARS, an individual criterion ranking exercise, an individual performance evaluation exercise and inter-group differences discussions are each described below.

BARS Development

BARS methodology was originally described by Smith and Kendall (1963) and their claim that the technique produced an instrument with superior scale properties stimulated much research interest and its application in many occupational areas. Periodic reviews (Schwab et al, 1975a, 1975b, Jacobs et al, 1980, Kingstrom and Bass 1981) have demonstrated that while BARS may not be a panacea for all rating scale problems it does provide a means of criterion clarification and agreement, rater training, securing rater commitment and has special properties to recommend it over other formats when instrument utility and information quality are considered. It is for these reasons that BARS suggested itself as a suitable vehicle for examining inter-group differences in Criterion and Standard judgement.

134

TABLE 6.1

Sequence of Research Activities

Phase 1 — Consecutive meetings with rater groups involving
Criterion generation (Stage 1 BARS)
Incident generation (Stage 2 BARS)
Criterion ranking exercise I.

Phase 2 — Editing of non-behavioural incidents (Stage 3 BARS)

Phase 3 — Consecutive meetings with rater groups involving
Retranslation of incidents (Stage 4a BARS)
Criterion ranking exercise II.

Phase 4 — Reduction of incident pool by consensus agreement
criterion (Stage 4b BARS)
Rephrasing of incidents (Stage 5 BARS)

Phase 5 — Consecutive meeting with rater groups involving
Incident Scaling (Stage 6a BARS)

Phase 6 — Reduction of incident pool by consensus agreement
criterion (Stage 6b BARS)
Preparation of ROP-specific BARS

Phase 7 — Individual performance evaluation exercise

Phase 8 — Consecutive meetings with rater groups involving
Inter-group differences discussions.

As there have been several procedural variations adopted in BARS development, an outline of the procedure used in this study, the purpose of
each stage and the control indices used are provided in Table 6.2 and
briefly described below.

Criterion generation. Following the original procedure, the three
groups of job-knowledgeable raters independently participated in naming
and defining the major components of job performance. Within each group
participants were asked "What distinguishes an effective from an ineffective mechanic?" Emergent criteria were posted on a list and the
group was asked to check that the agreed criteria were distinct, relevant and comprehensive in their coverage of the job performance domain.
This initial stage resulted in 14, 11 and 8 performance criteria generated by the FM, TS and TI groups respectively.

Incident generation. Raters were asked to draw on their individual ex-

TABLE 6.2

BARS Development Procedure

PURPOSE	DEVELOPMENT STAGE	INDEX USED
Increasing relevance through agreement on performance criteria	1. CRITERION GENERATION	Overt verbal agreement to the the meaning and comprehensiveness of criteria
Increasing relevance by the identification of specific performance indicators	2. INCIDENT GENERATION	Written examples of effective and ineffective performance
Elimination of ambiguous terms	3. EDITING OF INCIDENTS	Inspection for non-behavioural and non-specific terms
Controlling subjectivity through agreement on the performance criteria	4a. RETRANSLATION OF INCIDENTS	4b. Consensus agreement = $>$ 66% allocation to designated criteria
Standardization of incident format through use of the 'expectation' concept	5. REPHRASING OF INCIDENTS	Restatement of incident in terms of "could be expected to....."
Advancing the level of measurement by agreeing behavioural bench-marks for performance levels	6a. INCIDENT SCALING	6b. Consensus agreement = S.D. $<$ 10

136

perience to describe as many examples as possible of specific incidents of behaviour illustrative of effective and ineffective performance on each criterion. This stage yielded a pool of 445 incidents.

Editing of incidents. To ensure the behavioural nature and clarity of incidents those which were ambiguous (e.g. 'required only to be told once'), lacked behavioural specificity (e.g. 'displays a mature approach to life') or were duplicated, were removed from the incident pool. This process reduced the pool to 337 incidents.

Retranslation of incidents. The purpose of 'retranslation' is to control subjectivity and increase scale utility by ensuring agreement on the performance criteria illustrated by each behavioural example. Each participant was provided with a pack of randomly ordered cards (one for each generated incident relevant to the group's criteria), a list of group criteria and asked to indicate which criterion was illustrated by each incident.

Incidents were then selected for final scale inclusion according to a consensus agreement criterion. In practice this consensus criterion has varied from 100% (Maas 1965) through to 40% (Randell and Still 1973) but, based on Bernardin et al's (1976) study which found 60% agreement to be optimum, a consensus criterion of 66% was adopted here and less well-agreed incidents were discarded from the pool.

Rephrasing of incidents. At this stage incidents are transposed into a standardized format. Although there is a preference for 'observation' (BOS) versus 'expectation' scales (BES), Latham and Wexley (1977) found utility to depend on the rater's 'opportunity to observe'. As this factor was variable across the groups in this study, the latter format was adopted.

Incident scaling. Having obtained agreed performance criteria and constituent incidents participants were asked to locate each incident on the relevant criterion. Each criterion scale consisted of 60 subdivisions and was anchored at every 10 points by a label indicating degree of effectiveness i.e. the scale represented an effectiveness continuum. In order to arrive at final scale placements of incidents, for each rater group, the mean and standard deviation (S.D.) of each incident was calculated and a consensus agreement criterion of S.D. < 10 scale points was set such that incidents located with less agreement were discarded.

Interestingly, a significant proportion of incidents had S.D. < 5 scale points (61/133 FM incidents, 72/139 TS incidents and 25/158 TI incidents met the stricter criterion). Where raters are able to agree to within 8 scale points on a 60 point scale as to the placement of half of the incidents it is evident that they are capable of a level of discrimination not previously recognised in BARS studies. In contrast to the usual requirement that raters agree within 3 scale points on a 7point scale (Fogli et al, 1971, Goodale and Burke, 1975, Harari and Zedeck,

1973) this finding implies that rater discriminative ability on democratically-derived criteria is generally underestimated and supports Kafry et al's (1976) assertion that 'the application of more stringent criteria... can enhance the scalability' p.521.

Production of BARS. The BARS developed by each of the three groups were then constructed and the resultant instruments are included in Appendix A, B and C for the FM, TS and TI groups respectively.

Criterion Ranking Exercise

In order to measure and utilize perceived criterion importance as an independent variable and to check on its stability, each participant was asked, after both the criterion generation and incident retranslation stages, to rank the group-generated criteria in order of importance in determining job performance effectiveness. Where group rankings were required individual rankings were averaged.

Performance Evaluation Exercise

So as to provide data with which to analyse the effects of criterion importance on rating performance, participants were asked to use their group-derived BARS to assess the performance of individual mechanics (n = 91).

Strategies for avoiding the effects of other sources of subjectivity were built into the performance evaluation exercise. The factors which characteristically detract from rating ability were controlled here by the use of BARS which are assumed to embody commonly meaningful criteria and standards. Factors which detract from rater motivation were reduced by the raters' interest in discovering inter-group differences, by the prospect of achieving appraisal instruments which would facilitate feedback and through the provision of time and encouragement for the completion of this 'important task'. Cognitive affect factors were controlled by alerting raters to their potential bias and by providing a 'no-rating' alternative. A major perceptual factor, ROP, was of course an independent variable here but where raters felt they had insufficient opportunity to observe ratee performance they were provided with the 'no-rating' alternative.

In theory the ratee population numbered 91 but because of a split-shift system the potential ratee pool for any one rater was 45 mechanics. In addition, in light of the need to control subjectivity sources raters were invited to define their preferred rating pool. Table 6.3 indicates the number of ratings made by individual raters and it is included to show that, given the 'no rating' alternative, the rater's self-selected ratee pool is commonly smaller than normally required by the organisation.

138

TABLE 6.3

Number of Ratees selected per Rater

FM GROUP	TS GROUP	TI GROUP
FM(a) 17	TS(a) 22	TI(a) 15
FM(b) 15	TS(b) 34	TI(b) 49
FM(c) 32	TS(c) 20	TI(c) 18
FM(d) 20	TS(d) 25	
FM(e) 13	TS(e) 19	
FM(f) 19	TS(f) 25	

Intergroup Differences Discussions

In line with the underlying value placed on rater expertise, differences
and similarities between group criteria were explored with the raters
themselves. Each group was presented with a table of the 3 sets of
criteria and asked to explain the similarities and differences in content and perceived importance between groups. Although this is a subjective exercise, some confidence could be placed on resultant explanations as, for any one similarity or difference, three independent group
views were collected. Both the author and a colleague independently
annotated these discussions, focussing on identifiable reasons as they
emerged. These notes were later compared as a check on interpretation
and an agreed summary of substantive content is included below. (The
present author has provided a more detailed account of these discussions
elsewhere, Morrison 1981).

THE ANALYSES

The analyses are presented in three parts. First, to identify ROP-
related differences and similarities in preferred performance criteria,
the content, perceived importance and underlying dimensionality of the
three sets of independently generated criteria are compared by inspection, by reference to group discussion data and through factor analyses
of performance ratings. Second, to identify ROP-related differences and
similarities in performance standards, the behavioural content of shared
criteria, the value attributed to identical incidents and the application of standards on shared criteria are compared by a content analysis
of criterion inclusions, by an analysis of standard definition differences and by an analysis of performance evaluation data. Finally, to
examine the effects of PCI on rating performance, the stability of PCI,
the relationship between individual PCI and scale utilization, leniency
error and central tendency effect are explored.

139

ROP Criteria

The TI group generated and sustained 8 criteria, the TS group generated
11 but lost 2 through lack of agreement while the FM group generated and
maintained a more elaborated set of 14.   Among these criterion sets
there appeared to be some identical terms and several others which were
semantically similar.   There were, however, 14 terms, distributed
across the groups, which seemed to be semantically unique.   When identical criteria and those having close semantic similarity are considered
together the areas of intergroup agreement and disagreement can be more
clearly defined as criteria which are Common (to all groups), Shared (by
two groups) and Unique (to one group).   Table 6.4 shows the group-
generated criteria categorised in these terms, the group ranking for
each criterion and the average ranking of each category.

An initial inspection suggests that criteria apparently common to all
ROPs are those which are regarded as most important by each group.
Those shared by two groups seem to be located in the middle of each
ranking spectrum.   Unique criteria, accounting for approximately half of
each criteria set, are those which are regarded as least important by
the generating group.   In other words, there is substantial intergroup
agreement as to the most important performance criteria, some agreement
as to the slightly less important aspects but no agreement on the apparently significant but minor performance aspects.

Reasons for ROP criterion differences

During the intergroup differences discussions each of the three groups
was shown Table 6.4.   They were asked to focus on the shared and unique
criteria and to explain these apparent differences in concern.   In the
case of shared criteria participants were invited to account for their
inclusion by two groups and exclusion by the third.   The salient aspects
of each discussion are reported below.

Attendance (included by FM and TS, excluded by TI).   All participants
concurred that non-attendance (and lateness) caused problems for production personnel because of their responsibility to man the machines and
because of its implications for lost production, i.e. the TS and FM inclusion of attendance as a significant criterion was explained in terms
of implied consequences for the rater's task and his functional interest.   In contrast, comments such as 'TI's are not production oriented', 'Mechanic trainees come in whether they are ill or not', 'TIs
aren't bothered by attendance because non-attenders are sacked' suggested that the TI exclusion of attendance is explained in terms of functional interest and the low frequency of non-attendance behaviour in the
TI-ratee organisational context.

Safety Awareness (included by FM and TI, excluded by TS).   Reasons for
inclusion of this criterion centred on the rater's functional interest
(e.g. 'Safety awareness is a stated area of training') and rater responsibility (e.g. 'FM's carry-the-can for safety on the production floor',

TABLE 6.4

Common, Shared and Unique Criteria with Average Ranking for each Category

TRAINING INSTRUCTORS	TECHNICAL SUPERVISORS	FLOOR MANAGERS
COMMON CRITERIA		
Diagnostic Fault-Finding Ability (1)	Mechanical Aptitude (1)	Problem-Solving Ability (1)
Personal Application (2)	Dedication to work (2)	Attitude to Job (2)
Mechanical Aptitude (3)	Diagnostic Fault-finding Ability (3)	Practical Technical Ability (3)
(Av. Rank = 2)	(Av. Rank = 2)	(Av. Rank = 2)
SHARED CRITERIA		
-	Attendance (4)	Attendance (7)
-	Temperament/Disposition (6)	Temperament/Disposition (5)
Safety Awareness (6)		Safety Awareness (8)
(Av. Rank = 6)	(Av. Rank = 5)	(Av. Rank = 6.67)
UNIQUE CRITERIA		
Initiative (4)	Willingness to Learn (5)	Theoretical Technical Ability (4)
Resilience (5)	Personal Attitude to Others (7)	Confidence in Own Ability (6)
Use of Tools (7)	Advice Seeking (8)	Crew Confidence in Technical Ability (9)
Motivation (8)	Range of Interests (9)	Retention of Learning (10)
(Av. Rank = 6)	(Av. Rank = 7.25)	Housekeeping (11)
		Adaptability (12)
		Speed of Learning (13)
		Managing the Crew (14)
		(Av. Rank = 9.88)

'TI's are responsible for the safety of trainees'). The major reasons for the TS exclusion of this criterion appeared to be its interference with the achievement of the rater's task (e.g. 'TSs get battered for production and safety practices are one of the things that hold it up') and rater functional interest (e.g. 'TSs are more interested in production', 'My main concern is keeping the machines going').

Temperament/Disposition (included by FM and TS, excluded by TI). All groups explained the inclusion of this factor by FM and TS in terms of the organisational context (e.g. 'it's important when the mechanic has to work under pressure with a crew') and in terms of its implications for the rater's task (e.g. 'FMs have problems with male/female conflict between mechanic and crew', 'Mechanics cause trouble for me (TS) if they get too easily frustrated' etc). The TI exclusion of this factor was explained in terms of the TI's role relationship with the mechanic (e.g. 'TI's relationship is one of helping where he asks, for example, 'what's the problem?', rather than antagonistically asking, 'Why has the machine been down?' therefore he doesn't get an impression of how he reacts in a normal situation') and in terms of lack of opportunity to observe this behaviour (e.g. 'trainees are eager to make a good impression', 'TIs don't get to know the mechanics for long enough').

The reasons for inclusion and exclusion of uniquely-valued criteria are presented for 9 of the 14 which were generated. In the other 5 cases the non-generating groups were unable to identify or agree on inclusion or exclusion reasons. This indicated that some criteria not only lacked perceived value to other groups but also lacked any meaning. In the absence of this 'corroborative' evidence less confidence could be placed on the reasons offered. The 9 for which full data were available are briefly discussed below.

Use of Tools (Unique to TI) The agreed reason for TI inclusion and TS/ FM exclusion of this criterion was that poor performers had to be identified by the TI and either released or given remedial training before they progressed to the production floor. So while a critical aspect of training, the organisational context (after training) reduced observable variation in use of tools behaviour. These inclusion and exclusion reasons related to the TI functional interest and the FM/TS lack of opportunity to observe behaviour respectively.

Initiative (Unique to TI) The TIs justified their inclusion in terms of 'it reduces the call on my time' and 'it indicates learning is taking place'. In other words, initiative was valued because it reduced the rater's workload and was an index of rater success. The FM's exclusion came as no surprise to other groups as the FM-mechanic functional relationship precluded the opportunity to observe the relevant behaviour (e.g. 'FMs don't work as close', 'FMs don't get involved in sorting out a job', 'FMs knowledge of mechanics is restricted to exceptional cases'). The TS group originally generated an initiative criterion which didn't however survive development because TS's felt that a balance was needed between advice-seeking and initiative - 'too much or too little of either can cause problems'.

Resilience (Unique to TI). TIs maintained that this aspect was important in successful completion of training as perserverance in the early
days was crucial. The TS group supported their exclusion by the coverage of relevant behaviour by other criteria. It was agreed by all
groups that the FM group spent insufficient time with an individual
mechanic, i.e. Criterion inclusion was related to the rater's functional
objective and exclusion to lack of opportunity to observe.

Range of Interest (Unique to TS). The TS group appeared to value this
as it was a major feature of their social relations with the ratees
(e.g. 'its the most common area of conversation'), it was seen to be
predictive of other criteria (e.g. 'it tells you something about someone's mechanical aptitude', 'it tells you about his motivation') and it
was related to the rater's experience with an exceptional case (e.g. 'I
had one particularly bad mechanic in mind when generating incidents').
Both the FM and TI groups considered it either job-irrelevant or super-
fluous to other criteria.

Advice seeking (Unique to TS). The TS group explained their inclusion
of this criterion in terms of the implication that poor performance had
for the rater's workload (e.g. 'basically, too much of it bothers me
because it takes up my time'). FMs failed to include this factor
because they 'wouldn't expect a mechanic to come to me over the head of
the supervisor', i.e. lack of opportunity to observe behaviour because
of the functional relationship. TIs failed to include advice-seeking
for a different reason. They found detrimental levels of advice-seeking
difficult to discriminate because individual differences are non critical and expected within the TI-ratee functional relationship (e.g.
'asking and answering questions is a major part of training and some ask
a lot, some ask a little but it's usually important').

Housekeeping (Unique to FM). The groups concurred that as the FM is
held responsible by the organisation for this aspect, good mechanic performance in this area is valued because its absence reflects on the
rater (e.g. 'FMs are interested in the look of the place because out-
siders walk through', 'We're always being beaten over the head about the
state of the floor'). The reasons for TI exclusion of this factor may
be summarized in terms of the organisational context of TI-ratee contact
not providing the opportunity or need to observe (e.g. 'it's not a problem in the off-the-job situation'; 'it's part of our job to remind
them'; 'TIs have an easier area to clear'). The TS exclusion reasons
reflected the functional orientation of the rater, (e.g. 'a balance is
needed between housekeeping and efficiency because while they are clean-
ing up they could be losing production', 'providing it doesn't stop production I'm not bothered'), the rater's detailed knowledge of the real
situation (e.g. 'a lot of mess is created by others not mechanics'),
and the rater's perceived job responsibility (e.g. 'it's more the concern of the Administration Supervisor than mine').

143

Speed of learning (Unique to FM). The FM inclusion of this was based on a 'supposition that it was important in training'. This was criticised by the TS group who denied its practical relevance (e.g. 'they should have done their learning before they get on the floor') and its validity was questioned by the TI group (e.g. 'speed isn't important. I'd rather they learned slowly but retained it'.) TS and TI reasons for exclusion are perhaps most significant. In both cases the rater's knowledge ruled out its value.

Theoretical Technical Ability (Unique to FM). Similarly, this factor was included by FMs because of its 'supposed importance in training', but both TS and TI groups considered it to be more relevantly covered by mechanical aptitude and diagnostic fault-finding ability criteria.

Managing the Crew (Unique to FM). The major reason for FM inclusion related to its implication for rater workload (e.g. 'if mechanics do this well then it saves a lot of problems and managerial time'). This factor was not included by TS because, 'mechanics are not required to manage but co-operate and this is covered by personal attitude', 'a mechanic is finished if he isn't part of the crew'. Nor was it included by TIs because 'mechanics rarely work with the crew during training'. In other words reasons for exclusion again related to adequate coverage by other criteria, rater knowledge of job demands and lack of opportunity to observe.

In contrast to previous research this information provides some insight into the determinants of ROP criterion choice. Not only do there appear to be various reasons why specific rater groups prefer particular criteria but these go beyond the frequently quoted 'opportunity to observe' hypothesis. It's also apparent that the reasons for criterion exclusion by one group are not necessarily the inverse of the reasons for inclusion by another. A summary of frequently quoted inclusion and exclusion reasons brings this distinction into focus.

The six main reasons for criterion inclusion were:-

1. Criterion performance significantly effects rater workload e.g. Initiative (TI), Advice-Seeking (TS), Managing the Crew (FM).
2. Criterion performance reflects on the rater's performance e.g. Initiative (TI), Housekeeping (FM).
3. Criterion performance is associated with the rater's responsibilities, task or functional interest e.g. Attendance (FM), Temperament/Disposition (FM, TS) Safety Awareness (TI, FM), Use of Tools (TI), Resilience (TI).
4. The rater's experience with an exceptional case e.g. Range of Interests (TS).
5. Criterion performance is seen as a main feature of rater-ratee interaction e.g. Range of Interests (TS).
6. The rater's theoretical supposition e.g. Speed of Learning (FM), Theoretical Technical Ability (FM).

Outside the area of inter-group criterion agreement, differential ROP emphasis seems to be determined by individual factors such as personal experience, content of social interaction and personal theorising but also by the rater's functional relationship to the ratee. In particular, areas of ratee performance where deficiencies or excesses effect rater workload, perceived rater performance, achievement of rater objectives and rater's responsibilities, are valued by the rater.

In contrast, the seven main reasons for criterion exclusion were:

1. The rater-ratee functional relationship provides insufficient opportunity for relevant behaviour to be observed, e.g. Initiative (FM), Advice-Seeking (FM), Managing the Crew (TI), Temperament/ Disposition (TI), Resilience (FM).

2. Relevant behaviour is covered by another criterion e.g. Theoretical Technical Ability (TS/TI), Range of Interests (TI/FM), Resilience (TS).

3. Criterion performance is perceived as outside the rater's responsibility e.g. Housekeeping (TS).

4. Criterion performance interferes with the rater's objective, e.g. Safety Awareness (TS), Housekeeping (TS).

5. The organisational context reduces perceived criterion variation or importance e.g. Advice-seeking (TI), Use of Tools (TS/FM), Attendance (TI).

6. Rater knowledge of practical demands denies relevance e.g. Speed of Learning (TS), Housekeeping (TS/TI), Managing the Crew (TS).

7. Rater expertise denies relevance e.g. Speed of Learning (TI).

While there appear to be a variety of exclusion reasons the major determinants seem to be the lack of opportunity to observe behaviour and the inclusion of the performance aspect in another criterion. However, reasons related to rater knowledge of the ratee job, practical demands and his functional expertise are also evident as well as the influence of the organisational context in depressing the degree of inter-individual variation in performance. Finally, as with inclusion reasons some appear to relate to the rater's functional interest. In particular, raters talked in terms of their areas of responsibility and their task objective.

These analyses suggest that some ROP differences in preferred criteria relate to the rater himself.. Most of the reasons generated for criterion _inclusion_ were phrased in terms of the rater's task, responsibility or functional interest. While these factors were evident in reasons for criterion _exclusion_, the stronger theme related to opportunity to observe and the influence of the organisational context.

While these findings lend some support to the traditional hypothesis that ROP differences in criterion preference are due to differential opportunity to observe ratee behaviour, of greater significance is the apparently close relationship between what a rater perceives as critical in ratee performance and his own job task, function, responsibilities and interests. This seriously questions the utility of ratings which assume the rater to be a detached and objective observer when quite clearly the rater's own interests are influential factors.

Finally, it should be remembered that while this analysis focussed on differences between secondary and tertiary criterion priorities, there was substantial inter-group agreement on the primary criterion priorities.

The underlying dimensionality of criteria

The previous analyses focussed on semantic differences in group-generated criteria and the subjective perception of criterion choice determinants. In this analysis group criteria are compared in a more objective way by reducing the three criteria sets to underlying factors. The factorial structures were derived from the performance evaluation data. Individual rater's performance evaluations were normed and an average derived across each rater group for each ratee such that one set of ratings were available per ratee per group and the three ratee x criteria matrices subjected to factor analysis (S.P.S.S. Version 6.5 Principal Factor Varimax rotation). The factorial solutions for FM, TS and TI data are presented in Tables 6.5, 6.6, 6.7. respectively.

TABLE 6.5

Factor Analysis of FM BARS Ratings

	FACTOR I	FACTOR II
Problem Solving Ability	.82*	.36
Managing the Crew	.48	.61
Crew Confidence in Technical Ability	.74*	.41
Retention of Learning	.86*	.30
Theoretical Technical Ability	.79*	.33
Practical Technical Ability	.69*	.49
Attitude to Job	.27	.85*
Speed of Learning	.87*	.23
Adaptability	.67*	.47
Attendance	.39	.70*
Safety Awareness	.26	.61*
Temperament/Disposition	.23	.71*
Housekeeping	.26	.69*
Confidence in Own Ability	.75*	.28

*Denotes inclusion in factor.

The FM data, ratings of 91 cases on 14 criteria, collapsed into two relatively distinct factors. The constituents of Factor I (accounting for 62% variance) suggested an underlying Ability dimension. Those which load heavily on Factor II (accounting for 11% variance) suggested an underlying Motivation dimension.

TABLE 6.6

Factor Analysis of TS BARS Ratings

	FACTOR I	FACTOR II
Dedication to Work	.62	.56
Advice Seeking	.61*	.45
Mechanical Aptitude	.94*	.21
Attendance	.46	.24
Diagnostic Fault-Finding Ability	.87*	.23
Personal Attitude to Others	.29	.85*
Willingness to Learn	.69*	.55
Temperament/Disposition	.23	.77*
Range of Interests	.49	.36

* Denotes inclusion in factor

The TS data, comprising ratings of 91 cases on 9 criteria also collapses with two factors. Again, the main loadings on Factor I (accounting for 60% variance) suggested an Ability dimension. The significant constituents of Factor II (accounting for 11% variance) clearly suggested a Social dimension. Although Dedication to Work, Attendance and Range of Interests are divided between the two factors, the extraction of a third factor (accounting for 3% variance) only partialled out Range of Interests. Little is gained by this alternative solution except the additional information that an underlying dimension of Motivation is not readily accessible.

TABLE 6.7

Factor Analysis of TI BARS Ratings

	FACTOR I	FACTOR II	FACTOR III
Diagnostic Fault-Finding Ability	.65*	.46	.49
Use of Tools	.39	.28	.79*
Mechanical Aptitude	.62*	.34	.60*
Initiative	.69*	.39	.51
Safety Awareness	.19	.44	.50
Motivation	.43	.73*	.33
Personal Application	.41	.72*	.33
Resilience	.74*	.50	.29

*Denotes inclusion in factor

The TI data, comprising ratings of 91 cases on 8 criteria, collapsed into three factors. Factor I (accounting for 76% variance) was clearly ability-related and, when compared with Factor III appeared to be a dimension which taps the practical aspects of ability i.e. Practical Ability. Factor II (accounting for 8% variance) suggested an underlying dimension of Motivation. Factor III (accounting for 6% variance), comprising Use of Tools, Mechanical Aptitude and a slightly heavier loading of Safety Awareness than on other factors, appeared to indicate an underlying dimension of Technical Ability.

When factorial structures are compared across groups an Ability dimension appears to account for the majority of the variance in each set of ratings and includes two of the three criteria considered as most important by each group. Inter-group differences occur at the second and third factor level. FM and TI ratings both indicate a conceptually distinct but weak Motivation factor. The TS ratings do not yield a motivational dimension but do reflect a distinction made between behaviour towards the job and behaviour towards others. This is not surprising in view of the TS-ratee functional relationship. The TI ratings indicate that a distinction is made between problem-oriented and machine-oriented behaviour, a conceptual refinement which is again consistent with the TI's particular functional interest in ability.

ROP Standards.

The theme within this second set of analyses is guided by previous suggestions (Zedeck et al, 1974) and theory in Chapter 4 that different ROPs may maintain and use different behavioural standards. The common and shared criteria and their constituent behavioural benchmarks provide a means of assessing Standard judgement similarity and differences across groups in three ways.

First, if groups value different behaviours with respect to a common criterion then a comparison of group-specific criterion inclusions will yield different content. Second, if groups value the same behaviours differently then where common criteria include identical behaviours these will be scaled differently. Third, if groups rate according to different standards when using common criteria to rate the same ratee pool then rating means will differ.

Content analysis of shared criteria.

For each of the 5 shared criteria where groups had access to identical pools of behavioural examples, we are interested in the degree of overlap in the behavioural illustrations agreed by different groups as well as the nature of any differences. In the following analysis, based on the scale data included in Appendices A, B, and C, the number of common behavioural incidents per criterion are identified and semantic differences between unique content are explored.

Diagnostic Fault-Finding Ability. The common scales (TS and TI 15) include 8 and 19 behavioural incidents respectively, of which 6 are common. The TI criterion is therefore more elaborately defined than that of the TS. While unique TS content emphasises systematic analysis, data collection, diagnosis and speed, the TI examples emphasise fault-finding procedure (e.g. diagnosis before action), and the need to establish cures as well as provide remedies. These differences in behavioural definition are significant in their consistency. The TIs with a functional emphasis on working practice and complete fault elimination are likely to reflect these interests in the behaviours on which they assess mechanic performance. Similarly, with an admitted commitment to maintaining production it is not surprising that the TS tendency is towards achievement of results, without undue concern for the finer points of procedure.

Attendance. FM and TS 14 are anchored by 11 and 12 incidents respectively, of which 6 are common. There is considerable content similarity with a common focus on punctuality and reliability of attendance (it appeared that long or expected absences did not feature because they had less disruptive implications for the immediate supervisory personnel). There is also a suggestion that TSs, working in closer proximity to the ratees, are capable of finer discrimination of attendance behaviour. This is evident in the marginally greater dispersion of incidents, distinctions made between types of uncertified absence, and the FM scale being defined by more specific standards (e.g. 'could be expected to be late for work less than 4 times a year').

Safety Awareness. FM and TI 21 are anchored by 8 and 11 behavioural examples respectively of which 6 are common. Although TI 21 is slightly more elaborate in behavioural definition, scale inclusions are essentially similar and focus on safety procedures and practices. This similarity and the apparent ability to clearly define effective and ineffective performance (evident from the large mid-scale gap) perhaps reflects the availability of legislative guidelines with respect to this performance aspect.

Temperament/Disposition. FM and TS 25 are anchored by 8 and 11 examples respectively, of which 6 are common. Both sets of scale inclusions focus on patience and steadiness in approach to work and tolerance of others. A significant elaboration on the TS scale is the introduction of the concept of personal responsibility, a lack of which is seen to mark particularly ineffective performance. This unique concern may well reflect differences in working proximity and functional contact.

Mechanical Aptitude. This criterion is highly valued by both TS and TI groups. The scales (TS 13 and TI 19) are prolific in behavioural definition, both anchored by 16 behavioural examples, of which 5 are common. Although there is a mutual focus on evidence of mechanical comprehension, precision in tool use and accuracy in problem-solving procedures, TS 13 is differentiated by a concern for speed while the unique TI inclusions focus on mechanical knowledge. These different foci again may be explained in terms of ROP-specific functional interests.

This analysis of common scale inclusions indicates that there is a fair degree of inter-group similarity in the behaviours they value with respect to common criteria. The differences that do exist, however, lend support to the notion that behaviours which are valued reflect the rater's functional interest and organisational proximity.

This level of inter-group agreement on the kind of behaviours considered in assessing performance on the common criteria means that in general groups base their performance assessments, according to important criteria, on a common core of behaviours.

Standard definition differences in shared criteria

This analysis seeks to establish whether performance indicators are similarly valued i.e. do different groups assess a behavioural incident in the same way? Identical behaviour examples on shared criteria were rank ordered in terms of scale point allocation and a Spearman rank order correlation between common scales performed. The resultant co-efficient of correlation (ρ) is indicative of the extent to which the relative values placed on behavioural examples are similar and a test for the significance between means of paired scores, yielding a 't' statistic, is indicative of the extent to which the referent standard for different groups is similar.

TABLE 6.8

Rank Difference Coefficients of Correlation (ρ)
and Significance of Difference between Means (t)
of Scale Point Allocation of Identical Incidents

CRITERION	ρ	t
Diagnostic Fault-Finding Ability (n=6) (TS and TI Groups)	.8285*	.5711
Attendance (n=6) (FM and TS Groups)	.8857*	.1832
Safety Awareness (n=6) (FM and TI Groups)	.7142	.3337
Temperament/Disposition (n=5) (FM and TS Groups)	.9*	-4.2213*
Mechanical Aptitude (n=5) (TS and TI Groups)	.6	.4046

* significant at 5% level.

The results presented in Table 6.8 reveal a high degree of inter-group agreement on the relative value of identical behavioural examples and a substantial degree of agreement on the referent standards used by different groups. The notable exceptions are the referent standards used by FM and TS with respect to Temperament/Disposition where there is a significant difference in the scale placement of the behavioural examples. The mean difference indicates that FM evaluations of behavioural incidents were on average 4 scale points higher than those of TS. This suggests that, in evaluating Temperament/Disposition, the TS group adhere to stricter standards. This is consistent with both their focus on social aspects of performance and with a heightened appreciation of the criticality of Temperament/Disposition differences in the work place brought about by their functional proximity to ratees.

Standard application differences in shared criteria

The final analysis of inter-group differences in standards is based on the performance evaluation data where standards are, of course, put into practice. Group mean ratings on shared criteria were compared and the significance of their differences tested using a 't' test for independent samples, as there was some discrepancy in the ratee pools. The results presented in Table 6.9, indicating no significant differences in the application of standards, extends the empirical support that different ROPs apply similar standards when evaluating according to shared criteria.

TABLE 6.9

Significance of Difference between Group Means (t) of Independent Sample Ratings on Shared Criteria

Rater Groups	Criteria	t	df	Significance
FM & TS	Attendance	-.93	10	NS
FM & TS	Temperament/ Disposition	-.07	10	NS
TS & TI	Diagnostic Fault-Finding	.34	7	NS
TS & TI	Mechanical Aptitude	-.07	7	NS
FM & TI	Safety Awareness	-1.38	7	NS

These analyses of inter-group differences in shared criterion standards demonstrate that, although there are differences in group standard content and definition which can be explained in terms of rater group functional interest and organisational proximity, there is moderate agreement between functional groups on the behaviours they observe, the values they attribute to them and the standards they use (with the exception of Temperament/Disposition) in evaluating performance according to common and shared criteria.

It should be noted that as the focal criteria were not only _shared_ but also commonly regarded as the _most important_ such a level of agreement cannot be automatically assumed for criteria which are regarded of lesser importance. This qualification underlines the need for more information about the significance of criterion importance.

Perceived Criterion Importance (PCI) and Rating Performance.

There is a relationship between criterion importance and criteria commonality across ROP. The factor analyses also demonstrated a relation between those criteria perceived as important and those found to be statistically important. These findings and the qualification above add momentum to the initial interest in PCI.

Ultimately the author seeks to emphasise the arguments presented in Chapter 4, that certain aspects of the rating situation (in this case Rater Organisational Position) have sufficient influence on outcome to warrant a rethink of performance measurement methodology. Having investigated the relationship between ROP and criterion preference the final step is to examine the effects of perceived criterion importance on rating performance.

Stability of PCI

An index of PCI is given by the rank ordering of criteria generated by individual raters at the initial (R_1) and second (R_2) ranking stages. PCI stability was established by calculating within-rater PCI rank difference coefficients of correlation (ρ) over R_1 and R_2 and the results are given in Table 6.10. (R_1 ranking data was unavailable for FMa and FMe).

As all coefficients are positive and 75% are significant (at the 5% level at least) individual PCI appears to be relatively stable. Although the theory suggests that PCI varies according to experience and over time these results demonstrate that it has some stability over short periods of time (in this case 3 months) at least.

TABLE 6.10

Spearman Rank Differences Coefficients of Correlation (ρ)
of Perceived Criterion Importance (R_1 and R_2)

FM Group (N = 14)	$\rho R_1 R_2$	TS Group (N = 9)	$\rho R_1 R_2$	TI Group (N = 8)	$\rho R_1 R_2$
FMa	–	TSa	.48	TIa	.33
FMb	.82**	TSb	.73*	TIb	.81*
FMc	.55*	TSc	.92**	TIc	.19
FMd	.73**	TSd	.87**		
FMe	–	TSe	.97**		
FMf	.71**	TSf	.7*		

** significant at 1% level
* significant at 5% level

PCI and scale utilization

It has been suggested that criteria which are meaningful to the rater
yield greater rating accuracy because not only are they conceptually
well-defined but they are better discriminated and so permit greater
scale utilization. Having derived variably meaningful scales (indexed
by ranked importance) and samples of rater scale usage (from the performance evaluation exercise) this theoretical bridge can now be tested.
For each criterion and for each rater, a measure of scale utilization is
given by the rating range i.e. the difference between lowest and highest
ratings awarded across the ratee sample. Individual criterion rating
ranges were rank ordered and the rank difference coefficient of correlation (ρ) with PCI (R_2) was determined.

TABLE 6.11

Rank Difference Coefficients of Correlation (ρ) of Criterion Rating
Range and PCI (R_2)

FM Group (N = 14)	ρ	TS Group (N = 9)	ρ	TI Group (N = 8)	ρ
FMa	.04	TSa	.87**	TIa	.12
FMb	.34	TSb	.50	TIb	.76*
FMc	.51*	TSc	.77*	TIc	.19
FMd	.52*	TSd	.64*		
FMe	−.25	TSe	.70*		
FMf	−.38	TSf	.25		

** significant at 1% level
* significant at 5% level

Table 6.11 reveals 13/15 positive correlations, of which over half are significant at the 5%. These findings support the predicted relationship i.e. that PCI is positively related to scale utilization.

PCI and leniency error

It was earlier suggested that leniency error results where the criterion standard lacks meaning to the rater. If this is true then it would follow that criterion meaning and degree of leniency error are inversely related. We can therefore test the proposition by correlating measures of PCI with measures of leniency error.

As leniency error refers to the extent to which criterion performance is consistently over- or under-rated it can be defined as the distance between the rater's standard reference point and the criterion standard reference point. Assuming a normal ratee population distribution, leniency error can be operationally defined as the difference between the rater's rating mean and the criterion mid-scale point. However, as an initial examination of mean and standard deviation statistics for the ratee population showed a positive population skew on each of the rated criteria, the degree of leniency error per rater per criterion was taken as the difference between the rater's rating mean and the ratee population mean on that criterion. Positive and negative leniency error is indicated by positive and negative estimates respectively.

These rater leniency estimates for each criterion were then ranked (R_L) according to distance from the mean i.e. Rank 1 = closest to zero, Rank 2 = next closest to zero etc, and correlated with the individual PCI (R_1 and R_2) to yield rank difference coefficients of correlation ($\rho R_L R_1$, $\rho R_L R_2$). If increasing PCI is associated with decreasing leniency then the resultant correlation coefficient would be positive. Table 6.12 presents the results for individual raters and demonstrates that there is neither a consistent nor significant relationship between PCI and leniency error.

TABLE 6.12

Rank Difference Coefficients of Correlation (ρ) of Rater Leniency Error (R_L) and PCI (R_1 and R_2)

FM Group (N = 14)	$\rho R_L R_1$	$\rho R_L R_2$	TS Group (N = 9)	$\rho R_L R_1$	$\rho R_L R_2$	TI Group (N = 8)	$\rho R_L R_1$	$\rho R_L R_2$
FMa	–	.03	TSa	−.80**	−.28	TIa	.76*	.09
FMb	.28	.35	TSb	−.55	−.33	TIb	.14	.57
FMc	−.23	−.46*	TSc	.13	.23	TIc	−.33	−.17
FMd	−.20	−.41	TSd	−.32	.07			
FMe	–	−.39	TSe	.03	.17			
FMf	.09	.35	TSf	−.38	−.33			

** significant at 1% level
* significant at 5% level

While these results are disappointing it should be remembered that a
positive population skew was assumed, based on the observation of consistent differences between ratee population and criterion means. These
differences could however have been the result of individually consistent over-rating, indicating that the 'agreed' standards were not in
fact agreed. In the case of wide-spread and consistent leniency we cannot be surprised by a failure to find the relationship sought here and
indeed a subsequent analysis (see Morrison 1981) provided some support
for this alternative explanation of apparent skew. This analysis then
did not bear out the predicted relationship but it is included because
it ultimately suggests that the degree to which BARS is an adequate
method for deriving agreed and meaningful performance standards should
be questioned.

PCI and central tendency effect

Central tendency effect was argued to result where the rater adopts
standards which lack meaning to him. We would expect therefore that
central tendency is inversely related to scale meaning and we can test
this proposition by correlating PCI with degree of central tendency.

A suitable measure of rater central tendency effect on individual criteria is given by the standard deviation from the mean (S) of ratings
given. Criterion standard deviations (S) for each rater were ranked in
order of decreasing amplitude (R_s) and a rank difference correlation,
with ranked PCI (R_1 and R_2), performed to yield coefficients ($\rho_{R_s R_1}$,
$\rho_{R_s R_2}$). By calculating central tendency in this way, a positive co-
efficient indicates an inverse relationship between central tendency and
PCI. The results for individual raters are presented in Table 6.13

TABLE 6.13

Rank Difference Coefficients of Correlation (ρ) of Rater Central
Tendency (R_s) and PCI   (R_1 and R_2)

FM Group (N = 14)	$\rho_{R_s R_1}$	$\rho_{R_s R_2}$	TS Group (N = 9)	$\rho_{R_s R_1}$	$\rho_{R_s R_2}$	TI Group (N = 8)	$\rho_{R_s R_1}$	$\rho_{R_s R_2}$
FMa	–	.09	TSa	.31	.80**	TIa	.00	.31
FMb	.27	.22	TSb	-.25	.13	TIb	.67*	.74*
FMc	.32	.23	TSc	.87**	.92**	TIc	.83**	.38
FMd	.46*	.53*	TSd	.47	.38			
FMe	–	.23	TSe	.42	.48			
FMf	-.09	-.10	TSf	.78**	.49			

** significant at 1% level
 * significant at 5% level

Although the relation between central tendency and PCI (R_2) shows a wide variation in coefficients all but one are positive and, of these, approximately 38% are significant at the 5% level. In addition, of those lacking a significant relationship here 20% show highly significant correlations between central tendency and PCI (R_1). While neither result of its own provides strong evidence, together they indicate a trend in the predicted direction, that central tendency effect does decrease as PCI increases.

The findings from this final set of analyses indicate that PCI is a relatively stable phenomenon and, in support of the theory, that it is positively related to scale utilization and inversely related to central tendency effect. However, within the limitations of the data collected in this study, no consistent nor significant relationship is evident between PCI and incidence of leniency error.

SUMMARY

Through this chapter inter-group differences and similarities in preferred performance criteria and standards have been explored and some effects of PCI on rating performance have been examined in order to underline the significance of ROP differences in criterion preference and the importance of adopting meaningful criteria to facilitate rating performance. From the results relating to ROP criteria, ROP standards and PCI the main findings can be summarized and their significance discussed.

ROP Criteria

There are systematic differences between the performance criteria preferred by different ROP in the evaluation of the same focal job performance. While this reinforces previous similar findings we are now able to identify the nature and extent of these differences.

The extent and nature of criterion similarities. In this study approximately half of the generated criteria were valued and used by more than one group so we can conclude that ROP selected criteria are by no means group-specific i.e. that some level of criterion agreement is to be found between raters in different organisational positions.

In addition, in examining the differences and similarities in ROP preferred criteria a relationship between criterion commonality and perceived criterion importance was found. Those with greatest commonality were also perceived as having greatest importance. Partially common criteria were seen to have secondary importance while ROP-unique criteria were perceived as least important. In other words criterion prioritization reflects a continuum of common, shared and unique criteria. So not only does an area of inter-ROP agreement exist but it focusses on those aspects of performance considered most important by all rater organisational positions.

<u>The dimensional structure of performance ratings</u>. As the factor
analyses yield a major underlying ability dimension, comprising the
group criterion priorities, in each set of ratings we can conclude that
criteria which have perceived importance also have statistical importance. This not only gives broad objective support for the subjective
ranking exercise but indicates that commonly-valued criteria are those
which focus on the ability component of performance. In reference to a
point made in Chapter 3 it should be noted that the adoption of a factor
analytically-derived dimension (in this case ability) would have masked
the significant conceptual distinctions made within and between groups
as to its constituents. Differences in factor analytic structure reflected differential ROP emphasis. At the second factor level FM and TI
groups favoured motivation variables while the TS group, in closer contact and in direct receipt of work group problems, valued social aspects. The TI group, with a detailed functional interest in ability distinguished between practical and technical aspects.

<u>The nature of ROP criterion differences</u>. In contrast to previous
suggestions it is now clear that differences in ROP criterion emphasis
are not just a matter of differential observation opportunities. ROP
differences in preferred criteria reflect individual and contextual factors and aspects of the rater-ratee functional relationship.

Most consistently, reasons for ROP criterion selection stem from the
rater-ratee functional relationship. The rater values criteria where
the functional relationship is such that variation in criterion performance effects rater workload, rater job performance, rater responsibilities and achievement of the rater's job objectives.

Criteria fail to be valued or to have meaning where there is a lack of
opportunity to observe relevant behaviour, where the organisational context depresses criterion performance variation or where the rater's
functional expertise provides knowledge which identifies criterion
irrelevance or contamination.

<u>The inevitability of subjectivity</u>. The most general conclusion that
must be drawn from the analysis of criterion inclusion and exclusion
reasons is that raters cannot be assumed to be detached and objective
observers. Given a free rein they conceptualize and assess performance
from their <u>own</u> point of view in a mode pervaded by subjective interests.
It is therefore unlikely that these tendencies are suspended when they
are asked to evaluate in different terms. Not only are resultant evaluations likely to be biased but they may be meaningless and this leads to
a central finding.

<u>The value of rater expertise</u>. The distinction between criterion in-
clusion and exclusion reasons not only clarifies the role of behaviour
observation opportunity in criterion selection but adds weight to the
argument that raters have a legitimate expertise which should be recognised and valued. Their particular functional relationship with the
ratee provides a unique opportunity to identify and observe critical

performance behaviours which are perhaps context-specific. The rater can define and use criteria which are, in his terms, functionally relevant, important and rateable. As important perhaps is the fact that he has knowledge and expertise which qualifies him to identify criteria which are irrelevant or unassessable. It should be remembered that in this case the exclusion reasons came from discussions where raters focussed on the job-specific criteria developed by functionally close job-knowledgeable others and yet all exclusions were readily justified. Drawing from this, the utility of non-job-specific criteria derived by functionally distant non-job-knowledgeable others must be seriously questioned.

The value of ROP-specific criteria. Remembering that this study was in part undertaken in response to an organisational problem there is an additional index with which to gauge the value of ROP-specific criteria. The differences between ROP-specific criteria were seen as an answer to the previous inter-group disagreements about performance assessments. Individual raters said that they now appreciated the problems that other groups faced and expressed how knowledge of ROP differences in emphasis would enable them to give mechanics qualified performance feedback. As such, the process of developing and comparing ROP-specific criteria proved to be an experience that widened their concept of subordinate performance and added to their appreciation of other functional interests.

ROP standard similarities. In examining the content of shared criteria a fair degree of similarity was found such that in assessing performance on commonly valued criteria there appeared to be behaviours which were commonly regarded as important indicators. However the differences between ROPs in degree of scale elaboration and in additionally-valued behaviours were seen to be consistent with functional interest.

Focussing then on the identical scale inclusions high agreement was found on the relative value of behavioural incidents and substantial agreement on referent standards. However the notable exception could be explained in terms of differences in the ROP-ratee functional relationship. The fact that no significant differences were found between ROPs in the application of standards suggests that on shared criteria, differential content may only serve the purpose of ROP-specific conceptual clarification.

The stability of PCI. Although perceived criterion importance is expected to vary between and within individuals according to experience and over time intra-individual PCI was seen to be relatively stable over a three month period. This suggests that, for most individuals, PCI does not change rapidly and so should PCI prove to be a critical factor in criterion utility then confidence can be placed in derived criteria over short periods at least.

PCI and scale utilization. In support of the theory which suggests that criteria which are meaningful to the rater are better discrimin-

ated and therefore more carefully utilized, the results showed a positive relationship between PCI and scale utilization. This means that
raters make better use of criteria which they perceive as important and
so strengthens the case for taking account of rater Criterion judgement
in measurement development.

PCI and leniency error. While neither a significant nor consistent relationship was found between PCI and leniency error there is some reason
to question whether BARS, as a Democratic Criterion development method,
adequately achieves within-group standard agreement. If substantiated,
this would be a serious weakness of BARS methodology and has specific
implications for its development which are outlined below.

PCI and central tendency effect. The findings give general support to
the hypothesis that rater judgements about criteria and standards influence the incidence of rating error. In this particular case it was
found that the use of criteria and standards meaningful to the rater
reduced a tendency to cluster ratings. This suggests that the use of
meaningful criteria and standards facilitate rater discriminative ability and so improve the utility of performance assessments.

The significance of PCI. The findings here suggest that employing criteria which are meaningful to the rater increases scale utility and decreases some forms of rating error.

IMPLICATIONS

This study was designed to illustrate and reinforce earlier theoretical
conclusions and to highlight their academic and practical significance
at both a general and specific level. While general implications for
the main theoretical themes are discussed in the final chapter, some
specific implications illustrative of general themes, can be drawn from
this study for ROP choice in an organisational context, the development
of BARS methodology and the elaboration of the Rater Subjectivity
model.

Implications for ROP choice.

As there appears to be some agreement between different ROP with respect
to preferred performance criteria, standard definition and application
then it seems that the choice of rater group is unimportant if performance measurement focusses on mutually-valued criteria. However, as seen
in this study, the resultant performance construct (including only the
ability components) would be deficient. For some measurement purposes
perhaps such a deficiency would not be critical, (e.g. for training need
diagnosis or for predictor validation purposes) but for others (e.g.
promotion, reward or feedback purposes) a construct which fails to reflect motivational or social factors must be regarded as seriously deficient. When performance information is to be used in these ways then
ROP choice becomes a major issue because, according to functional in-

terest, expertise, responsibilities and objectives, different raters are attuned to different motivational and social aspects, able to define these in differing levels of detail and able to assess these with varying degrees of accuracy.

As most organisations use performance information for one or some of these latter purposes, ROP differences have major practical significance. How then might the fact of ROP differences effect the practice of performance measurement? The two competing methodological responses can now be easily evaluated.

Bearing in mind the level of agreement between preferred criteria and standards of different ROPs, to follow Guion's (1965) suggestion that performance ratings be obtained from all significant organisational positions would lead to needless duplication of information on core criteria and so would seem to be wasteful of time and effort. In addition some of the ROP-specific criteria are context-dependent (for example Use of Tools) and the utility of this performance information would depend on the purpose of measurement.

In contrast, Klimoski and London (1974), who advocated purpose-dependent rater group choice, seem to offer a methodological response which would actively capitalize on differential conceptual clarity and rating performance. This study has now identified rater function, responsibility and objectives as primary indicators of the rater's Criterion and Standard judgements and thus provides a point of departure for making decisions about appropriate ROP choice.

Implications for BARS

Contrary to previous assumptions (noted by Jacobs et al, 1980) it is evident from this study that raters do prioritize criteria and that PCI is a significant factor in explaining scale usage and the rating error of central tendency. This suggests that in future research on the psychometric properties of BARS, an index of PCI should be included as a potential moderator.

Second, in as much as organisational position is recognised as a factor in rating accuracy and ROP-specific BARS research is a foreseeable interest, then BARS developers should pay more specific attention to the rater's functional relationship with the ratee as a source of conceptual and perceptual influence.

Finally, and perhaps most significantly, leniency error appeared to be widespread and individually consistent despite the democratic derivation of performance standards in BARS development and this suggests that the BARS methodology is not fully effective in deriving standards which are commonly useful across raters. If we look at BARS development procedure then this is not perhaps surprising. Criterion derivation can be regarded as democratic because it involves a process of concept-sharing and clarification, resulting in mutually understood and agreed criteria. The selection of representative behaviours can be regarded as quasi-democratic because the retranslation process and consensus agreement criterion ensure mutual understanding and agreement of scale inclusions. However, in establishing absolute performance standards the scale point allocation of incidents is achieved through a process of statistical averaging with no guarantee that the resultant standard concurs with the Standard judgement of any one individual.

This would not be important if the consensus agreement criterion (S.D.) was substantially lower than the inter-incident distance on scales, because relative scale positions would preserve judged standards. But even the stringent S.D. criteria used here was greater than the average inter-incident distances. As a result the relative scale placement of incidents may have differed considerably from any individual's relative placements and so it is not surprising to find widespread leniency error.

By implication, BARS record for dealing with leniency error might be considerably improved by the application of more stringent S.D. consensus criteria to scale point allocation. Perhaps there is also a need to apply the principles on which the Criterion judgement phase is built, to the Standard judgement phase as well, by incorporating a technique of standard-sharing.

Implications for the Rater Subjectivity model

The results show that ROP differences are not simply a function of differential opportunity to observe behaviour but, as predicted, are also due to other rater-specific and ROP-specific variables. These add to an understanding of the Rater x Organisation source of subjectivity. In particular, the relationships between the rater's role/functional expertise/areas of responsibility/task objectives/job criteria and the ratee's job appear to be central to what is regarded as important, what is perceived and what is assessed with greater discrimination.

Second, while the results bear out the theoretical propositions that the adoption of more meaningful criteria and standards is associated with greater scale utilization and less central tendency error, they cast doubt on the proposition that democratic standard agreement reduces leniency error. However, as it has been argued that the BARS method for deriving standard agreement may be inadequate, the relationship between standard agreement and leniency error must remain 'not proven' until it is clear that agreement has been democratically-derived.

Third, the relationships found between ROP, PCI and performance standard definition support the general contention that subjective variables play an important role in determining construct meaningfulness.

Finally, the relationship found between PCI, criterion selection, standard definition and rating performance supports the general subjectivity theme of Chapter 4. Subjectively-important criteria are also statistically important and have some common currency across groups. Important criteria show substantial intergroup agreement on standards and are also associated with better scale use and reduced central tendency effect. In short, the general theme that constructions which are meaningful to the rater are also significant for measurement accuracy is supported.

CONCLUSION

In Chapter 4 the value and legitimacy attributed to observer influence was seen to create a watershed in criterion development methodology. In choosing to look at the effects of PCI and the nature of ROP differences the author sought to accentuate the argument for the legitimacy of observer influence.

The results here support the authors contentions that at a general level, PCI is a significant factor in performance measure utility and therefore some attention should be paid to the observer in measurement methodology, and at the specific level that at least some subjectivity sources should be actively accommodated. In particular, Rater Organisational Position does have a systematic effect on the criteria valued and standards adopted but more generally, perceived criterion importance is associated with greater scale utilization and the reduction of some measurement errors. While the specific focus on ROP differences gives rise to specific implications, the results are intended as indicative rather than comprehensive so they provide the potential for wider methodological implications to be drawn. In the final chapter the theoretical themes are drawn together and, in the light of this empirical elaboration, the implications for performance measurement methodology are discussed.

7 Towards a Situation-Specific paradigm of performance measurement

With the ultimate aim of increasing the effectiveness of performance appraisal practice and the specific aim of increasing the understanding of problematic issues in job performance measurement, the author has chosen an approach in this book which differs in important respects from others that have been adopted. First, in an area where there is already a wealth of research but where the problem is one of integration, a theoretical stance has been adopted in an attempt to identify underlying themes and assimilate other major contributions. Second, whilst most of the performance measurement research has taken as its reference the psychological measurement field, the approach adopted here has delved deeper into the concept of measurement in order to establish more explicitly the reference points that have often remained at the level of implicit assumption. Third, the author has gone beyond the occupational psychology sphere to draw from other fields of psychology where similar measurement concerns are apparent and advances are being made.

The approach, then, is necessarily theoretical and whilst the author recognises the immediate needs of practitioners, she is committed to the view that pragmatic developments are likely to be haphazard and piece-meal until coherent theory and understanding is established. If an underlying understanding of organisational behaviour is to be achieved then it is vital that knowledge be developed outside of but related to such pragmatic attempts. The objective has therefore been to contribute to the development of this knowledge base through which pragmatic, piece-meal attempts, might acquire a quality that improves the practice of performance measurement and hence appraisal.

This theoretical ground-clearing progressed through five identifiable stages. In the initial stage, performance measurement was seen as a fundamental feature of performance appraisal which itself was described as a universal and necessary organisational process, having a large number of diverse decision-making objectives. Locating performance measurement in this way, the needs of practitioners for a valid, reliable, discriminating method of performance measurement which provides relevant bias-free information, were seen to be both salient and understandable. In recognising the failure of research to date to fully satisfy these needs the stage was then set for a new initiative.

The second stage sought to identify the underlying problems in performance measurement by analysing current methods with respect to accepted criteria. In this way the basic problem appeared to be the difficulty in achieving performance measures which were both methodologically pure and conceptually sound. This basic problem translates into two major areas of concern. Thus the problems of establishing appropriate performance measures and those of relying on subjective judgement were distinguished as the fundamental issues in performance measure development.

The third stage focussed on the former issue, analysed the measurement concepts, provided some integration of previous research, identified salient research directions and strengthened the impetus for an examination of the second issue.

At the fourth stage, the role of subjectivity in performance measurement was analysed and the sources and effects of subjectivity made explicit. This allowed practical conclusions to be made in Chapter 5 about appropriate strategies for dealing with subjectivity. At this point the inextricable relationship between subjective judgement and the choice of appropriate performance measures and its potential implications for methodology became more apparent and so, at the final stage, the author sought to accentuate both general and specific emergent themes in Chapter 6 by reference to an empirical study.

This approach has provided intermediate theoretical conclusions and recommendations with significance for particular areas of research and practice at each stage. These findings are worthy of comment here in order to bring into focus the salient theoretical conclusions and the cumulative theoretical conclusions will be addressed to the problems of performance measurement discussed in Chapter 2.

In this final chapter then, the individual contributions of Chapters 3, 4, 5 and 6 are reviewed, cumulative theoretical findings discussed, major methodological themes identified and implications for research and practice examined.

THEORETICAL CONCLUSIONS

Chapter 3 established that performance measures (criteria or dimensions) were matters of choice, subject to issues of convenience, and that convenience was defined by purpose, observability, conditions of observation, quantification, characteristics of criteria and behavioural assessment. The author concluded that methodological purity and conceptual soundness are to be gained by identifying job performance measures which are appropriate according to the purpose for which information is gathered, the perceptual and observation capacities of the appraiser and the conditions under which information is gathered.

In pursuing the apparent salience of the appraiser in the determination of an appropriate performance measure, Chapter 4 examined the influences on the appraiser which shape his perceptual, observational and conceptual capacities. It identified the processes through which conceptual clarity may be tapped and which are commonly overlooked, as Criterion and Standard judgement, as well as those sources and channels that give rise to undesirable forms of subjectivity. Chapter 5, through an analysis of strategic applicability, concluded with recommendations about strategic choice in attempts to deal with specific sources and effects of subjectivity but highlighted the legitimacy and status afforded to rater judgement as a basic issue in methodological choice. It was then argued that conceptual soundness was to be gained by the active management and utilization of appraiser expertise in Criterion and Standard judgement, and methodological purity through the elimination or reduction of subjectivity source influence on the Assessment judgement.

In the empirical study reported in Chapter 6 the fact that appraisers have valuable expertise which might be utilized was demonstrated by the concurrence across appraisers with respect to the conceptually and statistically most important aspects of a focal job performance. The fact that conceptual clarity is a determinant of rating accuracy was demonstrated by the relationship between perceived criterion importance (PCI) and rating errors. And the fact that situational variables act systematically to influence the areas of appraiser conceptual clarity was demonstrated through an analysis of reasons for inter-group differences in preferred criteria.

These cumulative findings lead to the conclusion that the achievement of performance measures which exhibit both methodological purity and conceptual soundness requires that measures be chosen with reference to particular aspects of the measurement situation and that one facet which is both significant and variable is the appraiser himself.

To address this conclusion to the problem initially defined, the answer must be that there is no answer: there is no one best way to measure performance. The definition of measures which are consistently valid, reliable, relevant, discriminating and free from bias in all situations where performance information is required, is an unrealistic aim which denies the complexity of the performance measurement phenomenon. Not only this but the continued pursuit of such an aim will inevitably result in measures which sacrifice conceptual soundness for methodological purity or vice versa. Most pertinently, this research seriously questions the concept of performance measure generalizability.

IMPLICATIONS FOR METHODOLOGY

This conclusion presents an awesome threat to the development of performance measurement if, and only if, the continued concern is with identifying universal performance laws. That is, if our efforts are governed by a belief that an ideal representation of job performance exists in some absolute form which can be discovered and a belief that this revelation will yield absolute measures to meet diverse decision-making needs. In other words, the conclusion is daunting if a Fundamentalist paradigm is maintained in our research pursuits and working practices.

It is clear from the research described here that there are significant and commonly overlooked factors in the measurement situation which need to be actively incorporated if performance measurement is to improve. Moreover, in the extreme there is perhaps sufficient evidence to warrant a re-evaluation of a Fundamentalist paradigm in performance measurement. The elaboration of the purpose-, appraiser- and context- dependency of appropriate performance measures suggests that a paradigm which accepts situation-specificity of performance criteria and dimensions may be more appropriate.

Which paradigm we choose to be governed by dictates our research objectives, activities and interpretations and the author suggests that the above theoretical conclusions are only consistent with a paradigm which acknowledges situational-determinism of performance measure appropriateness. The ultimate methodological implication then, is the advocacy of a Situation-Specific paradigm to guide research and practice in performance measurement.

To underline the utility of a Situation-Specific paradigm of performance measurement and demonstrate its consistency with the present findings, it is useful to contrast it with, what has been termed, a Fundamentalist paradigm.

A Fundamentalist Paradigm

The concept of Fundamentalism is in some sense related to a concept of 'universality' and is associated with 'objective, to-be-discovered' as opposed to 'subjective, to-be-derived' laws. Consequently, such a paradigm dictates a science of performance measurement which seeks to discover universal performance laws through the identification of variables and relationships. These are subsequently tested for their generality by devising instruments to measure variants in the relationships and by the application of these to situations by subjects.

Some writers have already argued against the utility of such a paradigm on philosophical grounds. For example, Herbst (1970), in describing his 'Behavioural World' model of social science, argued that the existence of universal laws in psychology would not only make it unique but is highly unlikely given psychology's subjective and reflexive nature. In addition it could be argued that purely pragmatic considerations also favour a Situation-Specific paradigm. For example, Fundamentalism can be dysfunctional in pursuit of knowledge in performance measurement and the dysfunction is manifest in reactions to non-successful applications of purportedly 'universal' laws. Within a Fundamentalist paradigm, if

a hypothesized relationship is not borne out in practice (i.e. if particular performance criteria or dimensions are found to be inapplicable or
inaccurate when applied to a focal performance) there are four possible
classes of explanation.

First, the relationship is held to lack universality. As this is more
often suggested by those who prefer an alternative explanation for the
behavioural event (another set of criteria or dimensions) it could be
ascribed to an element of vested interest. However, it is likely that
the relationship has been found to hold in some circumstances and if
failure at achieving universality is equated with lack of validity then
the researcher is placed in a difficult conceptual position, i.e. the
all-or-none nature of the test encourages researchers to up-hold (perhaps at all costs) or to doubt and discount their initial findings.
That is to say, contradictory findings pose a problem when Fundamentalism is the guiding perspective and it is a problem that leads perhaps to
erroneous findings being falsely protected or useful findings being neglected.

A second characteristic response is to draw the conclusion that the
application of the instrument to the situation has been inappropriate.
For example, the finding that a measure of managerial performance fails
to discriminate amongst a group of managers might be explained away in
terms of the group in question being non-representative. This, together with suggestions of instrument inaccuracy, is more readily put
forward than any other reason. The researcher is in effect protecting
the universal law by questioning the decision about its application.

Third, and perhaps most commonly, the instrument is held to be inaccurate. The frequency of this response is apparent in the wealth of performance measurement research which is concerned with instrument refinement.

Finally, it is sometimes suggested that human involvement in measurement
has distorted results. It is not surprising that this reason is seldom
given more weight than lip-service because logic would tend to under-
value the influence of the human element in the face of something as
conceptually strong as a universal law. When, however, it is admitted
it is invariably regarded as a source of error. Coupled with this reluctance to accept human element interference is the fact that there is
often an assumption that it is dealt with by focussing on the instrument. As documentary support, in the well-researched area of psychometric errors, there is a concentration on manipulating instrument
characteristics to minimise the influence of the rater.

These latter two potential responses demonstrate in the light of the
present findings that a Fundamentalist orientation implies both methodology and strategies which may place an artificial ceiling on the development of performance measurement. Having examined some of the broader
implications of the Fundamentalist orientation the nature and implications of a Situation-Specific paradigm can now be explored.

A Situation-Specific Paradigm

This paradigm dictates a science of performance measurement which seeks to establish universal generative laws through the understanding of situational dynamism, i.e. an understanding of how situations are defined according to significant situational influences and how these can be used to yield characteristic variants and relationships. Within such a paradigm the researcher's concern is not with the discovery of universal variables or relationships between them but with the derivation of universal methodologies which yield situation-specific variables and relationships.

When this paradigm is compared with the Fundamentalist orientation described above five important distinctions can be made which recommend its utility. First, unlike the Fundamentalist paradigm where the universal law is a central concept, the notion of universal behavioural variables and relationships is of peripheral concern in this. Second, situational-specificity allows for the apparent inconsistency of results derived in different situations. Third, unlike the Fundamentalist paradigm where progress is achieved through focussing on similarities of results, the Situation-Specific paradigm focusses on differences between findings as potential sources of theoretical development. Fourth, idiosyncratic influences and effects can be accommodated with legitimacy without fear of threatening a fundamental concept or without forcing influences into error terms. Finally, the concern of a Situation-Specific paradigm is not to establish universality *per se* but to establish limits to generalizability. However, neither is universality denied but rather it is seen as one end of the generalizability continuum. This is a particularly important feature for it means that there can be acceptance of less conceptually strong states and indeed, at the opposite extreme from universality it would be possible to locate individual-specific idiosyncratic relationships peculiar to one situation only. It is towards this extreme that methodologies such as those suggested by Personal Construct theory might perhaps be located.

These differences suggest that a major academic gain arising from the adoption of a Situation-Specific paradigm would be the increased utility of individual research effort as well as the benefits that are yielded by the acceptance of a wider array of methodologies. However, by far the most important gain, in line with the emphasis here on subjective variability and its effects, is the implied legitimization of observer influence.

Contesting Views of the Rater

The Fundamentalist and Situation-Specific paradigms have two quite different views of the role of the observer/rater in the measurement process and the legitimacy of his influence. With respect to the former, the rater is assumed constant, where the law and the instrument are universal. Except for deliberate contamination or interference, the rater's influence on the accuracy of instrument readings is regarded as a minor variant with minimal effect (usually insufficient to warrant consideration). Indeed, greater consideration would be inappropriate within a paradigm which seeks universal laws. However, it is worth noting that even in the physical sciences, where universal laws are more common, some writers are drawing attention to the importance of the human element. Discussing the subjective nature of measurement, Wertheimer (1972), Elliot (1974) and Natsoulas (1978) have pointed out that the assumptions of total objectivity must be invalid.

Conversely, within a Situation-Specific paradigm the rater assumes a greater importance. In considering a particular situation as a universe of variants, for which an ordering structure may be derived, the rater cannot be the detached observer, rather he plays a role in determining the situation by perceiving other variants from his unique standpoint and by contributing his presence to the interaction effects with other variants. In this way it matters very much who the rater is and that he differs from other raters as this makes a difference in determining the critical variants and relationships in the particular.

In summary, within a Fundamentalist paradigm it is inappropriate to be concerned with the observer as a determinant of measure appropriateness. That is to say, as long as research is concerned with discovering the universal measures of XYZ performance the implied methodologies will pre-empt appraiser influence. On the other hand, if the arguments set forth above are valued and the conclusion accepted, then it is clear that the attainment of performance measures which are both methodologically pure and conceptually sound would seem to be afforded by methodologies which seek to derive appropriate dimensions or criteria of XYZ performance, for ABC purpose under DEF conditions, and which accept the appraiser as a significant determinant of these conditions.

A Fundamentalist paradigm could of course be modified to accept qualified, restricted or even local universality but clearly this would be a retrogressive step. Without the implied goal of generalization, Fundamentalism is robbed of its strength and all research initiatives could only take single case status which is neither desirable nor necessary. The Situation-Specific paradigm in contrast opens a new vista for research initiatives.

IMPLICATIONS OF A SITUATION-SPECIFIC PARADIGM

Immediate implications ·of the specific themes that have been pursued have already been described in earlier chapters. In summary, the recommended direction for research activity was seen to be in the development of performance measures which adhere more closely to the requirements of a measure, criteria and behavioural assessment; to be in the refinement of methodologies which harness Criterion and Standard judgement; and in the identification of other situation variants which effect measurement outcome. Concurrently, the specific implications for practice were seen to be the separation of procedures by which information is gathered for different decision-making objectives; the active management and control of rater subjectivity through the use of Democratic Criterion and Standard methods; and the selective application of Instrument Design, Rater Training and Systems Design strategies for dealing with undesirable subjectivity.

Bringing these conclusions into focus, in the final chapter it has been argued that the cumulative conclusion supports a paradigm of performance measurement research and practice which acknowledges the situational determinism of appropriate performance measures. So it is appropriate to ask what implications this grander conclusion might have. How would such an orientation effect the activities of researchers and practitioners? Is such an orientation entirely necessary for all performance measurement activities? It is to answer these questions that we now turn.

Research Directions

Herbst (1970) considered that the appropriate activities of social scientists lay in the derivation of universal generative laws rather than the discovery of universal behavioural laws. With respect to performance measurement, the role of the researcher would therefore change from attempting to discover universal performance measures to: providing methods for deriving appropriate measures; identifying the situational aspects which effect measure appropriateness; and identifying ways of capitalizing on appraiser knowledge and expertise. In other words, the focus of research might shift from e.g. identifying universal criteria of management performance to identifying universal methodologies which when employed would yield criteria of management performance which are appropriate to a particular management job, within a particular organisation for particular purposes, at a particular time. The implied aim would be that such derivations would be more valid, relevant, reliable, discriminating and useful, but also more sensitive than the types of measures currently adopted.

This ultimate objective assumes a knowledge base, which has yet to be developed, about significant situational variables and their interrelationships and so the development of this knowledge must be the initial research focus. In this book the author has examined one situational variable, i.e. the rater, and with the level of detail adopted here it becomes apparent that there are gaps in our knowledge about the sources of subjectivity. But the measurement situation is not only defined by the rater and other significant aspects need to be identified. Kane and Lawler (1979) laid the ground for research of gross situational influences by enumerating some determinants of appraisal effectiveness which, together with the elaborations included here, provides the starting point for accumulating the detailed information which is required about situation variability.

In order to construct generative methodologies not only do we need to know what the significant situational variants are but how they interrelate. In this book the author has expressed situational variant relationships through their effect on the rater but other relationships may exist (e.g. Lawler 1971, suggested that an interaction occurs between appraisal method and ratee performance) and these need to be identified.

Apart from conducting such basic research to generate the necessary knowledge it is also the researcher's task to communicate that knowledge to the practitioner and provide techniques so that he is able to derive appropriate performance measures in the particular case. This secondary task in itself suggests necessary areas of research activity.

Given the situational variability of appropriate performance measures, then the practitioner needs tools to assess the state of variants within the particular situation. By analogy, Fiedler's (1967) theory of leader effectiveness provided a methodology for achieving effectiveness according to situational contingencies but it is only through the development of the LPC scale for measuring one particular situation variant (i.e leader-member relations) that the contingency theory could even start to have practical utility. Likewise with performance measurement, the practitioner needs techniques to assess rater task perceptions, cognitive complexity in the performance domain etc., and it is the task of the researcher to provide them.

Finally, it was seen in Chapter 3 that statistical forms of dimensional analysis have a significant role to play in the delineation of the underlying dimensionality of performance measures and the author suggested that a fruitful line of research may lie in the use of the principle of dimensional homogeniety. Dimensional analysis and the matching of different performance measures to different performance measurement purposes may provide distinct starting points for purpose-dependent measure development. For example, on determining that the required dimensionality of information to be used for training diagnostic purposes is, say, multiple, ability and behaviour-achievement defined then: the significance of particular situational variants may be enhanced or decreased; the choice of appropriate rater group may be facilitated; and the delineation of the appropriate criteria range preset. Whilst this yet remains at the hypothetical level the approach has some intuitive logic, appeal and promise.

The Role of the Practitioner

Traditionally, at the systems level, the practitioner's role with regard to performance measurement has involved the administration and surveillance of the appraisal system and the collection, analysis and recording of performance data for whichever decision-making purpose they are required. But with an emphasis on situation-specificity of performance measures, the task of measure development would now fall within the practitioner's realm. By implication his role would be extended to include: the choice of appropriate measure, method and appraiser group; the development of appropriate criteria or dimensions; the training of appraisers; and the design of supporting systems.

The need to make decisions regarding appropriate measures, methods and appraiser group stems from the fact that measurement purpose is a salient aspect of the measurement situation, which determines the suitability of the information gathered, its source and the method by which it is collected. The implied introduction of such a decision-making role is seen as being consistent with the increasing expertise of Personnel with regard to human resource management, where it is to be expected that they have specialist knowledge on which to base judgements about human resource management activities. And it is reasonable to expect this expertise to include a knowledge of which performance information has to be acquired and by what means, according to decision-making purpose.

The second implied practitioner activity, the development of performance measures, which arises directly from the situation-specific nature of appropriate measures, is one which is likely to bring problems. Specifically, whilst the provision of methodological expertise is a matter of adequate training, the mere time and implied costs that have been frequently noted in developing democratic criteria could be a real stumbling block. This creates another impetus for research to provide less cumbersome and more refined criterion development techniques. With respect to BARS methodology this is already a direction which has been advocated and is starting to be pursued.

But to view the measure development task, even by BARS methodology, in isolation from other human resource management tasks denies its necessary integration and falsely inflates the implied resource commitment. Most BARS studies have been conducted in an experimental environment and those that have been conducted within organisations have tended to assume 'carte blanche' in criterion development. For this reason the impression given of the resource commitment required may be misleading. As performance measurement has a central place in the human resource management activities of selection, training, placement, promotion, welfare, etc., each of which involve the collection and accumulation of performance-related information, much of the information required for determining appropriate measure choice may already reside within the system. For example, the job analyses and descriptions fundamental to the employee selection process may well embody information to guide optimum appraiser group choice in terms of identifying functional relationships, responsibilities, workload contingencies, etc. The availability of such information would inevitably reduce the resource commitment required for the measure development activity alone.

Thirdly, the need to design supporting systems arises out of the finding that undesirable forms of subjectivity may contaminate rater judgement in using measures unless the sources are identified and eliminated. It is the practitioner's task, therefore, to selectively apply strategies in the measurement situation, having identified prevalent forms of undesirable subjectivity. Chapter 4 provides a knowledge base for identifying potential sources of subjectivity and more recently, the author (Bailey 1983) described a questionnaire to aid practitioners in their diagnosis of active sources of rating contamination. And Chapter 5 provides an aid to strategic selection by recommending strategies for the elimination, reduction and control of specific sources and effects.

Finally, all of the above focus on the implied change of the practitioner's role at the systems level - but what of the appraiser's role? As it was argued that a Situation-Specific paradigm attributes legitimacy and value to the role of the appraiser then in real terms his role would change quite dramatically. No longer would he be the technician in the system but rather he would take a more active and important part in determining the system. And by involving the appraiser in this way it is not only expected that measures would exhibit more relevance, validity and reliability but that the perceived importance of human resource responsibility and active management would be reinforced.

To What Extent is a Situation-Specific Paradigm Necessary?

The Situation-Specific paradigm has arisen out of the search for ways of determining performance measures which exhibit both methodological purity and conceptual soundness. Quite clearly a Situation-Specific paradigm of performance measurement has enormous implications and ramifications for both research and practice. However, given the significance that purpose has as a determinant of measure appropriateness, an unqualified advocacy of these pursuits would be foolish without considering the objective of the performance information-gathering activity. In other words, is it the case that for all practical purposes the grand methodological and conceptual criteria need not be so strictly observed and therefore the Situation-Specific paradigm is not wholly applicable?

While there are apparently purposes for which one or other of the grand criteria might be waived, this is at least open to debate. For example, where the appraisal objective is purely employee development then the proponents of the Individual Standards Procedures, which seek neither inter-appraisee comparison nor inter-appraiser reliability, would argue that such procedures can obviate measurement and thus need not meet the criterion of methodological purity. However, whether in practice these techniques can function without the availability of some external measures on which to base expectations and gauge the reality of objectives, is open to debate. At the other end of the method continuum, the Direct Indices, whilst lacking conceptual relevance for some purposes, provide methodologically pure measures which, with their apparent objectivity, may well be acceptable as measurement tools for reward allocation purposes. But their frequent inapplicability and their insensitivity to performance-related phenomena which the organisation may want to reward, (e.g. work effort) must inevitably dictate the use of subjective judgement in performance measurement.

Even if it was accepted that purely development or reward-allocation purposes obviated the need to meet both the methodological and conceptual criteria, for most appraisal purposes these criteria would still hold and so the above conclusions are difficult to avoid.. For example, for training diagnostic and promotion purposes where detailed, comparative performance information is required, which indicates by how much and in what way an individual's performance is better/worse than standard or others, then clearly neither methodological purity nor conceptual soundness can afford to be sacrificed. And in view of the argued reliance of other methods on the availability of such measures, ultimately the acceptance of appraiser expertise and judgement as a significant situational variant must be inevitable.

In the light of the requirements which different purposes place on appropriate measures, the trend towards temporal and systems separation of appraisal activities, according to decision-making objectives, which was apparent in the early 60s but which has more recently appeared to backslide, needs to be strongly reinforced. Without detailed definition of measure purpose, the simultaneous gathering of information for more than one purpose may result in unnecessarily elaborate information for one and an inadequacy of detail for another.

CONCLUSION

Through this final chapter the author has tried to bring together what were earlier pursued as separate themes. Theoretical conclusions with regard to performance measure choice and to subjectivity have been addressed to the originally stated problems with performance measurement. Ultimately, we must conclude that there can be no one best way to measure job performance. Appropriate performance measures are to be derived not discovered and the determination of appropriate job performance dimensions or criteria is situationally-dependent. Although one significant determinant of measure appropriateness is measurement purpose, and so there is a variation in measure requirements according to purpose, some degree of conceptual soundness and methodological purity is always necessary. Following from this, the acceptance and utilization of appraiser judgement is necessary. Among the performance measurement methods currently available, the behavioural scaling methods appear to be the only ones which actively manage and utilize appraiser judgement in the dual pursuit of conceptual soundness and methodological purity, and so are to be recommended.

While the specific focus here has been on the effects and implications of subjective involvement in the measurement process, at a more general level the conclusions underline the importance of situational variables in attaining accurate performance measurement. So the wider conclusion for performance measurement methodology can be seen as the support for a paradigm of research and practice which recognises the situational determinism of performance measures. Whilst at first sight radical, this conclusion reflects a growing trend in the philosophy of social science (Guba 1979), it parallels moves in the clinical and educational measurement spheres (Sundberg et al, 1978, Hartmann et al, 1979) and perhaps most cogently, it is in keeping with the directions apparent in other fields of industrial and organisational psychology. As more sophistic-ated and advanced theories of leadership, decision-making, communication etc. are being developed, we have come to recognise that there is no one best way to lead, to decide, to interview etc. And it is evident that this recognition of their complexity as well as an explicit regard for situational determinism has led to a greater degree of understand-ing, explanation and success in these areas of organisational behav-iour.

There is a certain irony in the fact that of all the organisational con-cerns with human behaviour, the most basic need is for accurate perform-ance information and yet the research and practice of performance measurement is perhaps the theoretically least sophisticated, being practically unique in its perserverance with, what has been termed here, a Fundamentalist paradigm.

In a milieu which recognises organisational and behavioural determin-ation and complexity, the author's research strongly supports a Situation-Specific paradigm for the research and practice of performance measurement. And it suggests that, in striving to achieve measurement capability to satisfy the needs of practitioners, performance measure-ment research must adopt strategies which assume the multi-determinism of appropriate performance measures, that clarify situational determin-ants, and that provide measure development methodologies capable of addressing the known complexity of organisational and individual behav-iour.

By adopting such an orientation researchers can realistically hope to contribute to the effectiveness of this universal organisational activ-ity by providing the knowledge base and techniques which practitioners require in order to diagnose measurement needs, implement measure devel-opment strategies and to attain a level of measurement accuracy which allows them to fully realise the potential yielded by accurate, rele-vant, valid and reliable individual performance information.

APPENDIX A

Floor Managers' BARS for mechanic
performance

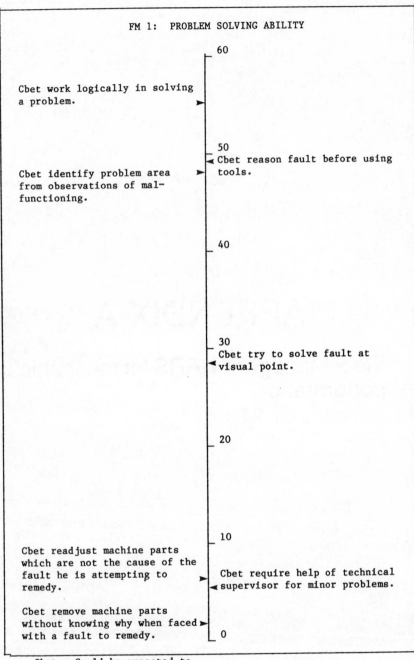

FM 1: PROBLEM SOLVING ABILITY

60

Cbet work logically in solving
a problem.

50
Cbet reason fault before using
tools.

Cbet identify problem area
from observations of mal-
functioning.

40

30
Cbet try to solve fault at
visual point.

20

10

Cbet readjust machine parts
which are not the cause of the
fault he is attempting to
remedy.

Cbet require help of technical
supervisor for minor problems.

Cbet remove machine parts
without knowing why when faced
with a fault to remedy.

0

Cbet = Could be expected to

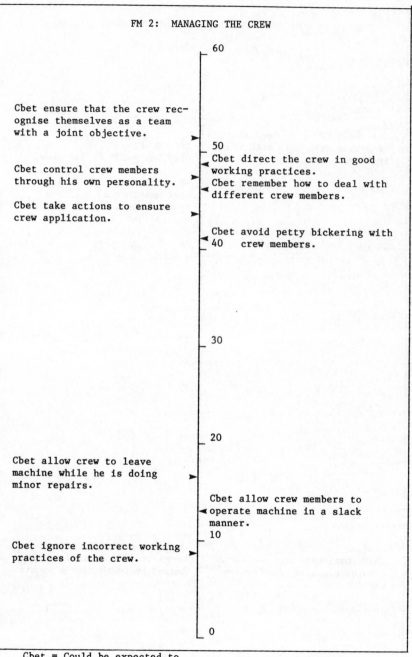

FM 2: MANAGING THE CREW

— 60

Cbet ensure that the crew recognise themselves as a team
with a joint objective.

— 50

Cbet direct the crew in good
working practices.

Cbet control crew members
through his own personality.

Cbet remember how to deal with
different crew members.

Cbet take actions to ensure
crew application.

Cbet avoid petty bickering with
40   crew members.

— 30

— 20

Cbet allow crew to leave
machine while he is doing
minor repairs.

Cbet allow crew members to
operate machine in a slack
manner.
10

Cbet ignore incorrect working
practices of the crew.

— 0

Cbet = Could be expected to

179

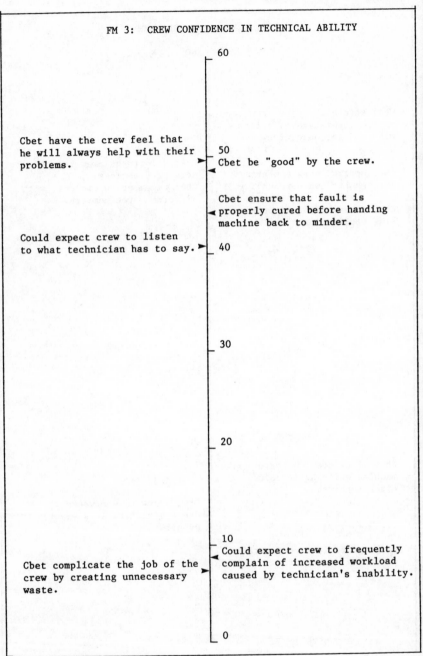

FM 3: CREW CONFIDENCE IN TECHNICAL ABILITY

60

Cbet have the crew feel that he will always help with their problems. ▶

50
◀ Cbet be "good" by the crew.

◀ Cbet ensure that fault is properly cured before handing machine back to minder.

Could expect crew to listen to what technician has to say. ▶

40

30

20

10
◀ Could expect crew to frequently complain of increased workload caused by technician's inability.

Cbet complicate the job of the crew by creating unnecessary waste. ▶

0

Cbet = Could be expected to

180

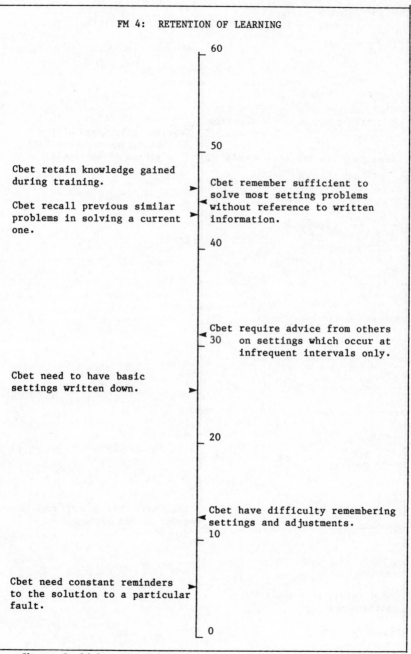

FM 4:   RETENTION OF LEARNING

60

50

Cbet retain knowledge gained
during training.

Cbet remember sufficient to
solve most setting problems
without reference to written
information.

Cbet recall previous similar
problems in solving a current
one.

40

Cbet require advice from others
30   on settings which occur at
infrequent intervals only.

Cbet need to have basic
settings written down.

20

Cbet have difficulty remembering
settings and adjustments.
10

Cbet need constant reminders
to the solution to a particular
fault.

0

Cbet = Could be expected to

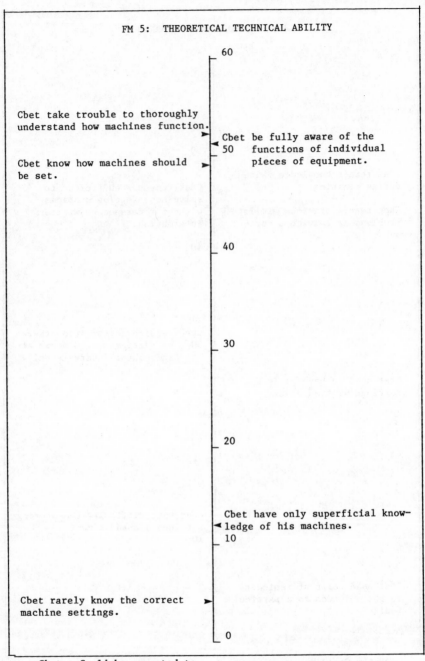

FM 5:   THEORETICAL TECHNICAL ABILITY

60

Cbet take trouble to thoroughly
understand how machines function.
              Cbet be fully aware of the
50   functions of individual
Cbet know how machines should   pieces of equipment.
be set.

40

30

20

              Cbet have only superficial know-
              ledge of his machines.
10

Cbet rarely know the correct
machine settings.

0

Cbet = Could be expected to

182

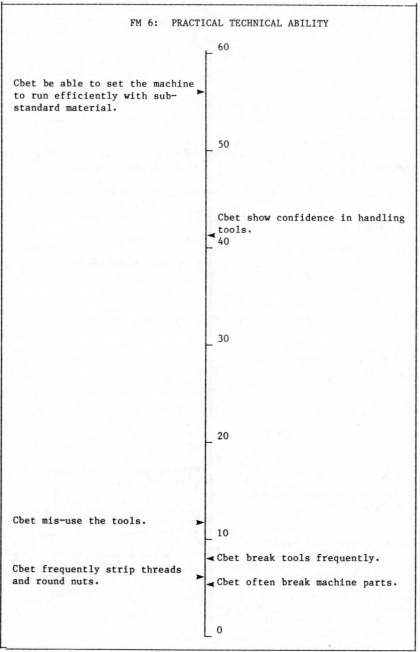

FM 6: PRACTICAL TECHNICAL ABILITY

Cbet be able to set the machine
to run efficiently with sub-
standard material.

60

50

Cbet show confidence in handling
tools.
40

30

20

Cbet mis-use the tools.
10

Cbet break tools frequently.

Cbet frequently strip threads
and round nuts.
Cbet often break machine parts.

0

Cbet = Could be expected to

183

FM 7: ATTITUDE TO JOB

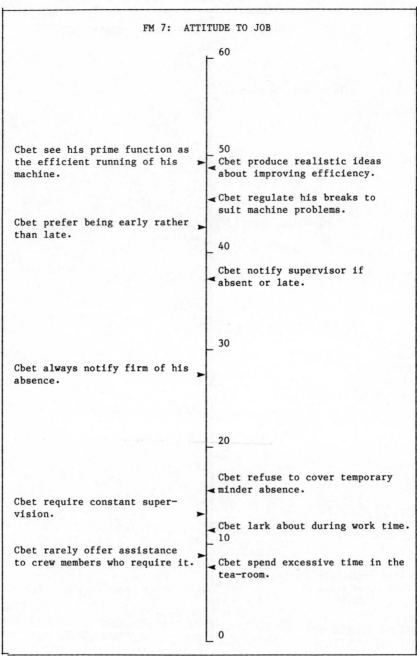

Cbet see his prime function as the efficient running of his machine.

Cbet produce realistic ideas about improving efficiency.

Cbet regulate his breaks to suit machine problems.

Cbet prefer being early rather than late.

Cbet notify supervisor if absent or late.

Cbet always notify firm of his absence.

Cbet refuse to cover temporary minder absence.

Cbet require constant supervision.

Cbet lark about during work time.

Cbet rarely offer assistance to crew members who require it.

Cbet spend excessive time in the tea-room.

60

50

40

30

20

10

0

Cbet = Could be expected to

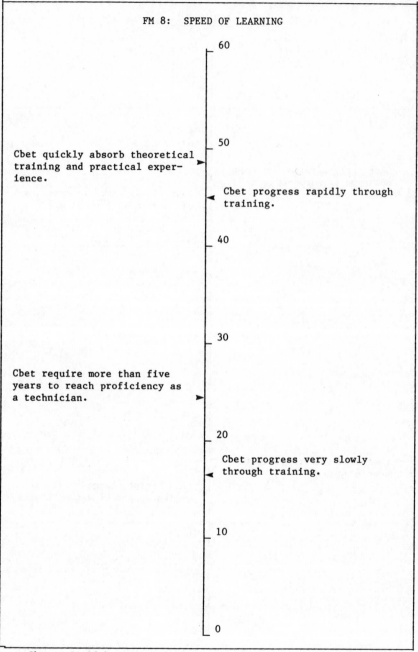

FM 8:   SPEED OF LEARNING

60

50

Cbet quickly absorb theoretical
training and practical experience.

Cbet progress rapidly through
training.

40

30

Cbet require more than five
years to reach proficiency as
a technician.

20

Cbet progress very slowly
through training.

10

0

Cbet = Could be expected to

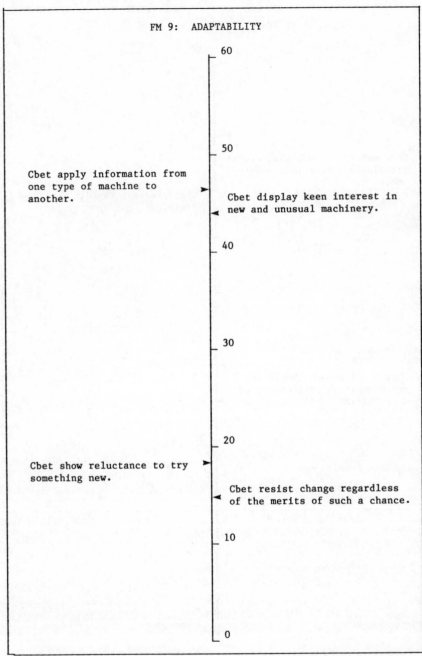

FM 9:   ADAPTABILITY

60

50

Cbet apply information from
one type of machine to
another.

Cbet display keen interest in
new and unusual machinery.

40

30

20

Cbet show reluctance to try
something new.

Cbet resist change regardless
of the merits of such a chance.

10

0

Cbet = Could be expected to

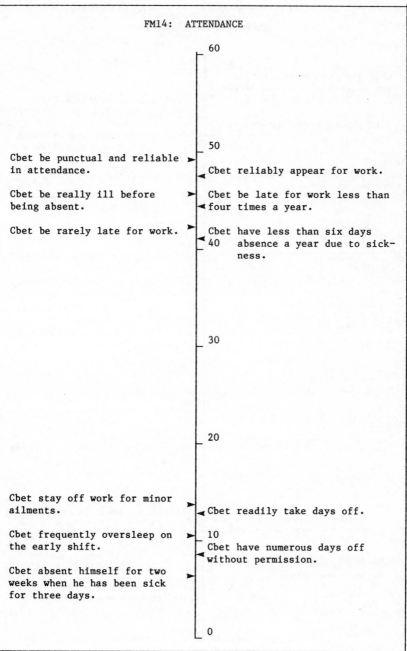

FM14:   ATTENDANCE

60

50

Cbet be punctual and reliable ►◄ Cbet reliably appear for work.
in attendance.

Cbet be really ill before ►◄ Cbet be late for work less than
being absent.   four times a year.

Cbet be rarely late for work. ►◄ Cbet have less than six days
40   absence a year due to sick-
          ness.

30

20

Cbet stay off work for minor ►◄ Cbet readily take days off.
ailments.

Cbet frequently oversleep on ► 10
the early shift.   Cbet have numerous days off
        ◄ without permission.

Cbet absent himself for two ►
weeks when he has been sick
for three days.

0

Cbet = Could be expected to

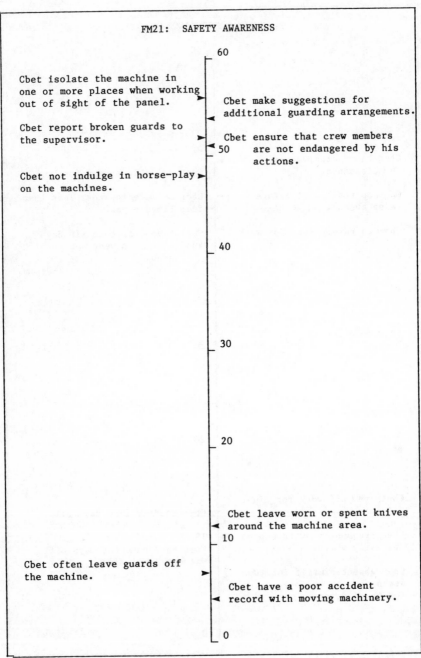

FM21:   SAFETY AWARENESS

— 60

Cbet isolate the machine in one or more places when working out of sight of the panel. ►

Cbet make suggestions for additional guarding arrangements.

◄

Cbet report broken guards to the supervisor. ►

Cbet ensure that crew members are not endangered by his actions.

◄ 50

Cbet not indulge in horse-play ► on the machines.

— 40

— 30

— 20

Cbet leave worn or spent knives ◄ around the machine area.
— 10

Cbet often leave guards off the machine. ►

Cbet have a poor accident ◄ record with moving machinery.

— 0

Cbet = Could be expected to

188

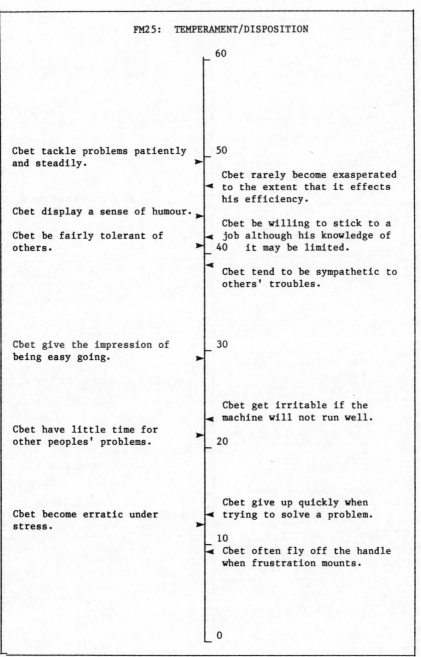

FM25: TEMPERAMENT/DISPOSITION

60

Cbet tackle problems patiently
and steadily.
▶
50
◀ Cbet rarely become exasperated
to the extent that it effects
his efficiency.

Cbet display a sense of humour.
▶
Cbet be fairly tolerant of
others.
▶
◀ Cbet be willing to stick to a
job although his knowledge of
40   it may be limited.

◀ Cbet tend to be sympathetic to
others' troubles.

Cbet give the impression of
being easy going.
▶
30

◀ Cbet get irritable if the
machine will not run well.
Cbet have little time for
other peoples' problems.
▶
20

◀ Cbet give up quickly when
trying to solve a problem.
Cbet become erratic under
stress.
▶
10
◀ Cbet often fly off the handle
when frustration mounts.

0

Cbet = Could be expected to

189

FM26: HOUSEKEEPING

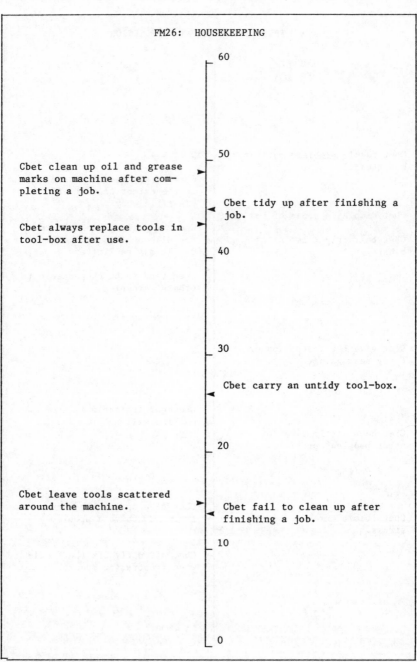

60

50

Cbet clean up oil and grease
marks on machine after com-
pleting a job.

Cbet tidy up after finishing a
job.

Cbet always replace tools in
tool-box after use.

40

30

Cbet carry an untidy tool-box.

20

Cbet leave tools scattered
around the machine.

Cbet fail to clean up after
finishing a job.

10

0

Cbet = Could be expected to

190

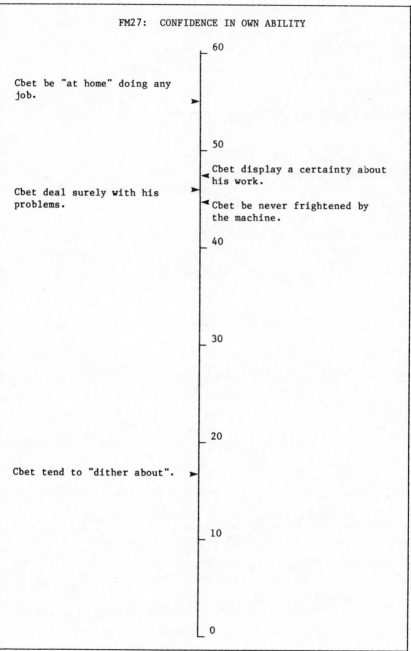

FM27:   CONFIDENCE IN OWN ABILITY

┌ 60

Cbet be "at home" doing any
job.
►

┌ 50

◄ Cbet display a certainty about
   his work.

Cbet deal surely with his
problems.   ►
◄ Cbet be never frightened by
   the machine.

┌ 40

┌ 30

┌ 20

Cbet tend to "dither about".   ►

┌ 10

┌ 0

Cbet = Could be expected to

APPENDIX B

Technical Supervisors' BARS for
mechanic performance

TS10: DEDICATION TO WORK

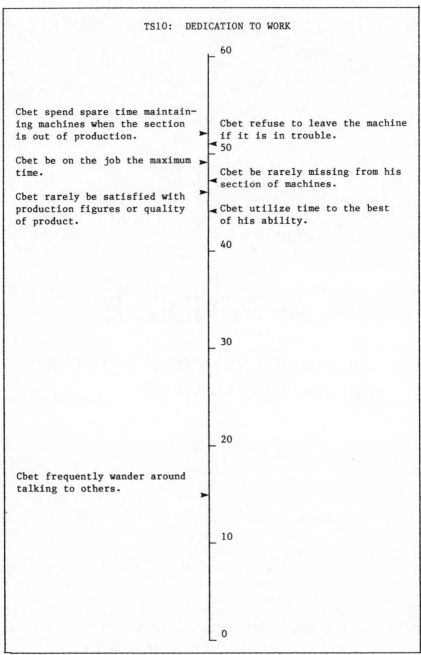

60

Cbet spend spare time maintaining machines when the section
is out of production.

Cbet refuse to leave the machine
if it is in trouble.

50

Cbet be on the job the maximum
time.

Cbet be rarely missing from his
section of machines.

Cbet rarely be satisfied with
production figures or quality
of product.

Cbet utilize time to the best
of his ability.

40

30

20

Cbet frequently wander around
talking to others.

10

0

Cbet = Could be expected to

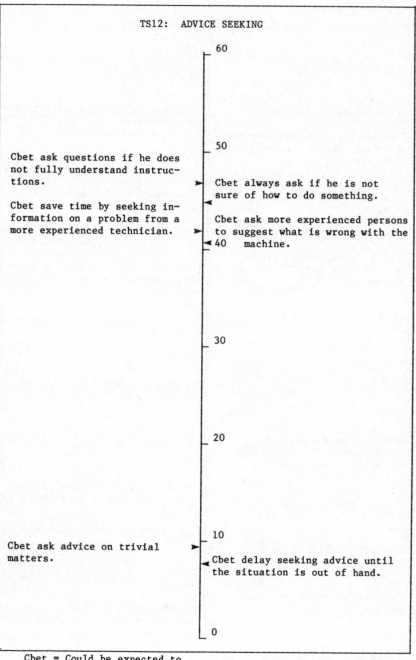

TS12: ADVICE SEEKING

— 60

— 50

Cbet ask questions if he does
not fully understand instructions.
                                    ► Cbet always ask if he is not
                                      sure of how to do something.
Cbet save time by seeking in-
formation on a problem from a   ◄ Cbet ask more experienced persons
more experienced technician.   ► to suggest what is wrong with the
                                   ◄ 40   machine.

— 30

— 20

— 10
Cbet ask advice on trivial   ►
matters.   ◄ Cbet delay seeking advice until
                                      the situation is out of hand.

— 0

Cbet = Could be expected to

195

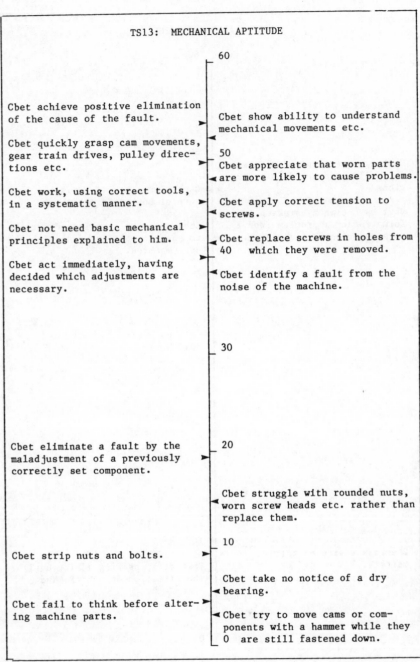

TS13: MECHANICAL APTITUDE

60

Cbet achieve positive elimination
of the cause of the fault.

Cbet show ability to understand
mechanical movements etc.

Cbet quickly grasp cam movements,
gear train drives, pulley directions etc.

50

Cbet appreciate that worn parts
are more likely to cause problems.

Cbet work, using correct tools,
in a systematic manner.

Cbet apply correct tension to
screws.

Cbet not need basic mechanical
principles explained to him.

Cbet replace screws in holes from
40   which they were removed.

Cbet act immediately, having
decided which adjustments are
necessary.

Cbet identify a fault from the
noise of the machine.

30

Cbet eliminate a fault by the
maladjustment of a previously
correctly set component.

20

Cbet struggle with rounded nuts,
worn screw heads etc. rather than
replace them.

10

Cbet strip nuts and bolts.

Cbet take no notice of a dry
bearing.

Cbet fail to think before alter-
ing machine parts.

Cbet try to move cams or components with a hammer while they
0 are still fastened down.

Cbet = Could be expected to

196

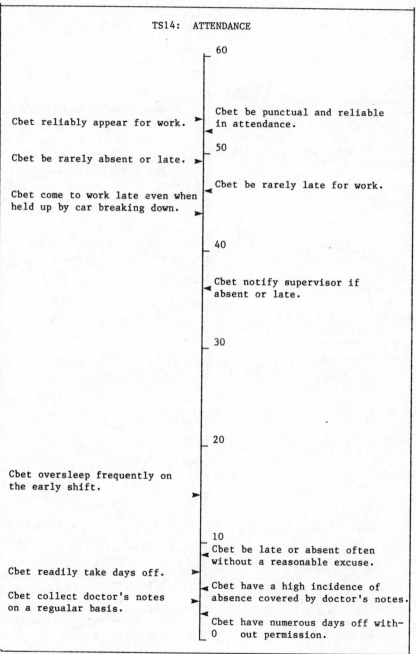

TS14: ATTENDANCE

60

Cbet reliably appear for work. ► ◄ Cbet be punctual and reliable in attendance.

50

Cbet be rarely absent or late. ► ◄ Cbet be rarely late for work.

Cbet come to work late even when held up by car breaking down. ►

40

◄ Cbet notify supervisor if absent or late.

30

20

Cbet oversleep frequently on the early shift. ►

10
◄ Cbet be late or absent often without a reasonable excuse.

Cbet readily take days off. ► ◄ Cbet have a high incidence of absence covered by doctor's notes.

Cbet collect doctor's notes on a regualar basis. ► ◄ Cbet have numerous days off without permission.
0

Cbet = Could be expected to

TS15: DIAGNOSTIC FAULT-FINDING ABILITY

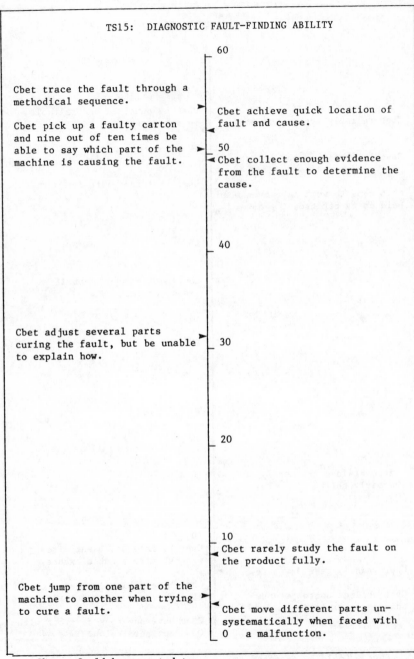

60

Cbet trace the fault through a
methodical sequence.

Cbet achieve quick location of
fault and cause.

Cbet pick up a faulty carton
and nine out of ten times be
able to say which part of the
machine is causing the fault.

50

Cbet collect enough evidence
from the fault to determine the
cause.

40

Cbet adjust several parts
curing the fault, but be unable
to explain how.

30

20

10

Cbet rarely study the fault on
the product fully.

Cbet jump from one part of the
machine to another when trying
to cure a fault.

Cbet move different parts un-
systematically when faced with
0   a malfunction.

Cbet = Could be expected to

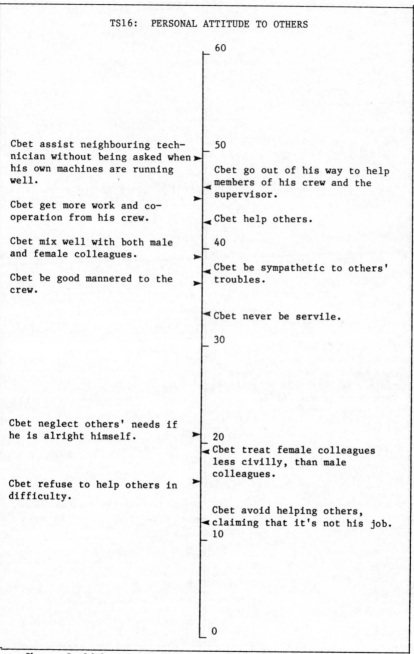

TS16: PERSONAL ATTITUDE TO OTHERS

— 60

Cbet assist neighbouring technician without being asked when ▶
his own machines are running
well.

— 50

Cbet go out of his way to help
◀ members of his crew and the
supervisor.

Cbet get more work and co- ▶
operation from his crew.

◀ Cbet help others.

Cbet mix well with both male
and female colleagues. ▶

— 40

Cbet be good mannered to the ▶
crew.

◀ Cbet be sympathetic to others'
troubles.

◀ Cbet never be servile.

— 30

Cbet neglect others' needs if
he is alright himself. ▶

— 20

◀ Cbet treat female colleagues
less civilly, than male
colleagues.

Cbet refuse to help others in ▶
difficulty.

Cbet avoid helping others,
◀ claiming that it's not his job.

— 10

— 0

Cbet = Could be expected to

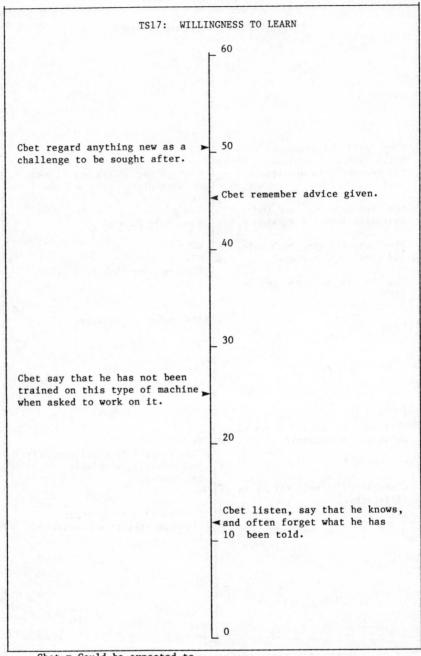

TS17: WILLINGNESS TO LEARN

— 60

Cbet regard anything new as a
challenge to be sought after. ► — 50

◄ Cbet remember advice given.

— 40

— 30

Cbet say that he has not been
trained on this type of machine ►
when asked to work on it.

— 20

Cbet listen, say that he knows,
◄ and often forget what he has
— 10 been told.

— 0

Cbet = Could be expected to

TS25: TEMPERAMENT/DISPOSITION

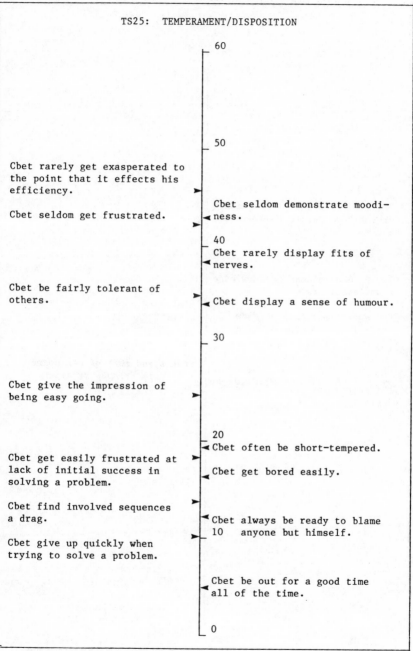

— 60

— 50

Cbet rarely get exasperated to
the point that it effects his
efficiency.

Cbet seldom demonstrate moodi-
ness.

Cbet seldom get frustrated.

— 40
Cbet rarely display fits of
nerves.

Cbet be fairly tolerant of
others.

Cbet display a sense of humour.

— 30

Cbet give the impression of
being easy going.

— 20
Cbet often be short-tempered.

Cbet get easily frustrated at
lack of initial success in
solving a problem.

Cbet get bored easily.

Cbet find involved sequences
a drag.

Cbet always be ready to blame
10   anyone but himself.

Cbet give up quickly when
trying to solve a problem.

Cbet be out for a good time
all of the time.

— 0

Cbet = Could be expected to

201

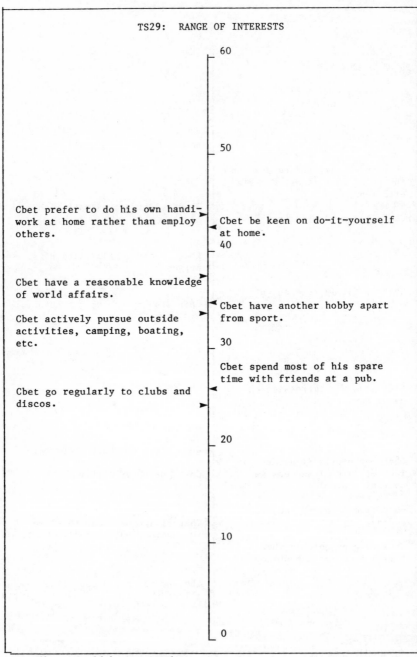

TS29:   RANGE OF INTERESTS

60

50

Cbet prefer to do his own handi-
work at home rather than employ
others.

Cbet be keen on do-it-yourself
at home.

40

Cbet have a reasonable knowledge
of world affairs.

Cbet have another hobby apart
from sport.

Cbet actively pursue outside
activities, camping, boating,
etc.

30

Cbet spend most of his spare
time with friends at a pub.

Cbet go regularly to clubs and
discos.

20

10

0

Cbet = Could be expected to

APPENDIX C

Technical Instructors' BARS for mechanic performance

TI15: DIAGNOSTIC FAULT-FINDING ABILITY

```
                                             ┌ 60
Cbet achieve positive elimin-                │
ation of the cause of a fault.    ──►        │  Cbet achieve quick location of
                                      ◄──     │  fault and cause.
Cbet pick up a faulty carton and             │
nine out of ten times be able to  ──►        │  Cbet go to great lengths to find
say which part of the machine is      ◄──     │  out not only the cure but the
causing the fault.                           │  cause of a malfunction.
                                             ├ 50
Cbet think the job out before         ◄──    │  Cbet return settings to status
altering any of the parts.                   │  quo if they have no effect in
                                             │  curing the fault.
                                  ──►        │
Cbet trace a fault through a                 │  Cbet make only the adjustments
methodical sequence.                         │  that are needed.
                                      ◄──    │
Cbet consider the possibilities              │  ◄─40  Cbet identify a fault from
of a specific situation before               │         the noise of the machine.
acting.                                      ├
                                             │
                                             │
                                             │
                                             │
                                             ├ 30
                                             │
                                             │
                                      ◄──    │
                                             │  Cbet remove quality faults without
                                             │  investigation into the mechanical
                                             │  cause.
Cbet approach a job with the                 │
right-in, direct, spanner-        ──►        ├ 20
flashing approach.                           │
                                             │  Cbet adjusts several parts, curing
Cbet rarely study the fault on        ◄──    │  the fault, but be unable to say
the product fully.                ──►        │  how.
                                             │  ◄──
Cbet jump from one part of the        ──►    │  Cbet eliminate a fault by the mal-
machine to another when trying to            │  adjustment of a previously
cure a fault.                                │  10 correctly set component.
                                             │  ◄──
                                             │  Cbet fail to think before altering
Cbet tend to alter the first part            │  machine parts.
of the machine nearest to the     ──►        │  ◄──
malfunction.                                 │  Cbet say 'I've moved all sorts and
                                             │  it still happens', when asking the
                                             │  supervisor for help with a problem
                                             └ 0
```

Cbet = Could be expected to

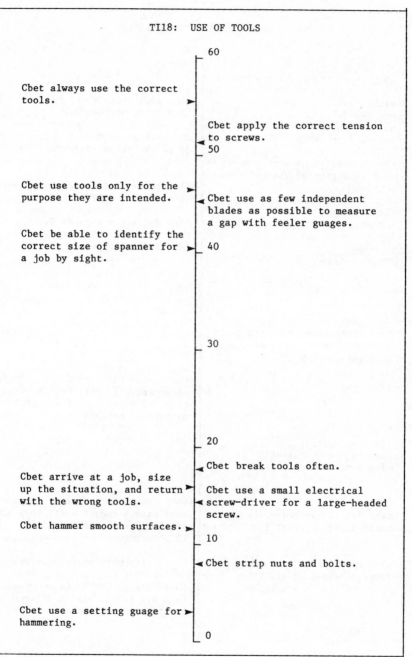

TI18: USE OF TOOLS

— 60

Cbet always use the correct
tools. ►

Cbet apply the correct tension
◄ to screws.
— 50

Cbet use tools only for the ►
purpose they are intended.
◄ Cbet use as few independent
blades as possible to measure
a gap with feeler guages.

Cbet be able to identify the
correct size of spanner for ► — 40
a job by sight.

— 30

— 20

◄ Cbet break tools often.

Cbet arrive at a job, size
up the situation, and return ► Cbet use a small electrical
with the wrong tools. ◄ screw-driver for a large-headed
screw.

Cbet hammer smooth surfaces. ►
— 10

◄ Cbet strip nuts and bolts.

Cbet use a setting guage for ►
hammering.
— 0

Cbet = Could be expected to

205

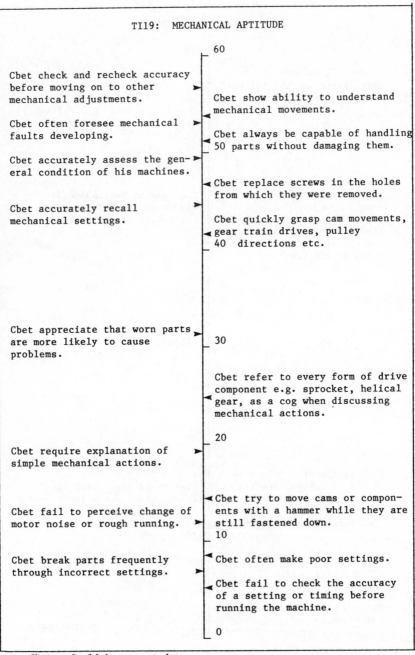

TI19: MECHANICAL APTITUDE

— 60

Cbet check and recheck accuracy
before moving on to other
mechanical adjustments.

Cbet show ability to understand
mechanical movements.

Cbet often foresee mechanical
faults developing.

Cbet always be capable of handling
50 parts without damaging them.

Cbet accurately assess the general condition of his machines.

Cbet replace screws in the holes
from which they were removed.

Cbet accurately recall
mechanical settings.

Cbet quickly grasp cam movements,
gear train drives, pulley
40 directions etc.

Cbet appreciate that worn parts
are more likely to cause
problems.

— 30

Cbet refer to every form of drive
component e.g. sprocket, helical
gear, as a cog when discussing
mechanical actions.

20

Cbet require explanation of
simple mechanical actions.

Cbet try to move cams or components with a hammer while they are
still fastened down.
10

Cbet fail to perceive change of
motor noise or rough running.

Cbet break parts frequently
through incorrect settings.

Cbet often make poor settings.

Cbet fail to check the accuracy
of a setting or timing before
running the machine.

— 0

Cbet = Could be expected to

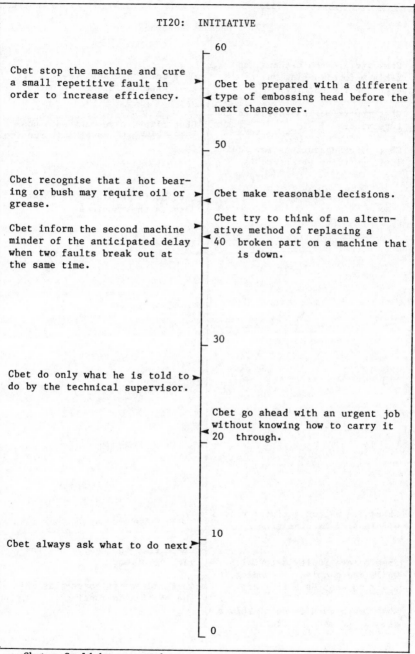

TI20: INITIATIVE

60

Cbet stop the machine and cure
a small repetitive fault in
order to increase efficiency.

Cbet be prepared with a different
type of embossing head before the
next changeover.

50

Cbet recognise that a hot bearing or bush may require oil or
grease.

Cbet make reasonable decisions.

Cbet try to think of an alternative method of replacing a

Cbet inform the second machine
minder of the anticipated delay
when two faults break out at
the same time.

40   broken part on a machine that
      is down.

30

Cbet do only what he is told to
do by the technical supervisor.

Cbet go ahead with an urgent job
without knowing how to carry it
20   through.

10

Cbet always ask what to do next.

0

Cbet = Could be expected to

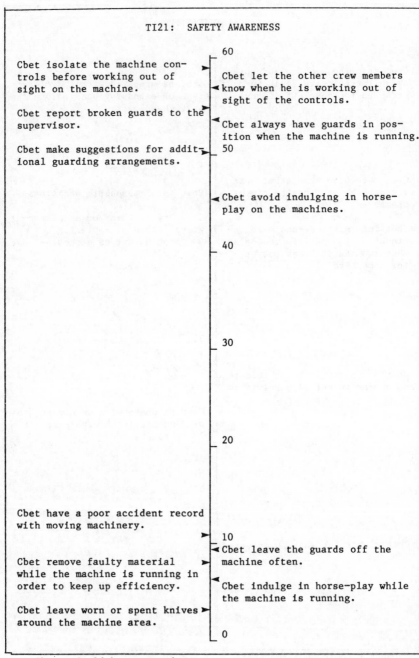

TI21: SAFETY AWARENESS

60

Cbet isolate the machine controls before working out of
sight on the machine.

Cbet let the other crew members
know when he is working out of
sight of the controls.

Cbet report broken guards to the
supervisor.

Cbet always have guards in position when the machine is running.

Cbet make suggestions for additional guarding arrangements.

50

Cbet avoid indulging in horse-
play on the machines.

40

30

20

Cbet have a poor accident record
with moving machinery.

10

Cbet leave the guards off the
machine often.

Cbet remove faulty material
while the machine is running in
order to keep up efficiency.

Cbet indulge in horse-play while
the machine is running.

Cbet leave worn or spent knives
around the machine area.

0

Cbet = Could be expected to

208

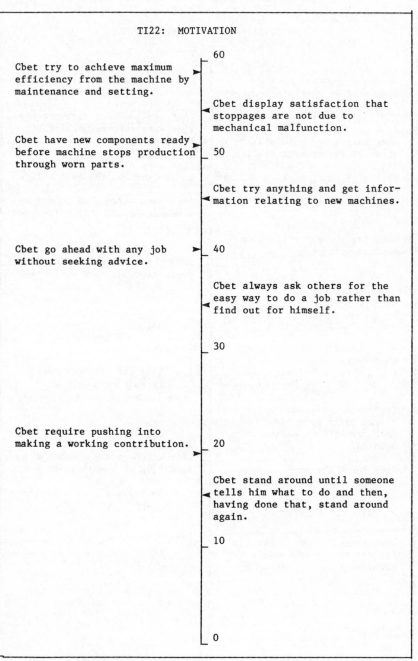

TI22: MOTIVATION

Cbet try to achieve maximum efficiency from the machine by maintenance and setting.

— 60

Cbet display satisfaction that stoppages are not due to mechanical malfunction.

Cbet have new components ready before machine stops production through worn parts.

— 50

Cbet try anything and get information relating to new machines.

Cbet go ahead with any job without seeking advice.

— 40

Cbet always ask others for the easy way to do a job rather than find out for himself.

— 30

Cbet require pushing into making a working contribution.

— 20

Cbet stand around until someone tells him what to do and then, having done that, stand around again.

— 10

— 0

Cbet = Could be expected to

TI23: PERSONAL APPLICATION

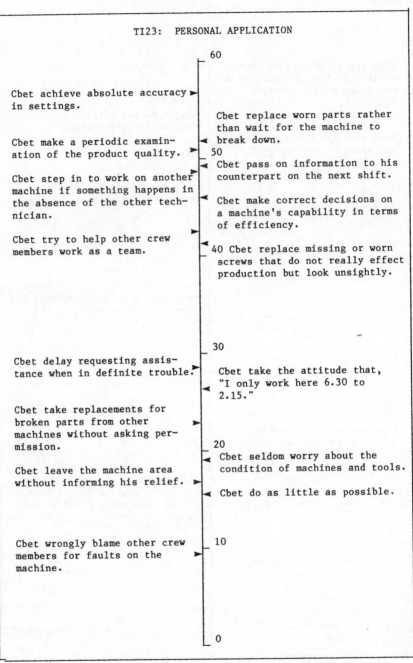

— 60

Cbet achieve absolute accuracy in settings.

Cbet replace worn parts rather than wait for the machine to break down.

— 50

Cbet make a periodic examination of the product quality.

Cbet pass on information to his counterpart on the next shift.

Cbet step in to work on another machine if something happens in the absence of the other technician.

Cbet make correct decisions on a machine's capability in terms of efficiency.

Cbet try to help other crew members work as a team.

— 40 Cbet replace missing or worn screws that do not really effect production but look unsightly.

— 30

Cbet delay requesting assistance when in definite trouble.

Cbet take the attitude that, "I only work here 6.30 to 2.15."

Cbet take replacements for broken parts from other machines without asking permission.

— 20

Cbet seldom worry about the condition of machines and tools.

Cbet leave the machine area without informing his relief.

Cbet do as little as possible.

Cbet wrongly blame other crew members for faults on the machine.

— 10

— 0

Cbet = Could be expected to

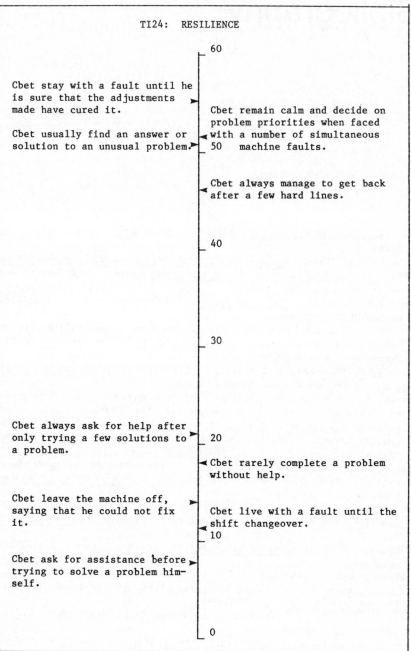

TI24: RESILIENCE

— 60

Cbet stay with a fault until he is sure that the adjustments made have cured it. ➤

◄ Cbet remain calm and decide on problem priorities when faced with a number of simultaneous machine faults.

Cbet usually find an answer or solution to an unusual problem. ➤ — 50

◄ Cbet always manage to get back after a few hard lines.

— 40

— 30

Cbet always ask for help after only trying a few solutions to a problem. ➤ — 20

◄ Cbet rarely complete a problem without help.

Cbet leave the machine off, saying that he could not fix it. ➤

Cbet live with a fault until the shift changeover. — 10 ◄

Cbet ask for assistance before trying to solve a problem himself. ➤

— 0

Cbet = Could be expected to

Bibliography

Anastasi, A. (1964), Fields of Applied Psychology, McGraw-Hill: New York.

Anastasi, A. (1972), An Investigation of Sources of Bias in the Prediction of Job Performance: A Six Year Study, Educational Testing Service: Princeton, New Jersey.

Anastasi, A. (1979), Fields of Applied Psychology, 2nd Revised Edition, McGraw-Hill: London.

Andersson, B-E & Nilsson, S-G. (1964), 'Studies in the reliability and validity of the Critical Incident technique', Journal of Applied Psychology, 48, (6), 398-403.

Anstey, E., Fletcher, C. & Walker, J. (1976), Staff Appraisal and Development, Allen and Unwin: London.

Arvey, R.D. & Hoyle, J.C. (1974), 'A Guttman approach to the development of behaviourally based rating scales for Systems Analysts and Programmer/Analysts', Journal of Applied Psychology, 59, (1), 61-68.

Astin, A. (1964), 'Criterion-centred research', Educational and Psychological Measurement, 14, (4), 807-822.

Bailey, C.T. (1983), 'A model of critical factors in performance rating', Paper presented to the BPS Occupational Psychology Conference, (Jan.), Warwick.

Baldwin, B.A. (1972), 'Change in interpersonal cognitive complexity as a function of a training group experience', Psychological Reports, 30, 935-940.

Barrett, R.S. (1966), Performance Rating, Science Research Associates: Chicago.

Barrett, R.S., Taylor, E.K., Parker, J.W. & Martens, W.L. (1958), 'Rating scale content: I. Scale information and supervisory ratings', Personnel Psychology, 11, 333-346.

Bass, B.M. (1954), 'The Leaderless Group Discussion', Psychological Bulletin, 51, 465-492.

Bass, B.M. & Norton, F.T.M. (1951), 'Group size and leaderless discussion', Journal of Applied Psychology, 6, 397-400.

Bayroff, A.G., Haggerty, H.R. & Rindquist, E.A. (1954), 'Validity of ratings as related to rating techniques and conditions', Personnel

Psychology, 7, 93-113.

Beatty, R.W., Schneier, C.E. & Beatty, J.R. (1977), 'An empirical investigation of perceptions of ratee behaviour frequency and ratee behaviour change using Behavioural Expectation Scales (BES)', Personnel
Psychology, 30, (4), 647-659.

Bechtoldt, H.P. (1947), 'Problems in establishing criterion measures',
in Stuit, D.B. (ed.), Personnel Research and Test Development in the
Bureau of Naval Personnel, Princeton University Press, 357-380.

Bechtoldt, H.P. (1951), 'Selection', in Stevens, S.S. (ed.), Handbook
of Experimental Psychology, Wiley: New York.

Bechtoldt, H.P. (1959), 'Construct validity: A critique', American Psychologist, 14, 619-629.

Bellows, R.M. (1954), Psychology of Personnel in Business and Industry,
(2nd edition), Prentice-Hall: Englewood Cliffs, New Jersey.

Bem, D.J. & Allen, A. (1974), 'On predicting some of the people some of
the time: the search for cross-situational consistencies in behaviour', Psychological Review, 81, 506-520.

Bendig, A.W. & Hughes, J.B. II (1953), 'Effect of amount of verbal anchoring and number of rating-scale categories upon transmitted information', Journal of Experimental Psychology, 46, (2), 87-90.

Bernardin, H.J. (1977), 'Behavioural Expectation Scales versus Summated
Scales: A fairer comparison', Journal of Applied Psychology, 62, 422-
427.

Bernardin, H.J. (1978), 'Effects of rater training on Leniency and Halo
errors in student ratings of instructors', Journal of Applied Psychology, 63, 301-308.

Bernardin, H.J., Alvares, K.M. & Cranny, C.J. (1976), 'A recomparison of
Behavioural Expectation Scales to Summated scales', Journal of Applied
Psychology, 61, (5), 564-570.

Bernardin, H.J., LaShells, M.B., Smith, P.C. & Alvares, K.M. (1976),
'Behavioural Expectation Scales: Effects of developmental procedures
and formats', Journal of Applied Psychology, 61, (1), 75-79.

Bernardin, H.J. & Walter, C.S. (1977), 'Effects of rater training and
dairy-keeping on psychometric error in ratings', Journal of Applied
Psychology, 62, 64-70.

Berry, N.H., Nelson, P.D. & McNally, M.S. (1966), 'A note on supervisor
ratings', Personnel Psychology, 19, 423-426.

Bieri, J. (1955), 'Cognitive complexity-simplicity and predictive behaviour', Journal of Abnormal and Social Psychology, 51, 263-268.

Bieri, J. (1966), 'Cognitive complexity and personality development', in
Harvey, O.J. (ed.), Experience, Structure and Adaptability, Springer:
New York.

Bieri, J. (1968), 'Cognitive complexity and judgement of inconsistent
information', in Abelson, R.P., Aronson, E., McGuire, W.S., Newcomb,
T.M., Rosenberg, M.J. & Tannenbaum, P.H. (eds.), Theories of Cognitive
Consistency, Rand McNally: Chicago.

Bigoness, W.J. (1976), 'Effect of applicant's sex, race and performance
on employers' performance ratings: some additional findings', Journal
of Applied Psychology, 61, 80-84.

Blum, M.L. & Naylor, J.C. (1968), Industrial Psychology, Harper & Row:
New York.

Borman, W.C. (1974), 'The rating of individuals in organisations. An alternate approach', Organizational Behavior and Human Performance, 12, 105-124.

Borman, W.C. (1975), 'Effect of instructions to avoid Halo Error on reliability and validity of performance ratings', Journal of Applied Psychology, 60, 556-560.

Borman, W.C. (1977), 'Consistency of rating accuracy and rating errors in the judgement of human performance', Organizational Behavior and Human Performance, 20, (2), 238-253.

Borman, W.C. (1978), 'Exploring the upper limits of reliability and validity in job performance ratings', Journal of Applied Psychology, 63, (2), 135-145.

Borman, W.C. (1979a), 'Individual difference correlates of accuracy in evaluating performance effectiveness', Applied Psychological Measurement, 3, 103-115.

Borman, W.C. (1979b), 'Format and training effects on rating accuracy and rating errors', Journal of Applied Psychology, 64, (4), 410-421.

Borman, W.C. & Dunnette, M.D. (1975), 'Behaviour-based versus trait-oriented performance ratings: An empirical study', Journal of Applied Psychology, 60, 561-565.

Borman, W.C. & Vallon, W.R. (1974), 'A view of what can happen when Behavioural Expectation Scales are developed in one setting and used in another', Journal of Applied Psychology, 59, (2), 197-201.

Bray, D.W. & Grant, D.L. (1966), 'The assessment center in the measurement of potential for business management', Psychological Monographs, 80, (17, Whole No. 625).

Brogden, H.E. & Taylor, E.K. (1950), 'The dollar criterion: Applying the cost accounting concept to criterion construction', Personnel Psychology, 3, 133-154.

Brown, E.M. (1968), 'Influence of training, method and relationship on the Halo effect', Journal of Applied Psychology, 52, 195-199.

Browning, R.C. (1968), 'Validity of reference ratings from previous employers', Personnel Psychology, 21, 389-393.

Burnaska, R.F. & Hollmann, T.D. (1974), 'An empirical comparison of the relative effects of rater response biases on three rating scale formats', Journal of Applied Psychology, 59, (3), 307-312.

Butcher, D.J. (1982), Organisational Boundaries and Determinants of Behaviour in Organisations: A Situational Analysis, Unpublished Ph.D. thesis, University of Bradford.

Byrne, D. (1971), The Attraction Paradigm, Academic Press: New York.

Campbell, D.T. & Fiske, D.W. (1959), 'Convergent and discriminant validation by the Multitrait-Multimethod Matrix', Psychological Bulletin, 56, (2), 81-105.

Campbell, J.P., Dunnette, M.D., Arvey, R.D. & Hellervik, L.V. (1973), 'The development and evaluation of behaviourally based rating scales', Journal of Applied Psychology, 57, (1), 15-22.

Campbell, J.P., Dunnette, M.D., Lawler, E.E. III & Weick, K.E. Jr. (1970), Managerial Behavior, Performance and Effectiveness, McGraw-Hill: New York.

Campbell, J.T. (1972), An Investigation of Sources of Bias in the Prediction of Job Performance: A Six Year Study, Educational Testing

Service: New Jersey.

Campbell, V.N. (1960), <u>Assumed Similarity, Perceived Sociometric Balance and Social Influence</u>, Unpublished doctoral dissertation, University of Colorado.

Carlson, R.E. (1972), 'The current status of judgemental techniques in industry', Paper presented at the symposium <u>Alternatives to Paper and Pencil Personnel Testing</u>, University of Pittsburgh, May.

Carroll, S.J. & Nash, A.N. (1972), 'Effectiveness of a forced-choice reference check', <u>Personnel Administration</u>, <u>35</u>, 42-46.

Cascio, F. & Valenzi, E.R. (1977), 'Behaviourally Anchored Rating Scales: Effects of education and job experience of raters and ratees', <u>Journal of Applied Psychology</u>, <u>62</u>, (3), 278-282.

Cattell, R.B. (1967), 'The three basic factor analytic research designs - their interrelations and derivatives', in Jackson, D.N. and Messick, S. (eds.), <u>Problems in Human Assessment</u>, Krieger: New York.

Chapman, L.J. & Chapman, J.P. (1969), 'Illusory correlation as an obstacle to the use of valid psycho-diagnostic signs', <u>Journal of Abnormal Psychology</u>, <u>74</u>, 271-280.

Cline, M.E., Holmes, D.S. & Werner, J.C. (1977), 'Evaluation of the work of men and women as a function of the sex of the judge and type of work', <u>Journal of Applied Social Psychology</u>, <u>7</u>, 89-93.

Cone, J.D. (1978), 'Truth and sensitivity in behavioural assessment', Paper presented at the <u>Annual Meeting of the Association for the Advancement of Behaviour Therapy</u>, Chicago.

Cooper, W.H. (1979), 'Ubiquitous halo: implicit construct correlation theory vs BARS', Paper presented at the <u>Meeting of the American Psychological Association</u>, September, New York.

Cozan, L.W. (1955), 'Forced Choice: Better than other rating methods?', <u>Personnel</u>, <u>36</u>, (3), 80-83.

Crockett, W.H. (1965), 'Cognitive complexity and impression formation', in Maher, B.A. (ed.), <u>Progress in Experimental Personality Research</u>, (Vol. 2), Academic Press: New York.

Crockett, W.H., Mahood, S. & Press, A.N. (1975), 'Impressions of a speaker as a function of set to understand or to evaluate, of cognitive complexity, and of prior attitudes', <u>Journal of Personality</u>, <u>43</u>, 168-178.

Crooks, L.A. (ed.) (1972), <u>An Investigation of Sources of Bias in the Prediction of Job Performance: A Six Year Study</u>, Educational Testing Service: Princeton, New Jersey.

Crow, W.J. (1957), 'The effect of training upon accuracy and variability in interpersonal perception', <u>Journal of Abnormal and Social Psychology</u>, <u>55</u>, 355-359.

Cummings, L.L. & Schwab, D.P. (1973), <u>Performance in Organizations: Determinants and Appraisal</u>, Scott, Foresman & Co., Illinois.

Dailey, W.W. (1961), 'Needed: A new manifesto for performance evaluation', <u>Personnel Administration</u>, <u>24</u>, 41-46.

Dean, J. (1957), 'Profit performance measurement of division managers', <u>The Controller</u>, <u>25</u>, (9).

Deaux, K. & Emswiller, T. (1974), 'Explanation of successful performance on sex-linked tasks: what is skill for the male is luck for the female', Journal of Personality and Social Psychology, 29, 80-85.

DeJung, J.E. & Kaplan, J. (1962), 'Some differential effects of race of rater and ratee on early peer ratings of combat aptitude', Journal of Applied Psychology, 46, 370-374.

De Nisi, A.S. & Pritchard, R.D. (1978), 'Implicit theories of performance as artifacts in survey research: A replication and extension. Organizational Behavior and Human Performance, 21, (3), 358-367.

Dickinson, T.L. & Tice, T.E. (1977), 'The discriminant validity of scales developed by Retranslation', Personnel Psychology, 30, 217-228.

Dingle, H. (1953), in Focken, C.M., Dimensional Methods and their Applications, Arnold and Co: London.

Distefano, M.K. & Pryer, M.W. (1975), 'Work behaviour dimensions of psychiatric attendants and aides', Journal of Applied Psychology, 60, 140-142.

Drucker, P.F. (1954), The Practice of Management, Harper & Row: New York.

Dubin, R., Porter, L.W., Stone, E.F. & Champoux, J.E. (1974), 'Implications of differential job perceptions', Industrial Relations, 13, 265-273.

Dunham, R. (1976), 'Measurement and dimensionality of job characteristics', Journal of Applied Psychology, 61, (4), 404-409.

Dunnette, M.D. (1963), 'A note on the criterion', Journal of Applied Psychology, 47, (4), 251-254.

Dunnette, M.D. & Borman, W.C. (1979), 'Personnel selection and classification systems', Annual Review of Psychology, 30, 477-525.

Dunnette, M.D., Campbell, J.P. & Hellervik, L.W. (1968), Job Behaviour Scales for Penney Co. Department Managers, Personnel Decisions: Minneapolis.

Einhorn, H.J. (1974), 'Expert judgement: some necessary conditions and an example', Journal of Applied Psychology, 59, (5), 562-571.

Elliot, H.C. (1974), 'Similarities and differences between science and common sense', in Turner, R. (ed.), Ethnomethodology: Selected Readings, Penguin Education: Middlesex, England.

Ellis, B. (1966), Basic Concepts of Measurement, Cambridge University Press: London.

Elser, J.R. & Osman, B.E. (1978), 'Judgemental perspective and value connotations of response scale labels', Journal of Personality and Social Psychology, 36, (5), 491-498.

Enell, J.W. & Haas, G.H. (1960), Setting Standards for Executive Performance, American Management Association: New York.

English, H.B. & English, A.E. (1958), A Comprehensive Dictionary of Psychological and Psychoanalytical Terms, Longmans, Green: New York.

Eysenck, H.J. (1952), The Scientific Study of Personality, Routledge and Kegan Paul: London.

Eysenck, H.J. (1967), 'The logical basis of Factor Analysis', in Jackson, D.N. and Messick, S. (eds.) Problems in Human Assessment, Krieger: New York.

Fiedler, F.E. (1967), A Theory of Leadership Effectiveness, McGraw-Hill: New York.

Finkle, R.B. (1976), 'Managerial Assessment Centers', in Dunnette, M.D.

(ed.), Handbook of Industrial and Organizational Psychology, Rand McNally: Chicago.

Fiske, S.T. & Cox, M.G. (1979), 'Person concept: The effect of target familiarity and descriptive purpose on the process of describing others', Journal of Personality, 47, (1), 136-162.

Flanagan, J.C. (1949), 'The quantitative measurement of employee performance', in Workshop Report on Performance Review, Industrial Relations Center, University of Chicago, 9-17.

Flanagan, J.C. & Burns, R.K. (1957), 'The employee performance record', Harvard Business Review, Sept.-Oct., 95-102.

Flaugher, R.L., Campbell, J.T. & Pike, L.W. (1969), Prediction of Job Performance for Negro and White Medical Technicians: Ethnic Group Membership as a Moderator of Supervisors' Ratings, (ETS Service Report PR-61-5), Educational Testing Service: Princeton.

Fleishman, E.A. & Fruchter, B. (1960), 'Factor structure and predictability of successive stages of learning Morse code', Journal of Applied Psychology, 44, 97-101.

Fleishman, E.A. & Hempel, W.E. (1954), 'Changes in factor structure of a complex psychomotor test as a function of practice', Psychometrika, 18, 239-252.

Fleishman, E.A. & Ornstein, G.N. (1960), 'An analysis of Pilot flying performance in terms of component abilities', in Ronan, W.W. & Prien, E.P. (eds.), Perspectives on the Measurement of Human Performance, Appleton-Century-Crofts: New York, 346-362.

Fletcher, C.A. (1973), 'An evaluation study of job appraisal reviews', Management Services in Government, 28, 188-195.

Fletcher, C.A. & Williams, R. (1976), 'The influence of performance feedback in appraisal interviews', Journal of Occupational Psychology, 49, 75-83.

Focken, C.M. (1953), Dimensional Methods and their Applications, Edward Arnold & Co: London.

Fogli, L., Hulin, C.L. & Blood, M.R. (1971), 'Development of first-level behavioural job criteria', Journal of Applied Psychology, 55, (1), 38.

Fox, W.M., Hill, W.A. & Guertin, W.H. (1973), 'Dimensional analysis of the least preferred co-worker scales', Journal of Applied Psychology, 57, (2), 192-194.

Fransella, F. (ed.) (1977), Personal Construct Psychology, Academic Press: London.

Frederiksen, N., Saunders, D.R. & Wand, B. (1957), 'The In-Basket test', Psychological Monographs, 71, (9), (Whole No. 438).

Freeberg, N.E. (1969), 'Relevance of rater-ratee acquaintance in the validity and reliability of ratings', Journal of Applied Psychology, 53, 518-524.

Friedman, B.A. & Cornelius, E.T. (1976), 'The effect of rater participation in scale construction on the psychometric characteristics of two rating scale formats', Journal of Applied Psychology, 62, 210-217.

Funk, S.G., Horowitz, A.D., Lipshitz, R. & Young, F.W. (1976), 'The perceived structure of american ethnic groups: The use of Multidimensional Scaling in stereotype research', Sociometry, 39, (2), 116-

217

130.

Garner, A.M. & Smith, G.M. (1976), 'An experimental videotape technique for evaluating trainee approaches to clinical judging', Journal of Consulting and Clinical Psychology, 44, 945-950.

Garner, W.R. (1960), 'Rating scales, discriminability and information transmission', Psychological Review, 67, (6), 343-352.

Ghiselli, E.E. (1956), 'Dimensional problems of criteria', Journal of Applied Psychology, 40, (1) 1-4.

Ghiselli, E.E. & Brown, C.W. (1955), 'Ranking Methods', in Whisler, T.L. & Harper, S.F. (eds.) (1962), Performance Appraisal: Research and Practice, Holt, Rinehart and Winston: New York, 203-208.

Ghiselli, E.E & Dunnette, M.D. (1970), Assessing Managerial Performance, Independent Assessment Research Centre.

Gill, D., Ungerson, B. & Thakur, M. (1973), Performance Appraisal in Perspective, Institute of Personnel Management: London.

Gill, R.W.T. (1980), The Trainability Concept for Management Potential, Unpublished Ph.D. thesis, University of Bradford.

Goldfried, M.R. (1977), 'Behavioral Assessment in Perspective', in Cone, J.D. & Hawkins, R.P. (eds.), Behavioral Assessment, Brunner/Mazel: New York.

Goldfried, M.R. & Linehan, M.M. (1977), 'Basic Issues in Behavioural Assessment', in Ciminero, A.R., Calhoun, K.S. & Adams, H.E (eds.), Handbook of Behavioral Assessment, Wiley: New York.

Goodale, J.G. & Burke, R.J. (1975), 'Behaviourally based rating scales need not be job specific', Journal of Applied Psychology, 60, 389391.

Gordon, M.E. (1970), 'The effect of correctness of the behaviour observed on the accuracy of ratings', Organizational Behavior and Human Performance, 5, 366-377.

Graen, G.B. (1967), 'Work Motivation: The Behavioural Effects of Job Content and Job Context Factors in an Employment Situation', Unpublished doctoral dissertation, University of Minnesota.

Graves, J.P. (1982), 'Lets put appraisal back in performance appraisal', Personnel Journal, 61, (11), 844-850.

Gravetter, F. & Lockhead, G.R. (1973), 'Criterial range as a frame of reference for stimulus judgement', Psychological Review, 80, (3), 203 216.

Greenwood, J.M. & McNamara, W.J. (1967), 'Inter-rater reliability in situational tests', Journal of Applied Psychology, 51, (2), 101-106.

Grey, R.J. & Kipnis, D. (1976), 'Untangling the performance appraisal dilemma: The influence of perceived organizational context on evaluative processes', Journal of Applied Psychology, 61, (3), 329-336.

Groner, D.M. (1974), 'Reliability and Susceptibility to Bias of Behavioural and Graphic Rating Scales', Ph.D. Thesis, University of Minnesota, Minneapolis, Minn.

Guba, E.G. (1979), 'Naturalistic Inquiry', Improving Human Performance Quarterly, 8, (4), 268-276.

Guilford, J.P. (1954), Psychometric Methods, (2nd edition) McGraw-Hill: New York.

Guion, R.M. (1961), 'Criterion measurement and personnel judgement', Personnel Psychology, 14, 141-149.

,, R.M. (1965), Personnel Testing, McGraw-Hill: New York.

Hackman, J.R. & Oldham, G.R. (1975), 'Development of the Job Diagnostic Survey', Journal of Applied Psychology, 60, 159-170.

Hackman, J.R. & Lawler, E.E. III (1971), 'Employee reactions to job characteristics', Journal of Applied Psychology, 55, 259-286.

Haeri, F.H. (1969), Performance Appraisal: What Managers Think, BIM: London.

Hake, H.W. & Garner, W.R. (1951), 'The effect of presenting various numbers of discrete steps on scale reading accuracy', Journal of Experimental Psychology, 42, 358-366.

Hamner, W.C., Kim, J.S., Baird, L. & Bigoness, W.J. (1974), 'Race and sex as determinants of ratings by potential employers in a simulated worksampling task', Journal of Applied Psychology, 59, 705-711.

Harari, O. & Zedeck, S. (1973), 'Development of behaviourally anchored scales for the evaluation of faculty teaching', Journal of Applied Psychology, 58, 261-265.

Hartmann, D.P., Roper, B.L. & Bradford, D.C. (1979), 'Some relationships between behavioral and traditional assessment', Journal of Behavioral Assessment', 1, (1).

Harvard Business Review (1973), Performance Appraisal Series, No. 21143, Harvard College.

Harvey, O.J. & Schroder, H.M. (1963), 'Conceptual organization and group structure', in Harvey, O.J. (ed.), Motivation and Social Interaction, Ronald Press: New York.

Hebb, D.O. (1974), 'What psychology is about', American Psychologist, 29, 71-79.

Heneman, H.G. III (1974), 'Comparisons of self and superior ratings of managerial performance', Journal of Applied Psychology, 59, 638-642.

Herbst, P.G. (1970), Behavioural Worlds: A Study of Single Cases, Tavistock: London.

Heslin, R. and Streufert, S. (1968), 'Task familiarity and reliance on the environment in decision making', Psychological Record, 18, 629-637.

Hilgard, E.R. & Atkinson, R.C. (1967), Introduction to Psychology, (4th edition), Harcourt Brace & World: New York.

Howell, R.A. (1967), 'A fresh look at MBO', Business Horizons, Autumn, 51-58.

Hulin, C.L. (1962), 'The measurement of executive success', Journal of Applied Psychology, 46, (5), 303-306.

Humble, J.W. (1970), 'Avoiding the pitfalls of the MBO trap', European Business, Autumn, 13-20.

Hunt, D.E. (1966), 'A conceptual systems change model and its application to education', in Harvey, O.J. (ed.), Experience, Structure and Adaptability, Springer: New York.

Irwin, M., Tripodi, T. & Bieri, J. (1967), 'Affective stimulus value and cognitive complexity', Journal of Personality and Social Psychology, 5, 444-448.

Ivancevich, J.M. (1979), 'Longitudinal study of the effects of rater training on psychometric error in ratings', Journal of Applied Psychology, 64, 502-508.

Jacobs, R., Kafry, D. & Zedeck, S. (1979), 'Consistency in multidimensional performance evaluations: An analysis of raters and dimensions', Journal Supplement Abstract Service, 9, (25), (Ms. 1834).

Jacobs, R., Kafry, D. & Zedeck, S. (1980), 'Expectations of Behaviourally Anchored Rating Scales', Personnel Psychology, 33, 595–640.

James, L.R. (1973), 'Criterion models and construct validity for criteria', Psychological Bulletin, 80, 75–83.

Jensen, B.T., Coles, G. & Nestor, B. (1955), 'The Criterion Problem in guidance research', Journal of Counselling Psychology, II, 58–61.

Jessup, G. & Jessup, H. (1975), Selection and Assessment at Work, Methuen: London.

Johnson, S.L. & Ronan, W.W. (1979), 'An exploratory study of bias in job performance evaluation', Public Personnel Management, Sept., 315–323.

Johnson, S.M. & Boldstad, O.D. (1973), 'Methodological issues in naturalistic observation: some problems and solutions for field research', in Hamerlynck, L.A., Hardy, L.C. & Mash, R.J. (eds.), Behavior Change: Methodology, Concepts and Practice, Research Press: Champaign, Ill.

Jones, L.V. (1976), 'The Nature of Measurement', in Thorndike, R.L. (ed.), Educational Measurement, (2nd edition), American Council of Education: Washington.

Kafry, D., Zedeck, S. & Jacobs, R. (1976), 'The scalability of Behavioural Expectation Scales as a function of developmental criteria', Journal of Applied Psychology, 61, 519–522.

Kafry, D., Jacobs, R. & Zedeck, S. (1979), 'Discriminability in multidimensional performance evaluations', Applied Psychological Measurement, 3, 187–192.

Kane, J.S. & Lawler, E.E. III (1979), 'Performance appraisal effectiveness: its assessment and determinants', Research in Organizational Behavior, 1, 425–478.

Karlins, M. (1967), 'Conceptual complexity and remote associate proficiency as creativity variables in a complex problem–solving task', Journal of Personality and Social Psychology, 6, 264–278.

Kavanagh, M.J., MacKinney, A.C. & Wolins, L. (1971), 'Issues in managerial performance: multitrait–multimethod analysis of ratings', Psychological Bulletin, 75, 34–49.

Kearney, W.J. (1979), 'Behaviourally Anchored Rating Scales – MBO's missing ingredient', Personnel Journal, 58, (1), 20–26.

Keaveny, T.J. & McGann, A.F. (1975), 'A comparison of Behavioural Expectation Scales and Graphic Rating Scales', Journal of Applied Psychology, 60, (6), 695–703.

Kelly, G.A. (1955), The Psychology of Personal Constructs Vol I: A Theory of Personality, W.W. Norton: New York.

Kelly, P.R. (1958), 'Reappraisal of appraisals', Harvard Business Review, 36, 59–68.

Kent, R.N., Kanowitz, J., O'Leary, K.D. & Cheiken, M. (1977), 'Observer reliability as a function of circumstances of assessment', Journal of Applied Behavioral Analysis, 10, (2), 317–325.

Kingstrom, P.O. and Bass, A.R. (1981), 'A critical analysis of studies comparing Behaviourally Anchored Rating Scales (BARS) and other rating formats', Personnel Psychology, 34, (2), 263–289.

Kipnis, D. (1960), 'Some determinants of supervisory esteem', Personnel Psychology, 13, 377–391.

Kirchner, W.K. & Reisberg, D.J. (1962), 'Differences between better and less effective supervisors in appraisals of subordinates', Personnel Psychology, 15, 295-302.

Kleber, T.P. (1972), 'The six hardest areas to Manage by Objectives', Personnel Journal, 51, August, 571-575.

Klimoski, R.J. & London, M. (1974), 'Role of the rater in performance appraisal', Journal of Applied Psychology, 59, 445-451.

Koontz, H. (1972), 'Short-comings and pitfalls in Managing by Objectives', Management by Objectives, 1, (Jan.) 6-12.

Kryger, B.F. & Shikiar, R. (1978), 'Sexual discrimination in the use of letters of recommendation: A case of reverse discrimination', Journal of Applied Psychology, 63, 309-314.

Landy, F.J. & Guion, R.M. (1970), 'Development of scales for the measurement of work motivation', Organizational Behavior and Human Performance, 5, 93-103.

Landy, F.J., Farr, J.L., Saal, F.E. & Freytag, W.R. (1976), 'Behaviourally anchored scales for rating the performance of police officers', Journal of Applied Psychology, 61, 750-758.

Landy, F.J. & Trumbo, D.A. (1976), Psychology of Work Behaviour, Dorsey Press: Homewood, Illinois.

Landy, F.J. & Farr, J.L. (1978), Performance Ratings, Unpublised manuscript, (Available from F.J. Landy, Dept. of Psychology, The Pennsylvania State University, University Park, pa. 16802).

Lasagna, J.B. (1971), 'Make your MBO pragmatic', Harvard Business Review, 40, (Nov.-Dec.) 64-69.

Latham, G.P., Wexley, K.N. & Purcell, E.D. (1975), 'Training managers to minimize rating errors in the observation of behaviour', Journal of Applied Psychology, 60, 550-555.

Latham, G.P. & Wexley, K.N. (1977), 'Behavior Observation Scales for performance appraisal purposes', Personnel Psychology, 30, (2), 255-269.

Lawler, E.E. III (1966), 'Ability as a moderator of the relationships between job attitudes and job performance', Personnel Psychology, 19, 153-164.

Lawler, E.E. III (1967), 'Multitrait-Multirater approach to measuring managerial job performance', Journal of Applied Psychology, 51, 369-381.

Lawler, E.E. III (1971), Pay and Organizational Effectiveness: A psychological view, McGraw-Hill: New York.

Lawshe, C.H., Kephart, N.C. & McCormick, E.J. (1949), 'The paired comparison technique for rating performance of industrial employees', Journal of Applied Psychology, 33, (1), 69-77.

Leskovec, E.W. (1967), 'A guide for discussing performance appraisal', Personnel Journal, 46, (3), 150-152.

Levine, J. & Butler, J. (1952), 'Lecture versus group discussion in changing behaviour', Journal of Applied Psychology, 36, 29-33.

Levy, S. (1960), 'Supervisory effectiveness and criterion relationships', Paper presented at the 68th Annual Meeting of the American Psychological Association, (May), Chicago.

Lissitz, R.W. & Green, S.B. (1975), 'Effect of the number of scale points on reliability: A Monte Carlo approach', Journal of Applied Psychology, 60, (1), 10-13.

Locke, E.A. (1965), 'The interaction of ability and motivation in performance', Perceptual and Motor Skills, 21, 719-725.

Lopez, F.M., Jr. (1966), 'Evaluating Executive Decision-Making: The In-Basket Technique, American Management Association Research Study, No. 75.

Lowenberg, G. (1979), 'Interindividual consistencies in determining behaviour-based dimensions of teaching effectiveness', Journal of Applied Psychology, 64, (5), 492-501.

Lumsden, J. (1976), 'Test theory', Annual Review of Psychology, 27, 251-280.

Maas, J.B. (1965), 'Patterned scaled expectation interview: Reliability Studies on a new technique', Journal of Applied Psychology, 49, 431-433.

Madden, J.M. & Bourdon, R.D. (1964), 'Effects of variations in rating scale format on judgement', Journal of Applied Psychology, 48, (3), 147-151.

Maier, N.R.F. (1955), Psychology in Industry, (2nd edition) Houghton Mifflin: Boston.

Maier, N.R.F. (1958), 'Three types of appraisal interview', Personnel, 34, 27-40.

Makin, P.J., Randell, G.A., Morrison, C.T., Taylor, D.S. & Wright, P.L. (1978), Selection and Validation of Psychological Tests for the Prediction of Cigarette Making and Packing Machine Mechanic Performance, Research Report, University of Bradford Management Centre, Human Resources Research Group.

Mandell, M.M. (1956), 'Supervisor characteristics and ratings', Personnel, 32, 435-440.

Mash, E.J. & Terdal, L.G. (1976), Behaviour Therapy Assessment Diagnosis, Design and Evaluation, Springer: New York.

Mayfield, E.C (1964), 'The selection interview: A re-evaluation of published research', Personnel Psychology, 17, 239-260.

Mayo, C. & Crockett, W.H. (1964), 'Cognitive complexity and primacy - recency effects in impression formation', Journal of Abnormal and Social Psychology, 68, 335-338.

McCall, M.W. & Devries, D.L. (1976), 'Appraisal in content: Clashing with organizational realities', Paper presented at the Meeting of the American Psychological Association, Sept. Washington, D.C.

McConkey, D.D. (1972), 'Writing measurable objectives for staff managers', Advanced Management Journal, 37, (Jan.) 10-16.

McGregor, D.M. (1957), 'An uneasy look at performance appraisal', Harvard Business Review, 35, 89-94.

McGregor, D.M. (1960), The Human Side of Enterprise, McGraw-Hill: New York.

McKelvie, S.J. (1978), 'Graphic Rating Scales: How many categories?', The British Journal of Psychology, 69, (2), 185-203.

McMurry, R.N. (1960), '17 ways to mismanage merit rating', Business, 82, (March).

McNemar, Q. (1946), 'Opinion-attitude methodology', Psychological Bulletin, 43, 289-374.

Mehrabian, A. (1965), 'Communication length as an index of communicator attitude', Psychological Reports, 17, 519-522.

Merrihue, W.V. & Katzell, R.A. (1955), 'ERI: Yardstick of employee relations', Harvard Business Review, 33, 91–99.

Messick, S. (1975), 'The standard problem: Meaning and values in measurement and evaluation', American Psychologist, 30, 955–966.

Metcalfe, R.J. (1974), 'Own versus provided constructs in Rep test measure of cognitive complexity', Psychological Reports, 35, 1305–1306.

Meyer, H.H., Kay, E. & French, R.P. Jr. (1965), 'Split roles in performance appraisal', Harvard Business Review, 43, (1), 123–129.

Meyer, H.M. (1970), 'The validity of the In-Basket test as a measure of managerial performance', Personnel Psychology, 23, 297–307.

Miller, H. & Bieri, J. (1965), 'Cognitive complexity as a function of the significance of the stimulus objects being judged', Psychological Re- ports, 16, 1203–1204.

Miner, J.B. (1968), 'Management appraisal: A capsule review and current references', Business Horizons, (Oct.), 83–96.

Mischel, W. (1968), Personality and Assessment, Wiley: New York.

Morrison, C.T. (1980), 'The Appraisal Interview – Evaluation or Development', Paper presented at Staff Development Seminar, Institute of Local Government, University of Birmingham.

Morrison, C.T. (1981), The Dimensionality and Subjectivity of Job Performance Measurement, Unpublished Ph.D. thesis, University of Bradford.

Mosel, J.N. & Goheen, H.W. (1952), 'Agreement among replies to an employment recommendation questionnaire', American Psychologist, 7, 365–366.

Mosel, J.N. & Goheen, H.W. (1959), 'The employment recommendation questionnaire: III Validity of different types of references', Personnel Psychology, 12, 469–477.

Muchinsky, P.M. (1979), 'The use of reference reports in personnel selection: A review and evaluation', Journal of Occupational Psychology, 52, 287–297.

Murrell, H. (1976), Motivation at Work, Methuen: London.

Myers, J.H. & Errett, W. (1959), 'The problem of preselection in weighted application blank studies', Journal of Applied Psychology, 43, 94–95.

Nagle, B.F. (1953), 'Criterion development', Personnel Psychology, 6, 271–289.

Natsoulas, T. (1978), 'Residual Subjectivity', American Psychologist, 33, (3), 269–283.

Naylor, J.C. & Wherry, R.J. (1964), 'Feasibility of distinguishing supervisors' policies in evaluation of subordinates using ratings of simulated job incumbents', USAF PRL Technical Documents Reports, No. 64-25.

Nealey, S.M. & Owen, T.W. (1970), 'A multitrait-multimethod analysis of predictors and criteria of nursing performance', Organizational Behavior and Human Performance, 5, 348–365.

Newcomb, T.M. (1961), The Acquaintance Process, Holt, Rinehart and Winston: New York.

Nidorf, L.J. (1961), Individual Differences in Impression Formation, Unpublished doctoral dissertation, Clark University.

Nieva, V.F. (1976), Supervisor-Subordinate Similarity: A Determinant of Subordinate Ratings and Rewards, Doctoral dissertation, University of Michigan.

Norman, W.T. & Goldberg, L.R. (1966), 'Raters, ratees and randomness in personality structure', Journal of Personality and Social Psychology, 4, 681-691.

O.S.S. Staff (1948), Assessment of Men, Rinehart: New York.

Otis, J.L. (1971), 'Whose Criterion?', in Ronan, W.W. and Prien, E.P. (eds.) Perspectives on the Measurement of Human Performance, Appleton-Century-Crofts: New York, 79-87.

Patton, A. (1960), 'How to appraise executive performance', Harvard Business Review, 38, (1), 63-70.

Peel, E.A. (1953), 'Factorial Analysis as a psychological technique', in Uppsala Symposium on Psychological Factor Analysis. Uppsala: Almquist and Wiksells.

Perry, A. & Freidman, S.T. (1973), 'Dimensional analysis of attitudes towards commercial flying', Journal of Applied Psychology, 58, (3), 388-390.

Peters, D.L. & McCormick, E.J. (1966), 'Comparative reliability of numerically anchored versus job-task anchored rating scales', Journal of Applied Psychology, 50, (1), 92-96.

Petronko, M.R. & Perin, C.T. (1970), 'A consideration of cognitive complexity and primacy-recency effects in impression formation', Journal of Personality and Social Psychology, 15, 151-157.

Porter, L.W., Lawler, E.E. III & Hackman, J.R. (1975), Behavior in Organizations, McGraw-Hill: Tokyo.

Poulton, E.C. (1977), 'Quantitative subjective assessments are almost always biased, sometimes completely misleading', The British Journal of Psychology, 68, (4), 409-427.

Quinn, J.L. (1969), 'Bias in performance appraisals', Personnel Administration, 32, 40-45.

Raia, A.P. (1966), 'A second look at goals and controls', California Management Review, 8, (Summer), 49-58.

Raia, A.P. (1974), Managing by Objectives, Scott, Foresman & Co.: Brighton.

Randell, G.A. (1973), 'Performance appraisal: purposes, practices and conflicts', Journal of Occupational Psychology, 47, 221-224.

Randell, G.A. (1975), 'Staff appraisal and development through interviewing', The Training Officer, 11, (6), 166-167.

Randell, G.A. (1976), 'A Management Skills Approach to developing people and organizations at work', Paper presented to the NATO International Conference on Coordination and Control of Group and Organizational Performance, July, Munich, West Germany.

Randell, G.A. (1978), 'Interviewing at work', in Warr, P. (ed.) Psychology at Work, Penguin: Harmondsworth.

Randell, G.A., Packard, P.M.A., Shaw, R.L., & Slater, A.J. (1974), Staff Appraisal, (revised edition), Institute of Personnel Management: London.

Randell, G.A. & Still, M.D. (1973), Management Training, Behaviour and Performance, Human Resources Research Group, Final Report, University of Bradford.

Richardson, M.W. (1962), 'The free-written rating', in Whisler, T.L. & Harper, S.F. (eds.), Performance Appraisal, Holt, Rinehart & Winston, New York

Rizzo, W.A. & Frank, F.D. (1977), 'Influence of irrelevant cues and alternate forms of Graphic Rating Scales on Halo Effect', Personnel Psychology, 30, 405-417.

Robertson, I. & Downs, S. (1979), 'Learning and the prediction of performance: Development of trainability testing in the United Kingdom', Journal of Applied Psychology, 64, (1), 42-50.

Robinson, Sq. Leader J.L. (1975), A Behavioural Approach to the Construction of Scales for Officer Assessment in the Royal Air Force, Report submitted in part fulfillment of the M.A. degree (Manpower Studies), Birkbeck College, University of London.

Ronan, W.W. (1970), 'Evaluation of 3 Criteria of management performance', Journal of Industrial Psychology, 5, (1), 18-28.

Ronan, W.W. & Prien, E.P. (1971), Perspectives on the Measurement of Human Performance, Appleton-Century-Crofts: New York.

Rosen, B. & Jerdee, T.H. (1973), 'The influence of sex role stereotypes on evaluation of male and female supervisory behaviour', Journal of Applied Psychology, 57, 44-48.

Rosen, B. & Jerdee, T.H. (1974), 'The influences of sex role stereotypes on a personnel decision', Journal of Applied Psychology, 59, 9-14.

Rothe, H.F. & Nye, C.T. (1959), 'Output rates among machine operators: II - Consistency related to methods of pay', Journal of Applied Psychology, 43, 417-420.

Rowe, K.H. (1964), 'An appraisal of appraisals', Journal of Management Studies, 1, 1-25.

Schinka, J.A. & Sines, J.O. (1974), 'Correlates of accuracy in personality assessment', Journal of Clinical Psychology, 30, 374-377.

Schleh, E.C. (1961), Management by Results, McGraw-Hill: New York.

Schneier, C.E. (1977), 'Operational utility and psychometric characteristics of Behavioural Expectation Scales: A cognitive reinterpretation', Journal of Applied Psychology, 62, (5), 541-549.

Schneier, C.E. (1978), 'Measuring human performance in organizations: An empirical comparison of the psychometric properties of two types of criteria content', Proceedings of National Meeting of Academy of Management, San Francisco.

Schneier, C.E. & Beatty, R.W. (1976), 'Performance appraisal in organizations: An empirical study of differences in rater's perceptions and performance due to level in the hierarchy', Proceedings of 13th Annual Eastern Academy of Management Meetings, Washington, D.C.

Schneider, G.A. & Giambra, L.M. (1971), 'Performance in concept identification as a function of cognitive complexity', Journal of Personality and Social Psychology, 19, 261-273.

Schroder, H.M., Driver, M.J. & Streufert, S. (1967), Human Information Processing, Holt, Rinehart and Winston: New York.

Schwab, D.P., Heneman, H.G. III & De Cotiis, T.A. (1975a), 'Behaviourally Anchored Rating Scales: A review of the literature', Proceedings of the 35th Annual Meeting of the Academy of Management, Auburn University, New Orleans.

Schwab, D.P., Heneman, H.G. III & De Cotiis, T.A. (1975b), 'Behaviourally Anchored Rating Scales: A Review of the Literature. Personnel Psychology, 28, 549-562.

Schwind, H.F. (1977), 'A new behaviour oriented evaluation scale to assess teaching & training effectiveness', Paper presented at the Evaluation Research Society Meeting, Oct., Washington, D.C.

Scott, W.A. (1962), 'Cognitive complexity and cognitive flexibility', Sociometry, 25, 405-414.

Scott, W.A. (1974), 'Varieties of cognitive integration', Journal of Personality and Social Psychology, 30, 563-578.

Scott, W.A. (1978), 'Cognitive Structure', in Streufert, S. & Streufert, S.C., Behavior in the Complex Environment, Halsted Press, New York.

Senger, J. (1971), 'Managers' perceptions of subordinates' competences as a function of personal value orientations', Academic Management Journal, 14, (3), 415-424.

Sharon, A.T. & Bartlett, C.J. (1969), 'Effect of instructional conditions in producing Leniency on two types of rating scales', Personnel Psychology, 22, 251-263.

Shaw, E.A. (1972), 'Differential impact of negative stereotypes in employee selection', Personnel Psychology, 25, 333-338.

Shimmin, S. (1955), 'Incentives', Occupational Psychology, 29, 240.

Shimmin, S. (1959), Payment by Results: A Psychological Investigation, Staples Press: London.

Shorter Oxford English Dictionary (1973), University Press: Oxford.

Shrauger, S. & Altrocchi, J. (1964), 'The personality of the perceiver as a factor in person perception', Psychological Bulletin, 62, 289-308.

Sieber, J.E. (1964), 'Problem-solving behaviour of teachers as a function of conceptual structure', Journal of Research in School Teaching, 2, 64-68.

Sieber, J.E. & Lanzetta, J.T. (1964), 'Conflict and conceptual structure as determinants of decision-making behaviour', Journal of Personality, 32, 622-641.

Sims, H.P., Szilagyi, A.D. & Keller, R.T. (1976), 'The measurement of job characteristics', Academy of Management Journal, 19, (2), 195-212.

Sisson, E.D. (1948), 'Forced Choice - The new army rating', Personnel Psychology, 1, (3), 365-381.

Sleight, R.B. & Bell, G.D. (1954), 'Desirable contents of letters of recommendation', Personnel Journal, 32, 421-422.

Smith, P.C. (1976), 'Behaviors, Results and Organizational Effectiveness: The Problem of Criteria', in Dunnette, M.D. (ed.), Handbook of Industrial and Organizational Psychology, Rand McNally: Chicago.

Smith, P.C. & Kendall, L.M. (1963), 'Retranslation of Expectations', Journal of Applied Psychology, 47, (2), 149-155.

Spriegel, W.R. (1962), 'Company practices in appraisal of managerial performance', Personnel, 39, 77-83.

Stark, S. (1959), 'Research criteria of executive success', Journal of Business, 32, 1-14.

Stewart, R. (1965), 'Reactions to appraisal interviews', Journal of Management Studies, 2, 83-99.

Streufert, S. (1966), 'Conceptual structure, communicator importance and interpersonal attitudes toward deviant and conforming group members', Journal of Personality and Social Psychology, 4, 100-103.

Streufert, S. & Streufert, S.C. (1969), 'Effects of conceptual structure, failure and success on attribution of causality and interpersonal attitudes', Journal of Personality and Social Psychology, 11, 138 147.

Streufert, S. & Streufert, S.C. (1978), Behavior in the Complex Environment, Halsted Press: New York.

Sundberg, N.D., Snowden, L.R. & Reynolds, W.M. (1978), 'Towards assessment of personal competence and incompetence in life situation', Annual Review of Psychology, 29, 179-221.

Taft, R. (1955), 'The ability to judge people', Psychological Bulletin, 52, 1-23.

Taylor, E.K. & Wherry, R.J. (1951), 'A study of Leniency in two rating system', Personnel Psychology, 4, (1), 39-47.

Teel, K.S. (1980), 'Performance appraisal: Current trends, persistent progress', Personnel Journal, (April), 296-316.

Tiffin, J. (1951), 'The Forced Distribution System', in Dooher, M.J. & Marquis, V. (eds.), Rating Employee and Supervisory Performance, American Management Association: New York. 17-19.

Tilley, K.W. (ed.) (1974), Leadership and Management Appraisal, English Universities Press: London.

Toops, H.A. (1944), 'The criterion', Educational and Psychological Measurement, 4, 271-297.

Turner, W.W. (1960), 'Dimensions of foreman performance: A factor analysis of criteria measures', Journal of Applied Psychology, 44, 216-223.

Ulrich, L. & Trumbo, D. (1965), 'The selection interview since 1949', Psychological Bulletin, 63, 100-116.

Vroom, V.H. (1964), Work and Motivation, Wiley: New York.

Wagner, E.E. & Hoover, T.O. (1974), 'The influence of technical knowledge on position error in ranking', Journal of Applied Psychology, 59, 3, 406-408.

Walker, J., Fletcher, C., Williams, R. & Taylor, K. (1977), 'Performance appraisal: An open or shut case?', Personnel Review, 6, (1), 38-42.

Warmke, D.L. & Billings, R.S. (1979), 'Comparison of training methods for improving the psychometric quality of experimental and administrative performance ratings', Journal of Applied Psychology, 64, (2), 124 131.

Watson, S.R. (1976), Counsellor Complexity and the Process of Hypothesizing About a Client: An Exploratory Study of Counsellors' Information Processing, Unpublished doctoral dissertation, University of California.

Weitz, J. (1961), 'Criteria for Criteria', American Psychologist, 16, 228-232.

Weitz, J. & Nuckols, R.C. (1953), 'A validation study of "How Supervise?"', Journal of Applied Psychology, 37, 7-8.

Wertheimer, M. (1972), Fundamental Issues in Psychology, Holt, Rinehart and Winston: New York.

Whisler, T.L. & Harper, S.F. (1962), Performance Appraisal: Research and Practice, Holt, Rinehart & Winston: New York.

Wiens, A.N., Jackson, R.H., Manaugh, T.S. & Matarazzo, J.D. (1969), 'Communication length as an index of communicator attitude: A replication', Journal of Applied Psychology, 53, 264-266.

Wiggins, J.S. (1973), Personality and prediction: Principles of Personality Assessment, Addison-Wesley: Reading, Mass.

Williams, W.E. & Seiler, D.A. (1973), 'A relationship between measures of effort and job performance', Journal of Applied Psychology, 57, 49 54.

Wish, M., Deutsch, M. & Kaplan, S.J. (1976), 'Perceived dimensions of interpersonal relations', Journal of Personality and Social Psychology, 33, (4), 409-420.

Wolf, M.M. (1978), 'Social validity: the case for subjective measurement or how applied behavior analysis is finding its heart', Journal of Applied Behavior Analysis, 11, (2), 203-215.

Wollowick, H.B. & McNamara, W.J. (1969), 'Relationship of the components of an assessment center to management success', Journal of Applied Psychology, 53, 348-352.

Yager, E. (1981), 'A critique of performance appraisal systems', Personnel Journal, 60, (2), 129-133.

Zedeck, S. & Baker, H.T. (1971), 'Evaluation of Behavioural Expectation Scales', Paper presented at the Meeting of the Midwestern Psychological Association, May, Detroit.

Zedeck, S. & Baker, H.T. (1972), 'Nursing performance as measured by Behavioural Expectation Scales: A multitrait-multirater analysis', Organizational Behavior and Human Performance, 7, 457-466.

Zedeck, S., Imparato, N., Krausz, M. & Oleno, T. (1974), 'Development of Behaviourally Anchored Rating Scales as a function of organizational level', Journal of Applied Psychology, 59, (2), 249-252.

Zedeck, S., Jacobs, R. & Kafry, D. (1976), 'Behavioural Expectations: Development of parallel forms and analysis of scale assumptions', Journal of Applied Psychology, 61, (1), 112-115.

Zedeck, S. & Kafry, D. (1977), 'Capturing rater policies for processing evaluation data', Organizational Behavior and Human Performance, 18, (2), 269-294.

Author index

229

Subject index